Great Stories of Hiking
the Appalachian Trail

Great Stories of Hiking
the Appalachian Trail

Edited by Debra Smith

STACKPOLE
BOOKS

Published by
STACKPOLE BOOKS
5067 Ritter Road
Mechanicsburg, PA 17055
www.stackpolebooks.com

Printed in the United States

10 9 8 7 6 5 4 3 2 1

First edition

Cover design by Caroline Stover
Cover photograph by Debra Smith

Library of Congress Cataloging-in-Publication Data

Great stories of hiking the Appalachian Trail / edited by Debra Smith. — 1st ed.
    p. cm.
  ISBN 978-0-8117-0598-1
  1. Appalachian Mountains—Description and travel. 2. Hiking—Appalachian
Mountains. 3. Trails—Appalachian Mountains. 4. Appalachian Trail. I. Smith,
Debra. II. Hiking the Appalachian Trail.
  F106.G74 2010
  917.4—dc22
                                    2009043119

This book is dedicated to Benton MacKaye
who dreamed of the Appalachian Trail,
to Myron H. Avery who brought it into being,
and to each of the hundreds of men and women
who have worked and are working
so hard to maintain it.

David Walp

Contents

Notes on this edition:

The following sections are not republished in their entirety. These longer stories were shortened so that we could bring you more of the legendary hikers and their tales. For the entire stories as originally published, see the original *Hiking the Appalachian Trail, Vol. 1 and 2*.

Early History of the Appalachian Trail
The Appalachian Trail and I
Friendly Little Markers
Following the Appalachian Trail; or Don't Spare the White Paint
A Mountain Every Morning: Margaret and Bump Smith's Hike

The map on page xiv is used with permission of the Appalachian Trail Conservancy.

Foreword

I salute Stackpole Books for reintroducing to a new generation of readers this collection of timeless stories that first appeared in the two-volume series, *Hiking the Appalachian Trail*, originally published by Rodale Press, Inc. in 1975.

In many respects, the Appalachian Trail is very different today than it was when many of the hikes described here took place. And, yet, many of the experiences described here are representative of the experiences enjoyed by contemporary adventurers: the opportunity to explore the natural and cultural richness of the greater part of the eastern United States; to discover—up close and personal—the flora and fauna and the geology of the ancient Appalachian Mountain range. Hikers still experience the awe-inspiring vistas of our eastern American landscapes as well as the macro-level view of the delicate intricacies of a lady's slipper orchid or a flame azalea. They endure hardships and challenges, but also the rewards that arise from overcoming them in order to escape—if only for a few months—from the frenzies of contemporary urban life to a simpler, more fundamental existence—one based on self-sufficiency with only the relative handful of possessions necessary for subsistence. Regardless of when they hiked, hikers still engage in hours of self-reflection and emotional and spiritual renewal and relish the richness of relationships—however transient—formed through encounters with other wayfarers as well as adjacent landowners and residents in dozens of trail-side communities and the "trail magic" that often arises from those encounters.

Several stories in this collection—Myron Avery, Earl Shaffer, and "Grandma" Gatewood—are not first-person accounts and yet it is altogether fitting to acknowledge those early pioneers because each of them is a legend in the rich tapestry of folklore that surrounds the Appalachian Trail. While Benton MacKaye, the visionary forester and regional planner who first proposed and popularized the concept of an extended trail spanning the Appalachians, is often credited as the "father" of the Appalachian Trail, it was Avery—the hard-charging maritime attorney from Lubec, Maine—who really spearheaded the effort to first scout and then to clear and mark the route of the Appalachian Trail and to organize the hiking and outing clubs whose volunteers have cared for the trail ever since. Shaffer, as the first individual to hike the trail from end to end in one continuous hike and whose last hike—his third—was completed at the age of 80, continues to serve as an inspiration for would-be "thru-hikers" today both through his deeds and through his prose, his poetry, and his photography. And, no collection of Appalachian Trail lore would be complete without some mention of "Grandma"—the indomitable flatlander from the Midwest who hiked the trail multiple times in her signature sneakers, sporting an assortment of funky hats, and carrying her few possessions in a denim shoulder bag.

Other stories in this collection describe section-by-section hikes and continuous end-to-end hikes, some south-to-north, some north-to-south, most from spring to fall, but one in the depths of winter. Some describe their experiences in great detail—almost as a travelogue—while others apply a broader brush. All of them describe their hardships, their chance encounters, the awe-inspiring scenery they experienced along the route, and the gratification of fulfilling an at-times seemingly impossible goal.

Many, if not all, of those authors would marvel—perhaps some with mild disdain—at the technological advances that have taken place in hiking equipment and clothing. Few hikers today, for example, are likely to carry a Hudson Bay ax. Gone are the days of heavy canvas rucksacks, kapok sleeping bags, or raingear fashioned from plastic shower curtains. But, now as then, long-distance hikers are a weight-conscious lot and the evolution in outdoor gear and clothing toward ultra-light packs, tents, sleeping bags, and cooking gear, freeze-dried foods, and synthetic Gore-Tex and fleece garments have made it far easier to achieve the elusive goal of a pack that weighs less than 25 pounds.

A number of the authors describe getting lost due to poor marking of the footpath or out-of-date guidebooks and maps, of slogging through sections overgrown with weeds and briars, of negotiating many fallen trees or "blow-downs," and of tramping sections of poorly drained, eroded or gullied footway. Such conditions are far less likely to be encountered on today's trail, which is well marked and graded. Our knowledge of trail-construction and erosion-control techniques evolved from the early days when the prime objective was to get from the base of any given mountain to the summit in the least amount of distance—usually directly up the fall line. In fact, the trail is longer today than when it was completed in 1937, by nearly 100 miles, and much of that increase is due to improved trail design, better grading, and the incorporation of switchbacks and drainage-control devices.

The system of more than 250 three-sided shelters or lean-tos along the trail today is more complete, with shelters spaced about 10 miles apart. Many include improvements such as cooking shelves, well-decked floors, and even skylights. The venerable pit privies of the past gradually are being replaced by more environmentally friendly and less odiferous composting privies. Campsite design has improved as we learn new techniques to minimize the impacts of overuse.

As several of the authors in this collection note, the Appalachian Trail project has been a volunteer-based project since its earliest beginnings in the 1920s. But, while that assemblage of dedicated volunteers may have numbered in the hundreds in the early years, today the trail project is supported by an "army" of more than 6,000 volunteers—men and women, young and not-so-young, from all walks of life. Most are members of one of the 30 trail clubs affiliated with the Appalachian Trail Conservancy, while others choose to engage on a more episodic basis. Together, they contribute more than 200,000 hours each year to a wide assortment of trail-management functions ranging from trail- and facility-maintenance and construction to natural-resource management, environmental-health monitoring, boundary maintenance, and visitor services.

Perhaps the biggest change affecting the Appalachian Trail arises from the long-term efforts by the Appalachian Trail Conference (now Conservancy) to secure federal recognition for the trail and ultimately to secure a publicly owned right-of-way and protective corridor or "greenway" bordering the footpath. In 1968, the U.S. Congress passed and President Lyndon B. Johnson signed into law the National Trails System Act, which designated the Appalachian Trail, along with the Pacific Crest Trail, as the nation's first national scenic trails and authorized federal and state land-acquisition programs to acquire a right-of-way for each trail. Ten years later, again at the urging of the Appalachian Trail Conference (ATC) and others, Congress amended the act to expand land acquisition authority and, in every year since, ATC has requested annual appropriations from the Land and Water Conservation Fund to support the A.T. land-acquisition programs of the National Park Service and USDA-Forest Service. In 1982, when it appeared that the administration and Congress might abandon federal land-conservation programs altogether, ATC formed its own privately-supported land trust program to assure that critical parcels of land would not be lost to development and that the continuity of the foot-path would not be severed.

The result of those efforts—spanning more than 40 years—surely ranks as one of the most successful land-conservation initiatives in the history of the United States: Nearly 200,000 acres in each of the 14 states crossed by the trail have been acquired since 1968 while other lands bordering the trail as it passes through existing public lands—including more than 25 congressionally designated wilderness areas—are managed under special-management prescriptions. Overall, about 270,000 acres form the 2,178-mile greenway surrounding the A.T. and fewer than 10 miles of the footpath are not yet in public ownership.

The Appalachian Trail is a unit of the National Park System, although it is unlike any park in that remarkable system. Not only is it the longest (and skinniest) national park, but it is a patchwork quilt of administrative jurisdictions. For example, more than half of the trail passes through lands administered by the USDA-Forest Service, while hundreds of additional miles traverse more than 60 state parks, forests, and game-management units.

Today, trail managers know much more about the rich natural and cultural heritage contained within the boundaries of the Appalachian Trail greenway. For example, natural-diversity inventories conducted in the 1980s and 1990s documented more than 2,200 occurrences of federal- or state-listed rare, threatened, and endangered species and critical habitats, ranking the trail among the most biologically diverse units of the national park system. Preliminary inventories suggest that it is equally endowed with significant historical and archeological resources.

How have all these changes affected the experience described by the authors in this collection? Perhaps the most tangible change is in the route of the footpath itself. About one-half of the footpath has been reconstructed and relocated in the past 30-plus years. In 1978, for example, more than 200 miles of the A.T. were situated along road shoulders, while about 600 additional miles crossed privately owned lands under constant threat of encroaching residential and commercial development. Today, all but a few miles of the trail—those that pass through a number of trail-side communities—are off the roads, resulting in an even more scenic experience than that described by these hikers. In some cases, those relocations have even added to the physical challenge of hiking the footpath by eliminating lowland road walks in favor of ridge-crest routes.

The protective corridor that now surrounds the trail is a buffer to the footpath—and that corridor averages only 1,000 feet in width. Gone are the days when the trail might be obliterated by incompatible land uses such as the chicken-farm operation that ultimately displaced the trail from its original southern terminus at Mt. Oglethorpe. Still, trail managers and supporters remain vigilant to new threats to the trail and its all-too-fragile greenway, threats arising from proposed highway expansions, wind-energy developments, wireless-communications facilities, off-road vehicle use, trespass and timber theft, invasive species, and acid-rain deposition.

The trail greenway can play an important role in connection with one of the greatest challenges facing our planet: global climate change. The mostly forested landscape that surrounds the trail is a significant repository for carbon sequestration, while its continuous greenway plays a role in adaptation to the effects of climate change for several animal, bird, and plant species. The trail greenway is home to the headwaters of many of the major watersheds of the eastern United States and helps assure the health of our lakes, streams, and great rivers as well as the quality of our drinking water. Through the Appalachian Trail MEGA-Transect environmental-monitoring program, supported by ATC, NPS, USGS, and many other public and private partners, the A.T. greenway already is serving as a laboratory for monitoring more than a dozen environmental indicators and thus is a barometer of the environmental health for much of the Eastern Seaboard.

Through still other programs, such as the ATC/NPS-supported Trail to Every Classroom program and the A.T. community-partner program, we also hope to cultivate a new generation of trail advocates and supporters to assure that the trail remains true to its traditions as a volunteer-based initiative.

Many of the developments in the trail project remain invisible to most trail visitors—even those who choose to walk its entire length. And, perhaps, that is at it should be. After all, one of the primary objectives of trail managers and supporters throughout the more than 80 years of its development has been to retain its simplicity and primitive, even wilderness-like qualities. The experience of hiking the length of the Appalachian Trail today is, in most respects, similar to the experiences described in the following pages by the early pioneers who first followed its undulating route across the ridge crests and valleys of the Appalachians. It remains today what some have described as "the experience of a lifetime," a journey of five million footsteps, and a pathway toward the discovery of the natural world and the inner self.

Dave Startzell
Executive Director
Appalachian Trail Conservancy

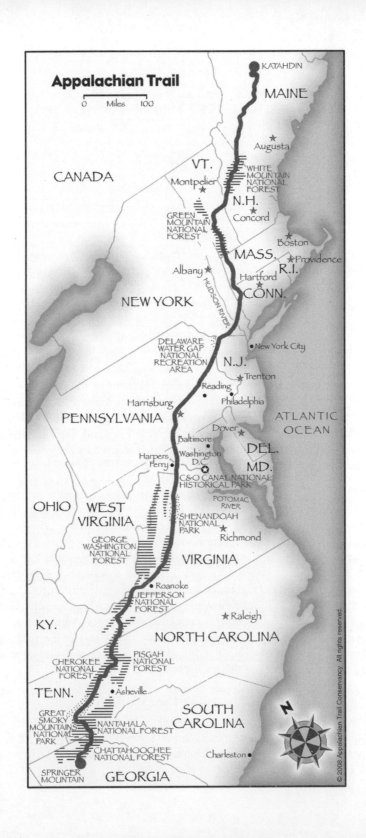

Appalachian Trail

0   Miles   100

KATAHDIN

MAINE

★ Augusta

VT.

WHITE
MOUNTAIN
NATIONAL
FOREST

Montpelier ★

N.H.

Concord ★

GREEN
MOUNTAIN
NATIONAL
FOREST

★ Boston

MASS.

★ Providence

CANADA

Albany ★

R.I.

Hartford
★

CONN.

NEW YORK

HUDSON RIVER

DELAWARE
WATER GAP
NATIONAL
RECREATION
AREA

N.J.

• New York City

★ Trenton

Reading •

Philadelphia

ATLANTIC
OCEAN

Harrisburg
★

PENNSYLVANIA

Dover ★

DEL.

Baltimore •

Harpers
Ferry •

Washington
D.C. ✪

MD.

C&O CANAL NATIONAL
HISTORICAL PARK

POTOMAC
RIVER

OHIO

WEST
VIRGINIA

SHENANDOAH
NATIONAL
PARK

★ Richmond

GEORGE
WASHINGTON
NATIONAL
FOREST

VIRGINIA

• Roanoke

JEFFERSON
NATIONAL
FOREST

KY.

★ Raleigh

NORTH CAROLINA

PISGAH
NATIONAL
FOREST

CHEROKEE
NATIONAL
FOREST

TENN.

• Asheville

SOUTH
CAROLINA

GREAT
SMOKY
MOUNTAINS
NATIONAL
PARK

NANTAHALA
NATIONAL FOREST

CHATTAHOOCHEE
NATIONAL FOREST

Charleston •

SPRINGER
MOUNTAIN

GEORGIA

N

Early History of
the Appalachian Trail

The origin of the Appalachian Trail can be traced directly to Benton MacKaye, a forester, author, and philosopher, of Shirley Center, Massachusetts. In October, 1921, MacKaye published in the *Journal of the American Institute of Architects* an article entitled "An Appalachian Trail, a Project in Regional Planning." In that article he proposed the trail as a sort of backbone, linking wilderness areas suitable for recreation and readily accessible to dwellers in the metropolitan areas along the Atlantic seaboard.

Several men had thought of a through trail in the northern states. Prof. Will S. Monroe, the revered seer of the Green Mountain Club, had proposed a trail from Delaware Water Gap to northern Vermont. Arthur C. Comey, chairman of the New England Trail Conference, had urged that a combination of trails maintained by the conference be linked into a through route from Maine to the Hudson River. Albert M. Turner, field secretary of the Connecticut State Park and Forest Commission, and J. A. Allis of New York City, a member of the Appalachian Mountain and Green Mountain Clubs, had also urged a long through-trail project and had contributed ideas as to a practicable route.

However, the idea for the Appalachian Trail was solely MacKaye's conception. MacKaye writes that he first thought of the project in the early 1900s, but refrained from announcing it until after the Long Trail in Vermont was begun in 1910. Observing from one of the peaks on that trail that the long straight ranges of the Green Mountains made feasible a through route, he expanded the proposal of the Long Trail into a footpath to link up the wilderness areas in the 13 original states and in Maine and Vermont.

Actually the trail traverses 14 states. Originally the northern terminus of the trail was to be Mt. Washington (the highest peak in the North) and the southern terminus was to be Mt. Mitchell (the highest peak in the South). Harlan P. Kelsey suggested that the southern terminus be the famous Lookout Mountain near Chattanooga, Tennessee, in

*Benton MacKaye
at eighty-five.
Photo courtesy of
Mrs. Henry Barnes.*

the Cumberland Mountains across the Great Appalachian Valley. Paul
M. Fink, an authority on the Great Smoky Mountains, developed in
1922 at Kelsey's request a route down the western range to Cohutta
Mountain and across the valley to Lookout Mountain. The necessity of
crossing a wide cultivated valley brought Lookout Mountain into disfa-
vor, and Cohutta Mountain was accepted as the proper southern termi-
nus of the trail until the activities of E. B. Stone, Jr., Charles N. Elliott,
Roy R. Ozmer, and other members of the Georgia Appalachian Trail
Club focused attention on the eastern Blue Ridge route, and on Mt.
Oglethorpe in Georgia as the trail's southern terminus.

MacKaye's article attracted the attention of many volunteer trail
workers and led to the first efforts toward the location and construction
of the Appalachian Trail. In April, 1922, at Washington, D.C., Mac-
Kaye organized a small group to further the Appalachian Trail project
south and north of the Potomac River. This group included Dr. L. F.
Schmeckebier, one of the founders and moving spirits in the Potomac

Appalachian Trail Club when it was formed later, and François E. Matthes, Louis F. Post, and Mrs. Alice Thatcher Post. However, other than a cursory examination of a trail route, little was accomplished at this time. Dr. H. S. Hedges of Charlottesville, Virginia, made a number of scouting trips in the region that is now the southern part of the Shenandoah National Park and his notes helped in the later location of the trail in this area.

The first actual field work was done in the Harriman and Bear Mountain sections of the Palisades Interstate Park of New York and New Jersey, where the Palisades Interstate Park Trail Conference, organized in 1920 for the extension of trails in that preserve, was already in existence. This work was under the leadership of Raymond H. Torrey. The Palisades Interstate Park section of the Appalachian Trail, from Bear Mountain Bridge to the Ramapo River south of Arden, was begun in 1922 and completed in 1923. It was followed by the building, in 1924, of the section from Arden to Greenwood Lake. These two sections were the first to be marked with the Appalachian Trail copper marker, which was designed by Major W. A. Welch, general manager and chief engineer of the Palisades Interstate Park.

The trail marker as first designed bore the Appalachian Trail monogram and the words APPALACHIAN TRAIL–PALISADES PARK. Later the words MAINE TO GEORGIA were substituted for the local reference. In 1931 Arthur Perkins designed a diamond-shaped marker made of galvanized sheet iron, with the same insignia. Somewhat less expensive and more durable, this marker has been used in later years.

Myron H. Avery: First to Hike the Entire Appalachian Trail

Started in Maine in 1920s, when trail was in formative stages. Finished last section in 1936.

Myron H. Avery was the first person to walk the entire Appalachian Trail. He started in Maine in the 1920s while the trail was in its formative stages, and finished in the fall of 1936.

Born in North Lubeck, Maine, of pioneer stock, Myron Avery attended secondary schools in his home community. At Bowdoin College he was elected to Phi Beta Kappa, and later received a law degree from Harvard. In 1926 Judge Arthur Perkins of Hartford, Connecticut, then chairman of the yearling Appalachian Trail Conference, enlisted the aid of Myron Avery in translating the proposed trail from wishful thinking into a reality. His love of the outdoors stood young Avery in good stead for this arduous task. In 1927 he was appointed assistant chairman (during Judge Perkins's illness), and then served as chairman from 1931 to 1952.

The first task facing Myron Avery was to form an organization of volunteers who were interested in the idea of a footpath along the Appalachian Range of the eastern United States. It was soon found that more was needed than a bare trail. Myron set to work writing and editing manuals on trail construction, on lightweight camping techniques, and on lean-to design and construction, as well as trail guidebooks. At first he paid for the printing of each publication out of his own pocket, recovering his outlay as copies were sold.

Myron Avery believed that trail travel filled a fundamental need in living, and that a properly maintained and marked trail was an object of beauty, in harmony with the surrounding woods and fields. Being a perfectionist, he had to know the trail firsthand. He scouted most of the new sections, pushed a measuring wheel over much of the footway, and took copious notes for the preparation of guidebooks. He hiked much of the trail many times, some of the trail twice,

*Myron Avery.
Photo courtesy of
Appalachian Trail
Conference.*

and all of the trail at least once. He organized trail clubs in key areas
and participated in their hiking activities. The normal speed of completion did not seem fast enough to a man who was anxious to finish
a dream project, and often his enthusiasm and urgency were misunderstood, especially by some members of the southern clubs.

Benton MacKaye advanced the idea of a wilderness footpath, and
Arthur Perkins resurrected the trail project when it had become mori-
bund and was in danger of degenerating into a fireside philosophy,
but it fell to Myron Avery to supply the driving force that would
make the Appalachian Trail a reality. His persistence and tremendous
drive often were misunderstood, but Myron was able to patch up the
differences that arose and go on to the completion of the project.

In his final report to the conference in 1952 Myron Avery wrote:
"The Appalachian Trail derives much of its strength and appeal from
its uninterrupted and practically endless character. This is an attribute
which must be preserved. I view the existence of this pathway and the
opportunity to travel it, day after day without interruption, as a distinct aspect of our American life." He completed his report with the
oft-quoted definition of the Appalachian Trail: "Remote for detach-
ment, narrow for chosen company, winding for leisure, lonely for con-
templation, it beckons not merely north and south but upward to the
body, mind, and soul of man."

—CONTRIBUTED BY LESTER L. HOLMES

Maine to Georgia—All the Way

By George W. Outerbridge

Started at LEHIGH GAP, PENNSYLVANIA, on October 30, 1932
Finished at DAMASCUS, VIRGINIA, on June 22, 1939

From *Appalachia* for December, 1939

A trip to Virginia and Tennessee in June, 1939, enabled Dr. Martin Kilpatrick, of the University of Pennsylvania, and me to complete our last lap of the Appalachian Trail. Mrs. Kilpatrick, who has been on most of our trips, has a few gaps totaling about 100 miles, but has done all the rest. We have done no skipping or shortcutting, but have stuck right to the trail the whole way, or as close to it as is humanly possible in those places where, because of overgrowth of the footway and deficient marking, recent lumbering, or road construction, bits of it could be said to be virtually nonexistent for the time being. We are certain that we have at no time deviated to any significant extent from the established route. This may seem to some to be merely something in the way of a "stunt," but we do not look on it in that light. The Appalachian Trail is a real entity, and we felt that if one set out to follow it, he should do just that, and not something "almost, but not quite."

Starting in a more or less desultory way by doing short bits fairly near at hand as a pleasant objective for an occasional weekend trip, we soon found ourselves getting more and more interested in it, so that a subtle shift of emphasis might be said gradually to have taken place—from doing a bit of trail because we wanted to take a trip, to taking a trip from time to time because we wanted to do another bit of trail. And, as the bits done in this way accumulated, it wasn't long before we began to think it would be fun to do it all, although at first that goal seemed nebulous and far away. Gradually, however, we found the gaps on our trail maps getting shorter and shorter—and finally vanishing altogether. When we had done perhaps somewhere around half of it, I formulated a little slogan for myself: "The AT before sixty;" and here it is accomplished—with a couple of years to spare! Doing it not only has been awfully good fun, every bit of it, but has supplied a very real motive for summer vacations and many delightful shorter trips. We feel, however, the greatest boon derived from doing the Appalachian Trail has been getting us into many parts of the country that otherwise we never would have seen. In this respect, I have in mind especially the whole of the trail in Maine, the apparently little-used link between the Appalachian Mountain Club bailiwick in New Hampshire and the Long Trail in Vermont, which, utilizing Dartmouth Outing Club trails part of the way, runs through lovely rolling New England country, bits in the Berkshires and the Kittatinnies, and above all, from my own personal point of view, the whole stretch from Harpers Ferry to Mt. Oglethorpe, which entire region had heretofore been (and without the Appalachian Trail would probably have remained) a complete terra incognita to me. Other districts, such as the White and Green mountains and Katahdin itself, are of course magnificent, but were well known and fairly accessible to climbers before the days of the Appalachian Trail. It is in opening up and making known these other areas, and linking them all together so enticingly, that I feel the Appalachian Trail has done such a grand job.

As stated above, we have enjoyed doing it *all*, though naturally some parts are more attractive and scenic than others. There are sections with too much road walking, notably east of High Point, New Jersey, in some parts of Massachusetts, and several other places. It is a pleasure to know that the two worst stretches, from Glenvar to Galax, in southern Virginia, and from Winner to Indian Grave Gap, in northern Tennessee, will be completely eliminated by the splendid rerouting projects now under way. It is to be hoped that elsewhere, as the trail grows older and the colossal problem of getting it through at all recedes into the background, the local clubs may be able to give some time and effort to rerouting road stretches into adjacent fields and woods. Of course, in some places this will never be possible, but it is an ideal well worth striving for. One particularly pernicious form of activity (from the viewpoint of the walker) is the construction in more or less wilderness areas of what are euphemistically known as "truck trails," in reality usually wide, straight, shadeless, hard gravel, or even stone-surfaced roads, replacing for many miles what had formerly been a pleasant woodland path. We have encountered these in Maine, Georgia, and elsewhere; here again fairly extensive rerouting projects may be in order. While welcoming enthusiastically the recently inaugurated half- to two-mile-wide Trailway project in state and national parks, we are certainly glad that we were able to do the section of the Blue Ridge south of Rockfish Gap, Virginia, and from Clingmans Dome to Deals Gap in the Smokies, before the construction of the contemplated parkways in those regions. I only wish we could have done the same in Shenandoah, where in the course of 100 miles the trail, splendidly reconstructed by the park service as to grades and footway, crosses the Skyline Drive 30 times and is within sight or sound of it much of the way.

Between Bear Mountain Bridge, New York, and northern Maryland, we have done the trail entirely on weekends from Philadelphia; from there to Galax, Virginia, on Christmas and Easter week trips, and all the rest in summer vacations of a couple of weeks to a month each. I have kept careful records of the dates of all Appalachian Trail hikes, and find that between my first piece of trail, Lehigh Gap to Bake Oven Knob, Pennsylvania, on October 30, 1932, and my last, U. S. Route 58 to Damascus, Virginia, on June 22, 1939, I have put in altogether 169 days or parts of days on it, many of these being only half-days, or less, of actual walking. The only parts I did separately from the Kilpatricks were the Shenandoah National Park and Long Trail sections, each about 100 miles, and some short bits in Pennsylvania and New Jersey, but their times on these were approximately the same as mine. We have in no sense, at any time, had the idea of making any records, but have merely gone along at such pace as happened to suit us, and have spent longer or shorter periods on the trail at such times as happened to be convenient. Nor have we, of course, made any attempt to do it consecutively, or all in the same direction. For the most part we have used the two-car system, planting one at each end of a trail section of suitable length, walking from one to the other and then driving around. Our winter trips to Virginia have been mostly by train.

We have encountered many vagaries of the weather, from a Christmas week blizzard and an Easter-time temperature of 12°F. in Virginia to such heat in Maine that we slept on, not in, our sleeping bags. Many of the "magnificent panoramic views" of the guidebooks we have had to imagine in the mist and the rain, but many, many more we have reveled in. Pleasant memories from our trail wanderings are of sunset and sunrise and the full of the moon seen from the balds of the Smokies and the Nantahalas; of Virginia hillsides in April clothed in Judas tree, dogwood, and apple blossoms; of flame azalea and 20-foot-high mountain laurel on Holston Mountain in June; of the russets and ochers and scarlets of autumn on the long ridges of our own state; of wild turkeys feeding in the snow on the Blue Ridge; of scores of miles of splendid virgin oak forest in Georgia and North Carolina; and of the endless profusion and variety of wild flowers on all portions of the trail in spring and summer.

Personal contacts along the way have been uniformly agreeable. Our single unpleasant adventure was the breaking into and pilfering of the Kilpatricks' car while parked at a lonely highway-trail intersection in Georgia in the summer of 1938. Among the most interesting and delightful of our experiences has been staying with natives living along the trail in the Rockfish Gap-to-Snowden and the Glenvar-to-Galax sections in Virginia on two Christmas weeks when camping out offered no attractions. On the former of these we were able to make complete arrangements in advance by writing, but on the latter this was only partly feasible. Several times we started off in the morning not knowing at all where we would stay that night, but we always were taken in, though it usually required quite a bit of persuasion, with one foot at least figuratively in the half-open door. Once accepted, however, nothing was too good for us. Without exception, we received charming hospitality, excellent food and plenty of it, and thoroughly comfortable sleeping accommodations with these people, no matter how unprepossessing their house might look from the outside.

We also greatly enjoyed staying at the "sporting camps" in Maine, and perhaps even more at the attractive open shelters between Orbeton Stream and Grafton Notch, which were spick-and-span new when we went through there in August of '37. Even packing one's own tent, as we did all the way between Galax, Virginia, and Mt. Oglethorpe, while it increases the load on one's back, has its charm too, permitting overnight stops at will, limited only by finding water and a possible campsite. Some of our pleasantest ones were entirely impromptu, when we found we couldn't comfortably reach an intended objective. In many parts of the southern Appalachians, however, water occurs none too frequently, and when it does, it may be in a steep-sided ravine, covered with rhododendron or other growth, and never a patch of cleared or level ground anywhere around big enough to lay out a pocket handkerchief, let alone put up a tent. It behooves the tramper, therefore, to watch his step pretty carefully as the day wears on, or he may find himself spending the night wrapped around a bush on a steep hillside, or making a dry camp. We never had to do this, but we did come fairly close to it once or twice. But we are all glad, I think, to have gone through this country before the erection of a chain of shelters; it *seemed*, at least, just that much less sophisticated. Only once north of Virginia did we have occasion to carry and use our tents—in Putnam

County, New York, where our friends had predicted we would find it so civilized as to be entirely uninteresting, which was most emphatically not the case.

From our experiences we feel that three is the minimum number for comfortable travel over those portions of the trail whose marking is (to put it politely!) a bit sketchy. This permits fanning out to look for the next blaze, or in heavy fog or dense bush one member of the party can hold the last mark while the other two circle ahead on either side of the assumed course until one or the other picks up the next mark. This is time-consuming, but infinitely less so than getting lost. Both the Kilpatricks have really uncanny noses for a trail; if there is the vestige of a rusty, battered-up old Appalachian Trail marker, or an almost faded-out paint blaze, half-hidden in foliage, within half a mile of the last one, they will surely find it! The places where we had the most difficulty in following the trail were in Connecticut (summer of 1937), in parts of Georgia, and a few sections along the North Carolina–Tennessee border (summer of 1938), but there were plenty of others where you could not just saunter nonchalantly along, head in air, musing on the higher things of life. On the other hand, I do not wish to convey the impression that a large portion of the trail is poorly marked, for such is not the case. Nearly all of the trail is perfectly easy to follow and is in excellent shape. And, after all, an occasional bit of uncertainty only adds spice to the game; if it were all *too* easy, perhaps it would not be quite so much fun.

The Appalachian Trail tramper, however, who knows the trail only in the more traveled portions of New England and the Middle states, and then turns his steps southward, must not expect to find the same conditions of clearance that he has been accustomed to. He must realize that for many long stretches the trail maintenance problems are almost insuperable. He must anticipate, therefore, not infrequent struggles through summer growth, often shoulder- or head-high, perhaps nettles or blackberry tangles (though, as a matter of fact, two of the worst brier patches through which the trail led us were near Cornwall, Connecticut, and Dalton, Massachusetts). He must be content if he finds sufficient blazes and markers to eke out the guidebook directions, and will feel that these slight discomforts are but a small price to pay for the pleasure of traveling through an unspoiled and fascinating region, quite different from that with which he has been familiar.

One thing has greatly impressed us—the paucity of others doing the trail. Of course, in the better-known regions, such as the Hunt Trail on Katahdin, the White and Green mountains, the Shenandoah and Great Smoky Mountains National Parks, Harriman State Park in New

York, etc., goodly numbers are encountered (sometimes almost *too* many!), but in many other districts all the way from Maine to Georgia we have walked for days on end without meeting a single hiker, a condition we hope and believe will be changed as the Appalachian Trail becomes better known and the stretches which now offer some difficulties are improved. All through the South so few have been over many parts of the trail that they are well remembered by the local people—the Mitchell brothers, who did more of the trail at one fell swoop than probably anyone else; Eiler Larson, the strange, wandering Dane with the shaggy hair, who has done most, if not all, of it; MacMullin, who went from Mt. Oglethorpe to Devil Fork Gap in the spring of '38—these about exhaust the list. The man who runs the ferry across the New River near Galax, Virginia, told us he had been there over three years, but had never before taken any trampers across. Although the white blazes are on fence posts right down his lane, he had no idea of their meaning.

One question we have been asked over and over and over again, from Katahdin to Oglethorpe: "What about snakes?" The answer—a couple of rattlers killed in Georgia (and a third, a huge fellow, lying stretched out right in the middle of the trail, and prodigiously belabored by Martin—until we realized that he was very dead before we ever saw him!), another big one, but alive, coiled, and ready for business, met by Martin and a friend (and very nearly stepped on by the latter) on their way to the Skyland conference in 1935, a few more encountered and dispatched on work trips to the short section of trail maintained by our club in Pennsylvania, and an occasional characteristic buzzing, "heard but not seen," elsewhere, constitute about the sum total of our experiences along this line—except for the fantastic tales that have been told to us by various and sundry individuals! We carried a snakebite outfit on all summer trips south of New England, but fortunately have never had occasion to use it. Of insect pests, chiggers in Georgia and blackflies in Maine have on occasion slightly (but only slightly) disturbed our equanimity; otherwise annoyances from this source have been practically negligible, mosquitoes in particular rather remarkably having failed to play a significant role on any of our trips except on a couple of warm days in Maine. For nearly all of our camping out I have used an unnetted Appalachian Mountain Club tent with perfect comfort.

Two other questions we have been asked repeatedly all through the South: "You-all get paid for doing this, don't you?" and, "Are you working for the government?" That we should be carrying heavy packs, sticking to the mountain trails, and camping out as we go, doing no hunting along the way, merely for *fun,* is of course completely incomprehensible! All through this region, nearly every man or boy encountered is carrying a gun; most of them say they would not think of venturing into the mountains without one, but except for copious bear droppings in the Smokies and the nearby wail of a bobcat while camping on Silers Bald, our contact with dangerous "varmints" has been absolutely nil.

In conclusion, all I can say is that we have had a grand time doing the trail, and will doubtless be tempted to start out again over some of the relocations when these have been completed. For there seems to be little danger of the Appalachian Trail ever becoming static. Not only will there always be the problem of upkeep, but major and minor re-routings are certain to be live questions for a long time yet. Portions of the trail that we have done are already practically obsolete, as for instance the Dead River route between Pierce Pond and Mt. Bigelow in Maine, and across the Housatonic from the washed-out Flanders Bridge in Connecticut, while others will soon become so. There used to be an idea that the human body is completely renewed about once every seven years; perhaps something of the same sort will hold for the Appalachian Trail!

If the aphorism is ever true that every human institution is but the lengthened shadow of one man, it certainly is so of the Appalachian Trail, only here we must say, of two men, not concurrently, but successively: Benton MacKaye, whose far-sighted vision and imagination conceived it, and Myron Avery, whose astounding energy and enthusiasm have transformed the Vision into Reality, and are maintaining it as such. To these men must go in unstinted measure the gratitude and appreciation of all those who have derived health and pleasure from hiking the Appalachian Trail or who shall do so throughout the years to come.

Earl Shaffer: Pioneer Through Hiker

Started at MT. OGLETHORPE on April 4, 1948
Finished at MT. KATAHDIN on August 5, 1948

Started at MT. KATAHDIN on July 19, 1965
Finished at SPRINGER MOUNTAIN on October 25, 1965

When Earl Shaffer set out to walk the entire Appalachian Trail *in one trip* he was undertaking a feat that many thought was impossible. It was 1948 and the trail had been in existence for 11 years. During those years no more than six or seven persons had walked its entire length, and each of them had done so by a series of comparatively short hikes with intervals of rest between the hikes. No one, as far as was known, had even attempted to do the trail all at once. It was generally felt that the 2,000-mile Appalachian Trail was too long and too difficult for such a hike.

Psychologically, Earl was well prepared to attempt this feat. He had served 4½ years in the army, much of the time in the Pacific. Now that World War II had ended he wanted to spend some time in the wilderness alone. In preparation for his hike Earl took exercises based in part on jujitsu training. He credited this preparation and abstinence from tobacco and alcohol as factors in his ability to meet the rigors of the Appalachians.

His clothing consisted of mountain cloth trousers, a U.S. Navy turtleneck jersey, a Marine Corps poncho, a rain hat, a long-sleeved shirt, T-shirts, part-wool socks, and moccasin boots with nine-inch tops. Earl chose the high tops because they gave extra protection against snakebite. The one pair of boots lasted for the entire 2,000 miles.

Earl began his hike with a small tent, but the weight was discouraging—really lightweight tents were not available at that time—and he soon mailed it home. If a storm came up at night, he would plug the head opening of the poncho with his rain hat and use sticks to support the poncho as a shelter cloth; sometimes the poncho would serve all day as a raincoat and all night as a shelter. Before sending the tent home he stripped it of its largest zipper and attached the zipper to his blanket, which had been trimmed down to fit his body like a mummy sleeping bag. A burlap sack proved useful to hold dry leaves for a bed, to isolate the fire-blackened cookpots from the rest of the gear in his pack, and to warm his feet on frosty nights.

On his first trip Earl's cooking kit was large for a solo hiker of otherwise Spartan tastes. Besides a cup and a spoon he carried a dish, two nested kettles of about two quarts capacity each, and a stainless steel frying pan. The day was begun with an oatmeal or cornmeal porridge sweetened with brown sugar. At noontime he panbaked bread over a fire. His recipe was essentially the same as for biscuits[1] except for the substitution of cornmeal for two-thirds of the flour. Whole wheat flour was preferred. On occasion, for variety, the mixture was two parts cornmeal and one part oatmeal. Honey, jam, or brown sugar were eaten with the bread.

Other staples were dried soups (particularly pea soup), potatoes, macaroni, peanut butter, dried or evaporated milk, and raisins. Food was bought at stores along the route. Canned meats and fruits were consumed on the spot, but seldom carried because of their weight. Beans were avoided. Earl had been forced to subsist on beans for a brief period on an island in the Coral Sea, and the memory was still painful.

Equipment was carried in a rucksack from which Earl had removed the large outside pocket and all but the most necessary straps. A hand ax and flat canteen were strapped to the rucksack. Nothing was carried on his belt. The trail guidebooks and maps that he had ordered were somehow mislaid in the mails. Without them he often had to use compass, logic, and instinct to find his way. The trail was in bad condition because work on it had been curtailed in wartime: entire sections were almost hidden by nettles, poison ivy, and briers; logging had destroyed blazed trees and left acres of slash to be navigated; signs were missing or undecipherable; blowdowns by the thousands lay on the path. When Earl lost the trail he would bushwhack until he had picked it up again.

It took Earl 124 days to hike from Mt. Oglethorpe to Mt. Katahdin. He averaged 16.5 trail miles a day, but because of detours and miles of walking off the trail for supplies, his actual daily mileage was probably 18 or 19. This was a remarkable feat, considering the condition

[1] A typical recipe for biscuits calls for 2 cups flour, 3 teaspoons double-acting baking powder, 1 teaspoon salt, 4 tablespoons shortening, and ¾ to ¾ cup milk or milk and water.

of the trail. The success of his solitary expedition was carried to the newspapers of America by the wire services. It caused a great stir in hiking circles. It was inevitable that someone would someday make a continuous through hike, but Earl Shaffer was the one who had the fortitude and imagination to do it first.

Seventeen years later, when he was 45, Earl hiked the trail again. This time he reversed his direction of travel. On July 19, 1965, as the rain came down in buckets, he started at Mt. Katahdin in Maine. Exactly 99 days later, on October 25, he finished in freezing weather on Springer Mountain in Georgia. He had averaged 20.5 miles a day and cut five weeks off his previous time. In addition to being the first person to walk the trail in one continuous journey, Earl was also the first person to walk the entire trail in both directions.

Earl found the trail to be much better on his second hike. There were fewer logs across the trail, less undergrowth to fight through, and generally good marking. There were dozens of new trail shelters and numerous hikers. Food and gear on the second trip were basically the same, but his canteen now was of plastic instead of metal and a plastic tarp had replaced his poncho. He found the plastic to be adequate as a cape during rain and thought it provided better shelter at night. Cooking utensils had been reduced to two stainless steel pans, a spatula, and an aluminum spoon. Pack weight ran about 30 pounds, including camera and hatchet.

Earl Shaffer described his second hike as "grueling." The three-mile-an-hour pace he set for himself was one factor, but another was that he found chasing Autumn to be a lot less pleasant than walking with Spring. In the fall the water sources tend to dry up, and Earl was often thirsty. Fewer birds cheerfully interrupted the silence, and blooming flowers were rare. The only advantage Earl found in north-to-south travel was the comparative scarcity of insects.

Editor's note: Earl Shaffer completed a third thru-hike in 1998 at the age of 79, fifty years after his original ground-breaking hike. Only his first two hikes are mentioned in the chapter in this book. For the fascinating story of Earl's first hike in 1948, read the now classic *Walking With Spring*.

Grandma Gatewood: A Legend Along the Appalachian Trail

Started at MT. OGLETHORPE on May 3, 1955
Finished at MT. KATAHDIN on September 25, 1955

Started at MT. OGLETHORPE on April 27, 1957
Finished at MT. KATAHDIN on September 16, 1957

Started at MT. KATAHDIN in 1954
Finished at RAINBOW LAKE, MAINE, in 1964

Mrs. Emma Gatewood, better known along the trail as Grandma Gatewood, is probably the best-known of all the hikers who have completed the 2,000 miles of the Appalachian Trail. Almost every through hiker has his favorite story about Grandma, which he has heard along the trail. She is the kind of personality about whom legends grow. The following story was obtained in an interview in January, 1973:

Grandma Gatewood climbed Mt. Katahdin for the first time in July, 1954. At the time she was in her late sixties, had born 11 children, was about five feet two inches in height, weighed around 155 pounds, and wore sneakers for hiking. Mt. Katahdin was the first mountain she had ever climbed, and this was her first extended hike.

When she reached the summit she put on a black wool sweater from the denim bag in which she carried her belongings and ate a lunch of raisins while she counted the lakes and ponds below. When she reached 100, she gave up counting, even though other ponds could be seen on the horizon.

At dusk Grandma was back at the foot of the mountain. She had hiked 10.5 miles, including 8,326 feet of rise and descent. People at the campground congratulated her, for many hikers who start out to climb Katahdin never make it to the top. A young couple invited her to share broiled hot dogs and pea beans baked with molasses and salt pork. Would she want a lift to Millinocket in the morning? No,

Grandma explained, she intended to hike "a ways" down the Appalachian Trail.

By first light she was gone. That day the trail was fairly level, and she did about 14 miles. She spent the night in a stand of birch near a brook. In the morning the trail took her up the Rainbow Ledges and down among blueberry bushes to the shore of Rainbow Lake. Here she came to a weather-rotted sign at a fork in the trail, could not decipher it, and took the wrong turning. She didn't realize that she must follow the white paint blazes which mark the Appalachian Trail. By afternoon her "trail" had disintegrated into wild animal paths in the vicinity of a fair-sized pond, and Grandma Gatewood knew that she was lost.

For a minute she experienced a surge of panic, but a mother who has raised 11 children is experienced in panics, great and small. Grandma Gatewood took a firm grip on herself. "If I'm lost, I'm lost," she told herself. "But it's not hurting any yet."

In the motionless air the blackflies were becoming bothersome. She tied a scarf around her head and made a pillow of the denim bag. Then, rolled up in a woolen blanket, she tried to sleep on a dry flat rock that protruded above the damp grass from which insects were swarming. During the night it rained, and at daybreak she was dismayed to find that a lens in her glasses was badly cracked. Apparently the glasses had been stepped on during the rain. While patching the lens with a Band-Aid, she remembered the rowboat she had seen yesterday, suspended upside down on ropes between trees. She remembered that it was near the shoreline of the pond. She began to retrace her steps and in a short while she arrived at the upside-down rowboat.

On first coming to the rowboat she was jubilant, thinking that since she had been able to backtrack this far she might be able to keep on backtracking to where she had lost the trail. At about that time she became conscious of the drone of an airplane, and soon a small floatplane came into sight overhead. It was flying low. Presently another small floatplane appeared, skimmed the trees, and vanished.

Grandma was certain that the planes were hunting for her, although she had no idea why she should be missed. Later she was to learn that a fire warden at a camp on Rainbow Lake had seen her as she hiked through. He had radioed the camp eight miles away on Nahmakanta Lake and asked for a report when she arrived. When Grandma did not show up, a search was started.

At the pond Grandma kindled a fire. A couple of hours later, as the floatplanes flew over again, she sprinkled water on the blaze from a rusting tin can she had found. She had remembered from her reading that during the daylight hours smoke is more easily caught sight of than fire. However, the planes did not see the smoke.

Grandma had read that a lost person should stay put and wait for rescue, so she waited and kept the fire going. She finished her small stock of peanuts and chipped beef. A plane was heard along toward evening. She threw wood on the fire till it roared and then drenched it with water. A spout of smoke rose above the trees, but the plane did not approach. That night, bedded down under the upside-down rowboat, Grandma was scarcely troubled by a light drizzle. The black-flies, however, persisted in their attacks until well after dark.

Next morning she ate a dozen raisins, all the food that was left. She looked for wood sorrel, whose leaves could be eaten, and teaberry, which could be steeped to make a refreshing drink. Both plants were familiar from her childhood, but neither was in evidence here. It was too early for raspberries, chokeberries, blueberries, and cran-berries that are plentiful in Maine in season.

Somewhere out of sight aircraft engines could be heard. Grandma was hungry, and became even hungrier as she realized that until she was rescued there would be nothing to eat. She thought the matter over. "If I'm going to starve, Lord," she said, "I might as well do it someplace else as do it here."

Having made her decision, Grandma packed her belongings and walked away from the upside-down rowboat. In a little while she happened upon a barely perceptible aisle in the forest. She followed it, and in a few hundred yards the aisle became wider and showed signs of recent use. Then, without warning, the aisle burst onto a lake. Cabins were clustered at the edge of the water, and the scene was somehow familiar. She was back at Rainbow Lake.

She saw a knot of men consulting a map. As Grandma approached, blue denim bag across her shoulder, they recognized her.

One of the men put a coffee pot on the stove. Grandma was given a wooden chair at a table covered with a checkered oilcloth. Through the window she watched a plane taxi to the landing dock. A man in the uniform of the Maine Forest Service stepped out of the plane and came to the cabin. For a moment he studied Grandma in silence.

"Welcome to Rainbow Lake," he said at last. "You've been lost."

"Not lost," Grandma said, "just misplaced."

The ordeal had undermined Grandma Gatewood's confidence in herself. From Katahdin's peak to Rainbow Lake is 24 miles, barely more than a hundredth part of the Appalachian Trail, so when the wardens of the Maine Forest Service suggested with considerable forcefulness that she give up hiking in the Maine wilderness until she was more experienced, she agreed. She returned to Ohio on the bus.

Grandma Gatewood had learned about the Appalachian Trail two or three years before from a magazine article. She remembered the description as being on the idyllic side: a smoothed footway with easy grades, a yard-wide garden path carefully blazed and manicured, with plenty of signs. She resolved to hike it all. She had always wanted to do something notable, and no woman had ever hiked the Appalachian Trail in one continuous journey. The length of the longest footpath in the world held an irresistible appeal for her. Her imagination was fired. It was a challenge worthy of the pioneer women of the last century, some of whom she had known well. She herself had come of a pioneer family, born October 25, 1887, one of 15 children, on a farm in Ohio. Most of her life had been lived on farms, where she had hoed corn, raked hay, chopped tobacco, and raised four sons and seven daughters of her own.

For her hike she had fashioned a bag from denim. In it she carried any clothing not being worn; food such as bouillon cubes, chipped beef, raisins, peanuts, powdered milk, and salt; items of first aid like adhesive tape, Band-Aids, and Mercurochrome; hairpins, safety pins, needles, thread, buttons, and matches in a plastic matchcase.

Her basic outer costume consisted of hat, skirt, blouse, and sneakers. She wore a single pair of socks, sometimes cotton, sometimes woolen. At night she would pull on a second pair of socks. She also had a scarf, a sweater, a jacket, and a light wool blanket.

Grandma had been a little cowed by the events in Maine; she knew it and she hated it. She traveled to California to visit with relatives, but as the months slipped by the pull of the trail became strong. One day in spring she boarded a plane bound for Atlanta, and a week later she signed the trail register on the summit of Mt. Oglethorpe in Georgia.

Her hiking gear had been increased by a flashlight, a Swiss army knife with nine miniature tools, a teaspoon, two plastic eight-ounce baby bottles for water, a rain hat and rain cape, and a plastic curtain. She had sewn a tail on the rain hat to shield her neck. The rain cape, made from two yards of plastic sheeting, protected herself and her denim bag when she walked in the rain. It was used as a ground cloth when she rested in some damp place or slept on the ground. The plastic curtain was used for shelter when it rained. A straw hat began the trip, but was lost when a stray wind blew it into Tallulah Gorge on the Georgia border. Other hats followed—a fisherman's cap, a man's felt hat, another hat with a green celluloid visor, and a knitted stocking cap. None lasted long before succumbing to some vagary of the trail, like being forgotten at a rest stop or falling into a mountain torrent. Grandma's pack seldom weighed as much as 20 pounds; 14 to 17 pounds were more usual.

A chilling fog was shrouding the famed rhododendron thickets on Roan Mountain on the North Carolina–Tennessee line when she arrived there at the end of a June day. She heated rocks in a fire, laid them on the grass, and went to sleep on top of the rocks, wrapped in her blanket. The rocks gave off warmth for hours and the night was tolerable. During a cold snap on another mountain she pulled a wide board from the ruins of a tumbledown cabin and toasted it over the embers. This became her bed, and if the board rather quickly lost its heat the night had at least begun cozily.

Like many a hiker before her, she made the discovery that picnic tables in forest and park campsites could be used as beds if the ground was soaked, and they were no harder than the floors of the lean-tos. She did not depend on lean-tos much; she was a woman and alone, and sharing such primitive accommodations with chance strangers was not always satisfactory.

Tiny wood mice pulled at her hair as she slept, no doubt regarding the strands as capital homemaking material. She thought of the mice as sources of amusement and company rather than as annoyances.

As she hiked through the southern hill country, Grandma soon learned that a stop at a home to inquire about the route or to fill her baby bottles at the hand pump in the yard was likely to make her the object of intense though well-mannered curiosity. She was often invited to stay for the night. While preferring the "company room" for slumber, she wasn't finicky; the hayloft would do nicely.

In Shenandoah National Park a black bear ambled onto the pathway. Its intentions seemed not unfriendly, although it was ambling her way. As the gap between them narrowed, Grandma let go with what she calls "my best holler."

" 'Dig,' I hollered, and he dug."

The episode seemed to release a little extra adrenalin into Grandma's system. Up till then she had been doing from 12 to 16 miles daily, but by nightfall on this particular day she had logged 27 miles.

West Virginia and Maryland sped by under Grandma's sneakered feet. By now she had switched to men's sneakers, having decided that the soles of women's sneakers were too light and thin. The rocks of Pennsylvania, which on the narrow ridgetops stand on end like the fins of the dinosaurs, put her choice of footwear to a stern test. In its 200 miles of trail, Pennsylvania accounted for about one and a half pairs of the five pairs of sneakers she was to wear out on her journey. Usually a pair of sneakers was good for from 400 to 500 miles.

For almost three months she had managed without utensils other than jackknife, teaspoon, and baby bottles. At a spring in New Jersey she picked up an abandoned tin cup and liked it so well that she never hiked without it afterwards.

Where the trail precariously negotiated a cliff on Kittatinny Ridge, a blacksnake practically stood on its tail in a fighting attitude, but Grandma Gatewood knew all about blacksnakes from her years on the farm. She simply waited until the creature subsided and fled into a crevice.

In New York a rattlesnake made the mortal mistake of shaking its tail at Grandma. And near the summer community of Oscawana Corners a German shepherd leapt a hedge and nipped the upper calf of her leg. As the skin was hardly broken, she painted the teeth marks with Merthiolate and hiked on, but more warily. When she ran into a patch of nettles she changed her mind about wearing a skirt on the trail. Dungarees became her usual garb after that.

In the Mohawk State Forest in Connecticut a bobcat circled around and "squeaked infernally" while Grandma was snacking from a can of sardines. "If you come too close I'll crack you," she warned. The bobcat kept its distance.

Coming down that choice little precipice in the Berkshires which Yankee humor has named Jug End, Grandma Gatewood slipped on the rain-wet slope. She grabbed at a tree limb; it broke and she slid hard against a rock. For some minutes she was unable to move and wondered if a shoulder was paralyzed, but the numbness ebbed and she went on.

In Vermont the porcupine thrives. Its flesh is said to be as toothsome as pork or veal. On learning this fact, Grandma cornered a porcupine and gave it a crack with a pole. Mindful of the quills, she skinned it with caution, then spitted the carcass over a fire. The flesh smelled lovely as it roasted, but the first forkful was another matter. "My imagination got away on me," Grandma said. "All at once the porcupine meat filled my mouth. I just couldn't swallow."

She had been carrying a walking stick, flourishing it at hostile dogs and using it as a third leg to ford streams; in the White Mountains she found it of particular help in descending barren ledges where her legs weren't long enough to make the step down without extra support.

As Grandma hiked, word of her progress ran ahead. She had become news, and reporters from local papers popped up at the road crossings to get her story. Heretofore only the children of her children had known her as "Grandma." Now "Grandma" was to become a fixed part of her name—and a part of the vocabulary of the Appalachian Trail.

The Maine Forest Service was on the alert as Grandma crossed the state line. If the service was astonished at seeing her again, after having issued a virtual writ of banishment, it managed to keep the emotion to itself, and was ready when she reached the Kennebec River at Caratunk. Waiting with a canoe to take her over were Chief Forest Warden Isaac Harris and Warden Bradford Pease. A dozen miles in the rain had soaked Grandma to the skin, and they brought her in some haste to Sterling's Hotel where Mrs. Sterling dried her out. A few days to the north Game Warden Francis Cyr rowed her across Nesowadnehunk Stream, thus sparing her the 10-mile detour made necessary by the recent collapse of the cable bridge.

On Mt. Katahdin Grandma signed the trail register while the low clouds hugged the summit and sprayed her with icy mist. She was wearing a plaid lumberman's jacket she had found back along the trail. The date was September 25.

When she returned to Katahdin Stream Campground, limping from a sore knee that had plagued her for days, she was met by Mrs. Dean Chase, a correspondent for the Associated Press. Mrs. Chase drove her to Millinocket, where she became the guest of the Chamber of Commerce and was interviewed by a reporter from *Sports Illustrated.* Grandma's time on the trail had been 145 or 146 days, depending upon whether the starting and ending days are counted as half-days or as full days. Exactly one month later she turned 68.

Grandma Gatewood was the first woman to walk the complete distance of the Appalachian Trail alone as well as the first woman to walk it in one continuous trip, straight through from one end to the other.[1] It was an exploit that only five others, all men, had ac-

[1] The first woman to complete the Appalachian Trail was Mary Kilpatrick of Philadelphia. She accomplished the feat by a series of trips with her husband and friends. She finished in 1939. The second woman credited with completing the trail was Mildred Lamb, also of Philadelphia. Her trip, made in 1952 with Dick Lamb, was made south-to-north from Mt. Oglethorpe to the Susquehanna River and then north-to-south from Mt. Katahdin to the Susquehanna, and included extended trips on side trails. Emma Gatewood is thus the third woman to have finished the Appalachian Trail, according to the records of the Appalachian Trail Conference. However, she is the *first* woman to walk the complete distance alone, as well as the first woman to walk it in one continuous trip.

complished at that time. Her weight had dropped to 120 pounds, 30 pounds lighter than when she started, and her feet had enlarged one size in width, from 8C to 8D.

The goal had been achieved, but if there was a glow of gratification, there was also the letdown. She told the news media that she had "had enough" and went home to Ohio and started a scrapbook.

Only 17 months passed before Grandma Gatewood was back on Mt. Oglethorpe's peak, poised for another go on the trail. From April 27 till September 16, from spring through the summer and into the autumn of 1957, she trod the trail energetically, to the delight of the manufacturer of Keds (six pairs) and of the many acquaintances on farms and in rural settlements along the way who marveled to see the 69-year-old lady once more.

Her second through journey was made in 142 days, at a daily rate of 14.5 miles. It was a trifle speedier and "no tougher" than before. She was the first person, man or woman, to hike the whole trail for the second time. (Three other persons have now hiked the trail more than once. Charles Ebersole and Earl Shaffer have done it twice. Another woman, Dorothy Laker, has walked it three times.—ED.) As always, there were days when she had to steel herself to continue. Aside from the love for the woods and the exhilaration that was hers on the trail, Mrs. Gatewood's reason for the second trip was simply to "see some of the things I missed the first time." As on previous trips, she didn't keep her family posted on her whereabouts, and was not nagged by the thought that she should dispatch a score of postcards from every country post office near the trail. Nor did her family worry; Grandma knew how to take care of herself.

When she wasn't invited to potluck in some mountain home, she was often content to dine upon the food that others had left behind in shelters. Certainly she didn't carry much food. Her pack of fewer than 20 pounds was probably the lightest burden ever taken on a through hike of the Appalachian Trail. She cared nothing for tea or coffee, and on the trail seldom cooked meals or even heated up prepared food. Even at home she had been out of the habit of cooking for several years. "Cold food is good enough for me," she said. "People eat things out of the refrigerator that are colder than just cold and think nothing of it."

Sometimes a fortnight would pass without a campfire. One of the few meals she cooked on the trail was a pancake supper. When the rafters of a lean-to in Maine yielded a box of Aunt Jemima pancake mix and some bacon she scoured off a piece of sheet iron that had been rusting in the weeds and greased it. The pancakes were turned with a piece of wood. There were even a few cold pancakes left over for breakfast.

Sassafras is a common plant in the Appalachians. She was fond of chewing its rich green leaves for their spicy taste. She also sampled ramps, or wild leeks, but judged them to be gamy.

The year after her second completion of the trail, Grandma began a series of walks that, added to her abortive attempt of 1954 in Maine (Mt. Katahdin to Rainbow Lake), were to lead to the completion of the trail for a third time. In 1958 she covered the distance from Duncannon, Pennsylvania, to North Adams, Massachusetts. The summer of 1960 saw her hiking between Palmerton, Pennsylvania, and Sherburne Pass, Vermont, and between Springer Mountain, Georgia (which had replaced Mt. Oglethorpe as the southern anchor of the trail), and Deep Gap, North Carolina. She made it from Duncannon back to Deep Gap in 1963. In a jaded moment she announced to her kinfolk (neither her husband nor her children were trail enthusiasts) that she was going to hang up her sneakers. The next summer, however, she laced them back on and in 1964, at the age of 77, finished what she had begun 10 years earlier by walking from Sherburne Pass to Rainbow Lake. She continued on to the top of Katahdin and then gingerly walked the Knife-Edge Trail, where in places the hiker, by merely leaning too far to either side, can risk a fall of 1,500 feet. Grandma Gatewood also tested her septuagenarian agility on other footpaths. There were the Long Trail in Vermont, parts of the Horseshoe and Baker Trails in Pennsylvania, the Chesapeake and Ohio Canal Towpath Trail in Maryland, and others.

Grandma always hiked by herself, rarely going with others for more than a mile or two, although one young lad, out on his first backpacking trip, kept her company for two days. She was comfortable only at her own pace, which included frequent pauses for rest, but was steady and generally began at five-thirty or six in the morning and kept on till three or four in the afternoon.

On none of her forays did she carry a sleeping bag, a tent, or a regular backpack with a frame, but remained faithful to her blanket (and didn't always take that), her rain cape and plastic curtain, and her homemade shoulder bag. Later she did add straps to the bag. Many times she was wet through from the plentiful Appalachian rain.

She used no guidebooks except once in New England, when a hiker who was leaving the trail presented her with his well-thumbed manual. Once she tried hiking in leather boots, but they gave her the only

Grandma Gatewood.
Photo by Elmer L.
Onstott.

blister of her career, and she was glad to get back into sneakers. Sneakers are not reckoned as suitable footwear for hiking by most people, and how her feet survived remains a mystery. A Boy Scout leader summed it up by saying, "Grandma, you've broken all the rules for hiking—but you got there just the same."

NOTE: Grandma Gatewood passed away on June 5, 1973. She was 85 years of age and had lived a full and colorful life. In addition to her hikes on the Appalachian Trail, Grandma Gatewood walked the Oregon Trail in 1959, at the age of 72, as a part of the 100th anniversary of the Oregon Trail.—ED.

The Appalachian Trail and I

By Max Bender, Ph.D.

Started in MAINE in 1939
Finished in NEW HAMPSHIRE in 1963

My first experience on the Appalachian Trail dates back to a two-week vacation in the early fall of 1939. My original idea had been to explore the Allagash Wilderness in Maine, but with the Maine requirement of a guide representing a prohibitive expense, I decided to go to Cyphers Sporting Camp at Ambajejus Lake, which is west of Millinocket in the Penobscot West Branch watershed. From this camp I made a three-day trip up the West Branch to the Appalachian Trail, and on the top of Mt. Katahdin and return. The view from Mt. Katahdin was nonexistent due to cumulus clouds. I was disappointed because I wanted to see the broken-mirror effect caused by the lakes, as described by Thoreau. (A few years later I did have the pleasure of this view.)

Since that time it has been a section of the Appalachian Trail here and there, year after year. At first I had no intention of covering the entire trail, but gradually I became a full-fledged Appalachian Trail devotee.

In 1940, while on an American Youth Hosteling trip, I climbed Mt. Greylock in the Berkshires via the Appalachian Trail. In September of 1941 I left Boston, where I had been born and brought up, and came to the New York metropolitan area to do defense work. I have been here ever since. As a result of all the wilderness country near the New York metropolitan area—the Ramapos, the Hudson Highlands, the Palisades Interstate Park, the Kittatinnies, the New Jersey Pine Barrens, the foothills of the Taconics in the Westchester area, and so on, with hundreds of miles of trails accessible, including some 200 miles of the Appalachian Trail, my interest in hiking increased a great deal.

My second backpacking trip on the Appalachian Trail occurred in the early forties and was combined with a bicycle trip in the Presidential Range of the White Mountains in New Hampshire. Leaving the bike in Crawford Notch, I took the Crawford Path up to the Appalachian Mountain Club's Lakes-of-the-Clouds Hut, stayed there two nights, and came back to Crawford Notch via the Webster Cliff Trail. It was my first experience in these mountains, and my first hike above timberline. I was impressed with what I saw in the Mt. Washington area during my three days of walking. It was fun to be hiking above thunderstorms, and I had a breathtaking view of Crawford Notch. The notch was filled with clouds as I walked along Webster Cliffs. Suddenly the clouds lifted and I had a dazzling view of the valley below, framed in mountains and clouds.

My first real Appalachian Trail backpacking experience occurred during a period of a week and a half in October, 1945. It was in the middle of a three-week vacation in which the first part was spent in bicycling and youth hosteling in Tennessee. Here are some excerpts from the diary I kept on this trip:

WEDNESDAY, OCTOBER 3. At Hot Springs I bought grub, left the bike with the ranger, and started off on the Appalachian Trail late in the afternoon. The trail goes up over Deer Park Mountain (2,600 feet) with a view of Hot Springs and the French Broad River. At the lean-to at Gragg Gap I cooked a meal and then went to bed and had a nice sleep.

THURSDAY, OCTOBER 4. Up early. Nice heavy breakfast. Went down Deer Park Mountain to Garenflo Gap to site of old abandoned farm, then up over Bluff Mountain (4,686 feet). It was a rugged climb. I puffed some and stopped here and there to ease the pounding of my heart. Then on to Kale Gap where, while bending over my map, I heard a growl and looked up to see a mountaineer and his dog. It was Elbert Wyatt, who lived in the gap below. He offered me the hospitality of his home, saying that the next lean-to at Walnut Mountain had a leaky roof and bad bunks. He also said it was going to rain, so I accepted his invitation.

Elbert lived with a young son. As the weather was raw, he made a fire and took pains to make me comfortable. Elbert had been married, had 10 or 12 kids, and then separated. His present philosophical attitude toward marriage was "nix." He had a cow and chickens and a vegetable garden and churned his own butter. He seemed to produce all the food he needed except flour and coffee, which he had to buy. He prepared a fine meal: milk, Irish potatoes, eggs, roasting ears

with very tasty butter, and corn bread. "Hep yo'self!" Elbert said. I
did. I ate and ate, and after supper I met some of Elbert's friends.

FRIDAY, OCTOBER 5. It did rain quite hard during the night. We had
a swell breakfast: three eggs, coffee, milk, biscuits and butter, and
corn bread. As I was leaving Elbert gave me food to take along.

On Walnut Mountain it started to rain again. The lean-to was in
bad shape and I began to appreciate how kind this fine mountaineer-
ing gentleman had been. There were horses on Walnut Mountain
(4,280 feet). Lemon Gap was a positively beautiful greensward with
grazing cattle. There were vistas of mountains and valleys and roads
and woods and fields. The greenness was an unusual lemon yellow-
green. The scenery was so beautiful that I shall never forget it.

I followed the dirt road past Max Patch Mountain and the lodge
where the American Youth Hostel used to be, and then climbed Max
Patch (4,629 feet) which was a bald and used to have an airfield on
it. Now bulls and cows were grazing there. I was scared of the bulls
but they moved out of the way. There was a fine view, even though
it was raining slightly. The clouds, which had been high, were getting
lower and the rain was increasing. I lost the trail going to Brown Gap
but finally found it. Then at Brown Gap I lost the trail to Deep Gap,
but found it again. The lean-to there was OK. I built a fire and had
a good meal in the rain, then a sound sleep. It rained that night and
on into the morning.

SATURDAY, OCTOBER 6. After a good breakfast I hiked to Turkey
Gap and up over Snowbird (4,263 feet). It was foggy so there were
no views. It was grueling, but good hiking nevertheless. I met a mountaineer and had his company for about half of the way; he shared
his soda crackers with me. We drank at Wildcat Spring and he found
some chestnuts (surviving American chestnuts) and chinquapin nuts
(dwarf chestnuts), which I enjoyed. We also found gooseberries.

I came to Waterville on the Big Pigeon River. The power plant here
is fed from a dam in the river some seven miles upstream. I had a
good meal at the boardinghouse for 75 cents. Meat and vegetables,
juice, cake, milk, honey in the comb, biscuits—all I wanted to eat. I
went a mile down the road to the village of Mt. Sterling, where I
stayed overnight. I picked up a little grub, just bread and condensed
milk. It was a small village and there was not much food to be had.

SUNDAY, OCTOBER 7. I had a heavy breakfast in the morning and
entered the Great Smoky Mountains National Park at Davenport Gap.
The clouds cleared off to afford views from Mt. Cammerer (5,025

feet). The views, over a full 360 degrees, were well worth the stiff climb. There was a beautiful blue sky. The terrain was rugged and rocky. The Appalachian Trail along here represented a fine job of grading and leveling and building up.

I was studying my map at Cosby Knob Trail Lean-to when Norman Bergendahl of Chicago, Illinois, came up. He had hiked the same trail that I had hiked from Mt. Sterling.

MONDAY, OCTOBER 8. I decided to go with Norman for a while. Some of the highest peaks were ahead—Old Black, Mt. Guyot, Tri-Corner Knob, and Eagle Rocks. There was beautiful scenery far and near, with rugged cliffs and rocks, broad slopes, mossy woods, ever-greens, and all kinds of trees and berries. We made it to Pecks Corner Lean-to.

TUESDAY, OCTOBER 9. It was cold last night; it rained and the temperature went down to 24°F. according to Norman's thermometer. There was frost on the fir trees and evergreens and on the ground this morning.

The view from Laurel Top was breathtaking with carpetlike ankle-deep moss, colorful alpine growth, hedges, and firs. Mt. Kephart and Charlies Bunion were rugged and breathtaking. The foliage was just turning color. All through this territory we found luscious berries of the blueberry-huckleberry species. Early in the morning the berries were partly frozen and tasted delicious. With respect to our camping and outdoor prowess a favorite joke developed. It involved Horace Kephart's book *Camping and Woodcraft* and how *he* would have done what we were doing. At Newfound Gap we saw people for the first time since Mt. Sterling.

WEDNESDAY, OCTOBER 10. We made it to Clingmans Dome, which at 6,643 feet is the second highest peak east of the Mississippi. As it was a clear day, the views were fine. Now the scenery changed; we were coming to the balds and the trees were deciduous hardwood. There was not so much evergreen, but lots of beech. We came to Silers Bald toward the end of the day; Norman wanted to take pic-tures of the sunset so we decided to sleep on top of the bald that night. Norman did not cook his meals, so I went down to the lean-to to cook. It was difficult to start a fire with beech wood but I had my supper in time to get back to the summit for the sunset. From this grassy treeless summit there was a wonderful panoramic view with beautiful red clouds. The east was purple, with peak rising on peak, including the highest of the Smokies—Clingmans Dome and Mt. Le

Conte. To the west the peaks diminished in altitude but presented a highly interesting array of balds and wooded tops with transverse ridges. Visible in the north was the broad expanse of the Tennessee River Valley with its many TVA reservoirs and towns. Mountain ranges occupied the immediate foreground and background. To the south, range after range of mountains eventually joined with the Blue Ridge. Nestling in the valleys could be seen large expanses of water, parts of the Fontana and Tapoco reservoirs. We slept in the open, on the grass. There was quite a frost that night, and we woke up every two hours or so. There were meteors and a beautiful moonset and in the star-studded sky I could see the various constellations.

THURSDAY, OCTOBER 11. We got up in time to see the sunrise. To the south there was a silvery bank of clouds in the valleys, with peaks showing through as islands. There was a quarter of an inch of frost on our ponchos, and with the frost making the grass slippery, I found I had slid downhill about 10 yards during the night. We had breakfast and were on our way after studying map and compass. We hiked through woods to Buckeye Gap, and then on to Cold Spring Knob and Chestnut Bald. It was quite a grueling hike. We came to Sugar Tree Gap and then to Maple Sugar Gap with its immense trees. There were cherry, oak, birch, sugar maple, and others we could not identify. There were loads of chestnuts to be had from the saplings that had come up since the blight. We made it to the top of Thunderhead after a strenuous climb and had a nice view of Le Conte and Clingmans to the east, with both balds and forested mountains in the foreground. The views north and south into the valleys were beautiful. It was nice in the sunset, even though we were tired.

FRIDAY, OCTOBER 12. Little Bald, Big Abrams Gap, Devils Tater Patch, Ekaneetlee Gap where the Indians used to trail through, more gaps and knobs, and on to the fine Gregory Bald Lean-to. Dead chestnut made a real good fire and there was a wonderful spring. The day's hike has been through interesting terrain and vegetation.

SATURDAY, OCTOBER 13. Breakfast, and a shave after seven days. Norman and I parted company here. He was to hike in the lowlands. I was going to Deals Gap and on south to Tapoco. There I would take a bus to Knoxville, and then another bus to Hot Springs, where I would pick up my bicycle.

My next Appalachian Trail backpacking trip was for eight days or so; it took place soon after I became engaged to be married. The wedding was to be a month and a half later (in September, 1947). I was tired from my work and studies towards my Ph.D., and who knows?—I may have been scared of getting married. May, my betrothed, was not inclined to go. While she loves the country, woods, nature, and scenery, she draws a line at the strenuous activity of backpacking and puffing up mountains.

Accordingly, I took off with good wishes from May, as well as remarks from friends to the effect that this would be my last hiking splurge. My future mother-in-law raised the question: "How is it that a man engaged to be married in only a month and a half can run off into the woods, leaving his sweetheart alone?" Oh, well. . . .

I took the train to Hanover, New Hampshire, and walked to Pinkham Notch, enjoying a mental rest and many interesting experiences. When I came back I was relaxed and probably much better company than I would have been otherwise.

That is the way I hiked the Appalachian Trail: solo one-week hikes once a year in Maine, Pennsylvania, Virginia, West Virginia, Tennessee, North Carolina, and Georgia; long weekend hikes in Pennsylvania, New England, New Jersey, New York; one-day, two-day, three-day, four-day hikes, alone or with comrades from my hiking club, the Woodland Trail Walkers, whenever I could get away. One of my best friends was Paul Reynolds, now deceased, with whom I enjoyed a fine companionship and with whom I did much of the trail in Pennsylvania and New England. Herb Hiller was another comrade. Herb has done the whole Appalachian Trail. We hiked together for a week in Maine and spent some time in the Virginia–West Virginia area.

My final miles completing the Appalachian Trail were accomplished when Paul and I set foot on U.S. Route 2 in New Hampshire, coming south from the Mahoosuc Mountain Range. With other Woodland Trail Walkers who were waiting for us, we made a great ceremony of kissing the road, taking photographs, sharing a crust of dry bread, and pinning on paper badges! I am not much as a diary keeper but it seems that this was in 1963.

Why Did I Walk the Trail?

My bout with the Appalachian Trail, or was it my embracement, represents many fulfillments. The following are not in any particular order of importance:

ACCOMPLISHMENT. There is an obvious satisfaction in being able to surprise people by saying that one did the trail "en toto," but in my judgment this is a minor satisfaction compared to others, which include:

1. Navigating the trail without ever becoming lost. There were many points where I couldn't find trail markings and had to explore, but at no time did I consider myself lost.

2. Providing myself with food, water, clothing, and shelter, but at the same time carrying a pack of minimum weight which allowed me to enjoy the hiking.

3. Climbing to the summits of a vast array of mountains of different shapes, heights, and topographical nature.

4. Walking across whole states or at least large sections of states as in Maine, New Hampshire, Massachusetts, Connecticut, New Jersey, Pennsylvania, Maryland, Virginia, Tennessee, North Carolina, and Georgia.

5. Putting up with hardships brought about by the terrain.

6. The simple fact of survival.

7. The feeling of resourcefulness which came from planning trips, being prepared, and meeting contingencies.

8. Walking a continuous stretch of 2,000 miles.

9. Gamesmanship. I made it a rule to walk every "legal" inch of the trail. Much as children play a game in which no stepping on sidewalk lines or cracks is allowed, I found myself avoiding all shortcuts and refusing to accept rides on roads or through towns. I even felt that I had to walk across every street. My Woodland Trail Walkers friends, seeing me walk around a puddle on one section of trail, argued that I should have gone through it. The matter of what was "legal" and official *vs.* what was permissible *vs.* what was "cheating" was the subject of many a discussion, although we all realized that no one could check on anyone else, and that it was strictly a matter of personal honor.

I could not rest until I had completed the missing links that had developed due to the way in which my hikes were begun and ended, or because of offsets on roads, detours on account of blowdowns, losing the trail, or trail rerouting.

RELAXATION. As much as I enjoy my work, mental relaxation is needed. Hiking, especially in wilderness surroundings, has been the best antidote for me. Just a one-day hike in country not far from New York City, where there are hundreds of miles of woodland trail, does wonders. It has been my practice to spend a solid week of vacation each year in walking, with either full pack or day pack, in an environment that is idyllic, wild, unobtrusive, mountainous, bucolic.

This, I can truly call a vacation. In such surroundings perspective is obtained, and peace and mental rest are the result.

The woods and the wilderness make it easy for me to relate to thoughts of a spiritual or philosophical nature. These feelings are beyond anything denominational, and no need is felt for any formal type of prayer. It seems easier to understand the rationale of man and his creation; his effect on himself and his surroundings, and the effect of his surroundings on him; his ambition or lack of it; and his very complex nature.

FULFILLMENT OF CHILDHOOD DESIRES. It is difficult to figure out exactly what in my youth led to my strong interest in the out-of-doors. Reading about Indians and pioneers in the wilderness was a factor. Movies were instrumental. Perhaps my association with the Boy Scouts played a part. My teachers certainly had an influence. Perhaps it was because my family hardly ever went to the country, or because I was scolded for getting my feet wet. Or it could have been a combination of all these and more. Who knows? In any case, as a boy I developed an acute desire to tramp around, wander, see, explore, travel. I envied the life of a tramp going from town to town, and of the Indian who traveled steadfastly and noiselessly through the forest, leaving scarcely any tracks. How I wanted to see, feel, smell, hear, satisfy all my senses, be in and wander through surroundings filled with woods, streams, mountains, fields, trails, trees, underbrush, cliffs, vistas, brakes, braes, wilderness! I itched to follow streams to their source, to hear them rushing over rocks, to bathe and swim in pools with gushing waterfalls or in the crystal clear lakes which they fed. I wanted to be free! I wanted to see wildlife in its primitive habitat, to see the stars and the moon over the wild places, to see caves, to sleep out, to camp and live on the food I could find around me! The forest pioneer, the woodsman-explorer-guide, always fascinated me. Here I was, a professional, with a love of my work which had developed over the years, still yearning for all of these out-of-door things! At least to some degree I was fulfilling my youthful desires by traveling over the Appalachian Trail.

AN INTEREST IN GEOGRAPHY AND SEEING THE WORLD. In the primary grades the courses in geography pertained to rivers, streams, lakes, mountains, towns, cities, people, industry, transportation; all of this I wanted to experience, to witness, to feel, to see. What better way, at least in the eastern half of the United States, than to travel the Appalachian Trail? I got to see and experience the height and location of the mountains and mountain ranges; I experienced the surface distinctions, the cliffs, rapids, falls, rock formations, boulder fields, glacial leavings, rocks (a most unusual one was Piazza Rock in Maine with trees growing on top of it in a bed of moss and evergreen tree needles). I learned about soils: gravel, sand, loam; about watersheds, swamps, streams, rivers, water supply; about lakes, natural and man-made.

In going to and from the trail I used different railroads and noted how they went through the mountains and along streams, and the geographical areas they served. The same was true for wagon and auto roadbeds and the canals along major rivers.

There were the water gaps of the Delaware, Lehigh, Schuylkill, and Potomac rivers, as well as many other water gaps and wind gaps and mountain passes and notches. These mountain "pass-throughs" saw the first signs of civilization, whether it was travel, settlement, agriculture, transportation, communication—or battle!

Industry, old and new, showed itself in terms of lumbering, papermaking, charcoal burning, coal, iron, asbestos, manganese, and copper mining, smelting, limestone, marble, and granite quarrying, cement, brick, and pottery works, transportation, farming, and even moonshining.

Of course the idea of the Appalachian Trail is that of a footpath through the wilderness. However, in my pursuit of the Appalachian Trail I became familiar with many towns and cities in each of the states through which the Appalachian Trail goes. I saw and enjoyed points of interest, street and town layouts, hotels and other places to stay, restaurants, even theaters.

In following the Appalachian Trail and in getting on and off of it there were many introductions, conversations, and acquaintances struck up with people who were different from me insofar as their locale had influenced them. Maine and the rest of New England *vs.* metropolitan New York *vs.* the Middle Atlantic states *vs.* Virginia and the Deep South. There was a wide spectrum of occupations, including inventors, rangers, farmers, foresters, laborers, inn-hotel-motel keepers, mountaineers in the true Appalachian sense, department store owners, rural and urban shopkeepers, hoboes, fellow hikers from different walks of life, lumbermen, vacationists, rich, poor, average. I met them in small villages, larger towns and cities, in the country, in cabins in the woods, in taxis, on hitched auto rides, on trains and buses. In other words, I saw the world!

CURIOSITY, ENLIGHTENMENT. I am a physical chemist with a

background in mathematics, physics, and colloid and surface chemistry. The latter deals with the science of particles and interfacial phenomena. For some time I have been interested in how biological as well as inanimate membranes function. It is fascinating to observe the manner in which given substances are absorbed into and on other materials and how given compounds pass through (diffuse through) membranes while other materials cannot pass through. What better place to observe such phenomena than the out-of-doors milieu of the Appalachian Trail? It is a showplace for the wondrous workings of Mother Nature.

All kinds of living things are everywhere and in abundance. The multitudinous manifestations of phenomena include bioluminescence in various forms, foam effects, atmospheric changes and surprises, ice formations, surface tension effects, light scattering, plant growth according to altitude, terrain, and particular environment, wetting phenomena, pollen and spore dusts, color effects, color changes, and so on. My science background helps me to understand and relate.

The trail has increased my appreciation and understanding in the general area of geology (minerals, rocks, land and mountain formations, erosion, sedimentation, glacial aspects), ornithology, animal life, fish, insects, plants (mosses, fungi, wild flowers, shrubs, trees). To say the least, observations in these varied fields have given me a broader outlook and have made it easier for me to carry on everyday work problems or just plain conversation.

I observed many animals and birds in their natural habitat. As I write my mind pictures the mother hen wild turkey and her brood that we surprised in an overgrown field in Pennsylvania, wild ducks swimming in quiet wilderness waters, beaver habitations, one moose trotting majestically along in the Maine woods and another clanking down a road just in front of us. In the mountains of Georgia and North Carolina I was surprised and scared by a herd of wild hogs (boar, if you will, and dangerous) coming up one side of the ridge in front of me and then crossing over the trail and going down the other side. And the hawks and other prey birds passing in the vicinity of Hawk Mountain, Pennsylvania, were truly memorable.

I saw grouse, fox, deer, eagles, geese, buzzards, bats, and bear. Every lean-to seemed to have its mice. They were cute, but of course had to be kept away from my food. One mouse in the southern Appalachians got into my knapsack and nibbled through a leather money pouch in which I had some chinquapin nuts. He took the nuts and left everything else intact.

More than once, when sleeping out under the stars, I have heard a slow steady shuffling in the leaves. My flashlight would show that skunks had come to look me over. Porcupines were a nuisance here and there. Other animal life included groundhogs, snakes (garter, black, rattler), turtles, and tortoises of huge size. One blacksnake imitated a rattler by rapidly shaking its tail against leaves and shrubs, possibly trying to scare me off.

NATURAL RESOURCES, POLLUTION, ECOLOGY. As a result of my wanderings on the Appalachian Trail and the areas around it my understanding of the need for our nation to preserve its natural resources became more realistic. Here was the source of pure water. The trees are the source of the important products of wood, cellulose, and paper, and it will be a long time before these products are replaced completely. The vegetation uses carbon dioxide and gives off oxygen. Dust particles, whether settling on the leaves or falling on the ground, become part of the soil. Even noxious gases like the nitrogen oxides are absorbed and contribute the nitrogen so essential to plant growth and protein formation. The benefits of this purification of the atmosphere should not be minimized.

Finally, there is the great respect I developed for the ecological cycles on which man is so dependent. These cycles involve plants, bacteria, fungi, insects, birds, animals, minerals, water, and atmosphere, all in such complex combination that elimination of any particular level could mean disaster.

On my Appalachian Trail walks I passed through many burned-out areas. Some of these burns had been recent, others were older. I could see the change in the terrain resulting from fire's devastation, and judge the time it would take for the original mature forest to grow again. At the time I went over White Cap Mountain in Maine a lumbering company had cleared off all the trees on one side of the mountain, leaving the slashings all around. These had caught fire, and the fire had also destroyed the moss and mulch and leaf mold, leaving raw earth exposed. Gullies and erosion were the result. The water-holding capacity of this mountainside was ruined and little soil was left for a new forest to begin.

In Washington, D.C., while en route to a hike in the southern Appalachians, I saw what had happened when some prankster had dumped detergent into one of the beautiful fountains. A mountain of foam had built up, covering the fountain. Something similar was happening to many of our streams!

MAPS, COMPASS. Another of my interests is maps. Paul Reynolds and I shared an often-repeated joke that we were so busy looking at maps while riding that we had no time to look at the scenery. For most of my Appalachian Trail walking I used U.S. Geological Survey maps along with maps furnished by the Appalachian Trail Conference in their guidebooks. It was a great pleasure to be able to identify brooks, streams, contours, mountains, roads, and so on, in terms of the maps. My compass saved me time more than once in finding the right trail and direction.

SCENERY, BEAUTY. The beautiful sights along the trail were sources of real pleasure. There were sunsets and sunrises under different conditions of terrain, weather, and cloud formations, as well as in the different seasons. There were farms and fields and woods; streams and lakes; waterfalls, babbling brooks, cascades, precipitous mountains and rolling hills; views down valleys, across ridges, up cliffs, down cliffs; southern Appalachian balds, snowcapped peaks; rhododendron bloom, azalea bloom, and forests and fields wild with spring flowers. I felt that I could not do this scenery justice with photography. There were just too many scenes that impressed me. If I had stopped to take all of the pictures I wanted to take, I never would have completed any significant fraction of the trail.

I enjoyed my share of beautiful fall colors. My Shenandoah–Skyline Drive hike was at the climax of foliage brilliance. My week in Georgia, from Mt. Oglethorpe to Deep Gap, North Carolina, was also at the height of fall foliage. This was in early November, and the hike afforded me the final entry in a "complete calendar" of fall foliage from north to south. It began with an Appalachian Trail weekend early in October in New England just when the foliage was exploding, the sugar maples being at their best. New Jersey, my home area, and the Appalachian Trail to the north of Arden, New York, were beautiful in middle and late October.

AMERICAN HISTORY. In walking the Appalachian Trail and going to and from access points, my knowledge of American history became greater, and I found considerable satisfaction in visiting historical places.

There are many manifestations of early industry. One often passes grown-over charcoal pits, the charcoal having been used in the early iron workings as far back as pre-Revolutionary days. Iron was mined in Pennsylvania, in the Ramapos of New Jersey, and the Hudson Highlands of New York. Many of the old mines still exist. Remains of the original iron-smelting furnaces are still present, including the enterprise of Peter Hasenclever in New York. Early coal mines are found in the Susquehanna region. Sites of old lumbering operations are found, especially in Maine.

In terms of transportation there are old Indian trails, and old canals such as those along the James, the Potomac, the Lehigh, and the Schuylkill. The Appalachian Trail utilizes old mining roads, old tote roads, lumbering roads, and charcoal-pit roads. There is the abandoned and overgrown stagecoach road in the Monson area of Maine. Now, even foot travel is difficult over parts of this old road. On either side are the typical New England stone walls, behind which the trees are old and large. In the roadway itself the trees are many years old and there are foundations and ruins of the dwellings of farmers who originally settled the country. In the Harriman State Park area of New York there is a road built (experimentally) of appropriate grade for crossing the mountains. In Maine and elsewhere the trail goes over the beds of early railroads used in connection with lumbering and mining.

In the matter of water supply and waterpower I saw primitive springs, reservoirs, filter beds for purification, and aqueducts. The waterwheels at Wesser, North Carolina, were fascinating.

All the way from Maine to Georgia there was Indian lore of one kind or another. I learned about the Cherokee in the South and talked with Indians themselves in Maine.

The mountain passes I traveled had seen early American pioneer migrations westward and Civil War battles. Davy Crockett had been at the Nolichucky River in Tennessee. In Maine, the Appalachian Trail near Flagstaff Lake crosses the route of the famous Revolutionary War expedition of Benedict Arnold and 1,000 men, a march which culminated in an unsuccessful attack on Quebec. The journey was heroic, especially since it occurred in the severity of a Maine winter. The expedition, begun in the fall of 1775, traveled up the Kennebec River and across the "Great Carrying Place" to the Dead River, past the mountains to Lake Megantic, and thence down the Chaudiere to Quebec (Flagstaff Lake is the dammed-up Dead River).

The Appalachian Trail goes through strategic country in New York, namely, the Bear Mountain–Popolopen Gorge–Hudson River territory where George Washington was active. General Mad Anthony Wayne took off from Fort Montgomery, near where the Appalachian Trail crosses the Bear Mountain Bridge, and followed Beechy Bottom Road around through the mountains to Stony Point, where he drove off the British. The Appalachian Trail crosses Beechy Bottom. The ironworks in New York and New Jersey were used to forge the links of the great chain which was stretched across the Hudson River to prevent the British fleet from capturing the waterways to Canada.

The Appalachian Trail goes through Civil War country in Pennsylvania, Maryland, West Virginia, and Virginia. Harpers Ferry is fascinating for the part it played in the Civil War, as well as in other periods of early American history.

MENTAL AND PHYSICAL HEALTH. No one questions the beneficial nature of the out-of-doors life with respect to one's health, as long as it is not overdone. Between the walking, climbing, exercising, fresh air, enforced abstinence, freedom from immediate concerns, pure water, and wholesome foods, one's health is bound to be better. Mentally, I found nothing more relaxing than to get out for a walk on the trail.

ADVENTURE, PIONEERING, EXPLORATION. We all crave adventure, and walking the Appalachian Trail has been a great adventure for me. I experienced a sense of pioneering as I tried different things, experienced new country, new people, new situations. There was a feeling of kinship to the first woodsmen of our country.

PURSUIT OF HOBBIES. Walking the Appalachian Trail helped satisfy numerous hobbies. For instance, I have a great interest in maps. I enjoy studying them and using them and am the owner of a goodly collection. My trail maps (including U.S. Geological Survey maps) were always a source of fascination. In connection with the broad vistas seen from the trail I used road maps (the Esso map is my preference) and other maps covering wide areas. I use the maps for exploration, for identification of mountains, lakes, streams, and boundaries, and to learn the "lay of the land."

LORE AND TRADITION. I became acquainted with some of the lore of the land I passed through, its legends, traditions, and historical events. In the South, for example, it was the lore of the Indians and the pioneers, the mountaineers and the moonshiners.

In Maine there was Indian lore, lumberjack lore, and sporting camps lore. Of special interest to me was meeting the Bodfish family at their old farmhouse in the beautiful intervale settled by their forebears some hundred years ago. The intervale is framed by Boarstone Mountain and the ledges of Barren Mountain, and there are beautiful broad level meadows with a stately elm here and there and clumps of white birches. The elderly occupants were quite hospitable as they told me about the local history.

SOCIAL. I have walked more than half of the trail alone, but I have never felt lonely. There have been many social moments. Most of the Appalachian Trail from southern Connecticut up into Maine was walked on two- or three-day weekends, usually with Woodland Trail Walkers members, among whom Paul Reynolds was my principal hiking buddy.

At the Devils Racecourse Shelter I met and stayed with Eugene Espy, who had started the Appalachian Trail in Georgia and was on his way to Katahdin. He was not nearly as tall as I was, but what a stride!

EXPERIENCES. My Appalachian Trail hiking experiences ranged from very pleasurable to serious hardship to some pretty scary affairs.

I had planned one of my week-long hikes to end on Roan Mountain, Tennessee, in late spring so that I could see the rhododendron in bloom. I had to guess at the timing. I started my hike some 100 miles to the south on a Saturday, hoping that the blooming would be at its height when I arrived on Roan Mountain the next Saturday.

Friday was a hot arduous day from Unaka Mountain over Little Rock Knob down to the Hughes Gap vicinity. I camped at an abandoned farmhouse that was practically in ruins. The spring which had originally served the farmstead was beautiful and deep with crystal clear cold water. The farmstead site itself was lovely. After I had explored my surroundings and had supper, I made my bed under the tumbled-down roof. The evening was very still and quiet with a loneliness and loveliness that was most enjoyable.

In the morning, with sorrow that this was the last day of my hike and with reveries of the solitude I had enjoyed at the farm, I started up Roan Mountain. The climbing seemed easy and I thought I had a long way to go. Suddenly I saw a fellow and a girl strolling arm in arm, as if they were on some city street. Farther along I saw other couples even more amorously engaged. Then my sense of privacy was completely destroyed as I came into crowds of people going, coming, sitting, lying everywhere. There was loud music and dancing and hawking and vending. I had arrived at the Roan Mountain Rhododendron Festival. My timing was perfect and I had beautiful weather to boot. I participated in the festivities, thus climaxing a fine week of hiking.

On another hike, in the Smokies, I was approaching the turnoff for the lean-to where I planned to stay. Right at the intersection, some 50 feet away, stood a giant black bear. I yelled at him. He wheeled around, glowered at me, and then ambled off into the woods. At the shelter I made sure to hang my pack from the rafters. I didn't hear a thing during the night, but next morning as I walked back to the trail I had to skirt around a huge pile of bear ordure deposited exactly in the center of the trail. It was the first time I had been told off by a member of the animal kingdom.

I spent a parched week hiking in Georgia. It was fall and very dry with hot sunny days. At one lean-to there was no water at all. I found a small can of evaporated milk which tasted good but didn't slake my thirst. I was quite dry and dehydrated. Going north I reached a vale where water dripped off ledges. I caught the water, drop by drop, until I had quenched my thirst and filled my canteen. Farther along the trail I came to a rhododendron thicket. I remembered that rhododendron thickets grow in wet areas, and sure enough, I found a little stream. I took out my Primus stove and cooked and drank nice hot noodle soup by the gallon. It was the best soup I ever had in my life. That week in Georgia was my driest hike.

I spent a very pleasurable evening on the Beauty Spot, a bald on the Unaka Mountain ridge near the Tennessee–North Carolina border. There was a 360-degree view and the scenery was wonderful in every direction. The bald itself, with its grass and shrubs, was beautiful to behold, and with horses and cattle grazing the effect was that of a bucolic heaven. As the weather was clear I decided to sleep under the stars. The sunset was impressive with contrasting colors. The grazing animals were inquisitive but minded their own business fairly well. After supper I enjoyed the scenery as day turned to evening alternately taking walks around the summit and lying down on my sleeping bag looking at the sky. As it grew dark the animals came nearer but still stood well away. I fell asleep, but not long afterward I was awakened by voices and lights. Some people with a large telescope had come up from nearby Erwin, Tennessee, to look at the stars. We talked and stargazed far into the night, exchanging all kinds of thoughts. Needless to say, my knowledge of astronomy was appreciably enhanced.

My scariest experience occurred in Pennsylvania. The trail, which slabbed a mountainside, was completely overgrown. The brush was chest-high and the footway barely visible. I always look where I place my feet, and through the brush I saw a big fat rattler. It slithered away, but in a short distance I came across another rattler. Apparently there were quite a few rattler dens on this mountainside. I proceeded carefully for fear of either surprising a snake or not giving him enough time to move off the trail. My mind was on snakes already, because I had almost stepped on one in the open just before I began to slab through the brush. The rattler struck at me but I was able to jump back out of reach. Although it is not my policy to kill rattlesnakes, I did kill that one by dropping rocks on it.

I had a most worrisome time when a friend and I began a hike from the east bank of the Lehigh River. We decided to walk the railroad trestle across the river. I don't know why he decided on this; perhaps he thought of it as a challenge. I know I looked on it as a way to save time. It turned out to be a terrifying experience for my friend. The height, seen through the open spaces between the ties and on both sides, practically paralyzed him. Absurdly, he continued to regard it as a challenge and kept walking, but at an extremely slow pace. Although I had been told that trains crossed this trestle only once or twice a day, I was afraid a train might come. I paced back and forth, carrying my friend's pack (I had deposited mine on the other side), and sometimes holding him by the arm or hand and looking for platforms to stand on if a train should come. It was a great relief when he finally got onto terra firma. He was really upset and we had to rest quite a while.

The day was hot and sunny. There was no water on the ridge west of the Lehigh River. We had a poor start and night came on us when we were still quite a distance from the lean-to where we had intended to camp. I spent the most parched night I had ever experienced on the Appalachian Trail, sleeping out under the stars on a hard rock ledge. Raw eggs and evaporated milk had to do us for food, and we had no water.

On a week-long trip north from Hot Springs, North Carolina, my first night out was in the open. There was no shelter and I had no tent. I came to a picnic area where there was a latrine. I decided to sleep in the vicinity so that if it rained I could take shelter in the outhouse. The night was balmy, and it was quite warm in my sleeping bag. The atmosphere became close and oppressive. I did not like the proximity of the latrine and could not fall asleep. I moved to a grassy spot on some ledges overlooking the deep wide valley below. I arranged my bed with my head practically sticking out over the ledges. The air was fresh and pleasant coming from the valley. With a view of the twinkling lights, the stars, and a beautiful cloud formation, I fell into one of the most pleasant sleeps I can recall on the Appalachian Trail.

I remember two nights that were stifling, malodorous, and uncomfortable. At Sams Gap, Georgia, I tried to sleep on the cold greasy concrete floor of a garage. There was no air, and the stench of years of automotive service was all over the place. The other bad night was spent in a small chicken coop. The space overhead was so low that I had to practically crawl to get in. The doors had to be closed, and the odor was something that I do not intend to put up with again.

My coldest night out without shelter was in the Mahoosuc Mountains of Maine, north of Mahoosuc Notch. It was in November and I was with Paul Reynolds. Paul's thermometer indicated a temperature of 10°–12° F. The deep balsam bough bed I prepared, plus all of my clothes and my 4½-pound down sleeping bag, were just enough to keep me from shivering.

Bly Gap, Georgia, had a couple of "mostests" which are indelible on my memory. My route was northward and up into the gap. It was about sunset and a thunderstorm was coming up just as I was leaving the woods and going into the open, with the panorama of the gap before me. Under the eerie light caused by the storm clouds, the view was awesome and desolate. The gap was boulder strewn, and with the cliffs and ledges it seemed vast. There was a feeling that some great spirit was present. Underneath my feeling of elation was my anxiety for shelter from the coming storm. I had a tent but the terrain was so boulder strewn I could find no place to pitch it. I could see woods up ahead on the ridge, but doubted if I could reach them before the storm reached me. There was no time to fix supper. I spent the night sitting on my poncho, with the tent draped over me. It rained all night. Rivulets ran under me and I got wet, but I did sleep some. It was my wettest night out without a shelter.

The most severe snowstorm I experienced on the Appalachian Trail was the "big snow" of the New York metropolitan area on December 26, 1947. A friend, who was a novice in hiking and backpacking, asked to come with me on a trip I was planning from Pawling, New York, south and west through the Clarence Fahnestock Reservation and on to Bear Mountain. We arranged to meet at the 125th Street railroad station in New York City and take the early morning train (around 5:00 A.M.) to Pawling. The evening before I had been impressed with the ring which was visible around the moon. When I left home in the early morning for 125th Street, snow was just beginning to fall. It was a light snow, but when we arrived in Pawling it had accumulated appreciably. Nevertheless, we headed for the mountain. We missed a turn and spent considerable time looking for the trail. By this time the depth of snow had built up greatly, and with snow still falling, my friend suggested we turn back. I felt we ought to complete the day's hike, so we walked on. We were enjoying ourselves, although the exertion was beginning to tell on my friend. We came to a hut and knocked on the door. The people were most cordial, and we rested by the fire and had tea. The snow was still coming down, so after being reminded by our hosts that this was a record snowfall, we headed back to Pawling. Our train took all night to get back to New York City. I finally appeared at home before my worried wife, having had a solid 24 hours of "adventure."

The deepest snow I ever traveled through on the Appalachian Trail, and this was without snowshoes, was on the Barren–Chairback Range in Maine in late May, 1969. I was with a friend. The winter's snow in Maine had been heavy, and there were still huge drifts, often more than hip-deep. Branches and bushes were weighted down with this snow, making a tangle under which we had to crawl. In some places the snow held our weight, but in other places we sank to our hips and had to crawl on our stomachs to make headway. My friend thought I was crazy when I argued that this was part of the Appalachian Trail experience, and that a hiker should be prepared for anything. It was strenuous, but we made it over the Barren–Chairback Range in three days, doing about four or five miles a day.

A short hike that took a long time was through Mahoosuc Notch, Maine, in November. This notch, which is strewn with huge boulders and rocks, is bad enough in any season. Now there was ice, and with the slippery conditions and our overnight packs, it took us all day to do the mile or so of the notch.

My longest hike with full pack was over Standing Indian Mountain. It ended at Deep Gap, North Carolina, after some 22 to 25 miles. The hike on which I carried the heaviest pack was my first Smokies jaunt. As a novice I carried a nine-pound kapok sleeping bag along with the other gear.

Vegetation often interfered with travel. I remember a stretch of trail in Maine, north of White Cap Mountain in the vicinity of the West Branch Ponds, which was so overgrown with young trees, alder bushes, grass, and brambles that I had to pick my way by looking for the slight indentations made by the feet of other hikers.

Hurricanes can really mess up a trail. Just one tree down results in an appreciable detour. Sometimes many trees are down, and they are interlaced with each other. In such cases the detour sometimes takes the hiker far off the trail, and as the blazes are down with the trees, pandemonium is not far off. I had such an experience in the Bigelow–Sugarloaf section in Maine. It was late in the fifties and hurricane damage had not been cleared away. Getting through the blowdowns and keeping on the trail was the roughest experience of its kind I ever had. I thought I was lost more than once, but my compass, maps, and circling method of finding a lost trail saved the day.

When was it most pleasant underfoot? That was when I was slabbing Mt. Guyot on the Appalachian Trail during my first Smokies hike. At that time I walked ankle-deep in moss. Since then the trail has been graded and the underlying gravel exposed.

About the most hospitable treatment I can recall was at Fatzinger's Hotel in New Tripoli, Pennsylvania. The management really went all out, and the food was marvelous and abundant, yet inexpensive. The steak was so huge it occupied a complete platter. The vegetables and other foods were on another platter. The apple pie, with a crisp crust and sweetness and tartness in exact balance, was out of this world. I was beginning a three-day hike west from the gap on Blue Mountain (U.S. Route 309) above New Tripoli. The owners drove me to the trail and also sent a car to pick me up at the end of my hike. They were most friendly.

I had some exhilarating hiking over the ledges on the summit of Mt. Lafayette in New Hampshire. A thunderstorm with hail and rain had just broken loose. Below me I could see swirling clouds and thunder and lightning. The whole thing was stimulating. I was happy and began to sing at the top of my lungs. It is not hard to understand, in terms of this experience and my experience at Bly Gap, the exaltation that the prophets of old felt under similar circumstances.

The Appalachian Trail: A Trip Made by James F. Fox and Paul A. Gerhard

By James F. Fox

Started at SPRINGER MOUNTAIN on June 7, 1963
Finished at MT. KATAHDIN on September 9, 1963

I found a world globe in a junk shop one day. A small battered remnant of some child's toy box. Dented and scarred, its paint colorfully symbolized strange places, cultures, and people. As I ran my fingers across its surface, my mind wandered back. Nepal, India, Iran. Across Asia and Europe, back to the United States. There, running north along the Atlantic, I could trace a line. A line from Georgia along the Appalachians to Maine. A line long enough to see on this tiny model of a vast globe. Could we, Paul and I, actually have placed our mark on this earth? Or, in attempting to do so, had we placed its mark on ourselves? I tossed the toy back into the box and wandered out for coffee, and reflection.

It began in the winter of 1963 at the University of Maryland. Paul, a math major, was president of the ski club, and I, studying civil engineering, was president of the trail club. We had climbed, caved, and hiked together, but though we knew and respected each other, we were not at that time especially close friends. One evening at a trail club meeting Paul tossed out the question, "Hey, anyone want to hike the Appalachian Trail?" After a few "sure, got my pack outside" comments, he continued with his idea. For most of us the next summer might be our last before becoming trapped in a full-time job. It would be a fantastic trip, as well as the biggest challenge around. It would take extensive planning and perfection in many aspects. He looked at me and I mused, "Yeah. Hmmm. It just might go." We decided to check it out.

During the next month we collected information, previous trip reports, maps, guidebooks, and equipment catalogs. In addition, we wrote to previous hikers and sought their advice. It soon became obvious that our greatest problem would be our available time and the total distance. Summer vacation gave us 106 days. The trail was 2,025 miles long. To finish, and we never considered doing otherwise, we would have to average 20 miles a day—every day. Such a pace would require exact planning and the best possible equipment. Once these two aspects were taken care of, the rest would simply be our own personal challenge.

Each of us took half the guidebooks and maps, and after adding revisions, studied each section in detail. We then prepared detailed lists of whatever logistical information we could find. We noted springs, shelters, and stores or towns along or near the trail. We also made notes of any special problems which might require advance planning. We began searching for equipment. We suspected that the weight factor would be important, if not critical, and we concentrated on finding the lightest and most efficient equipment available.

Finally the time came when we had to decide if we were really going to do it. From his initial suggestion until the end of our hike I suspect Paul was fully committed. If he ever questioned whether he could or would complete the trip in the time we had, I never knew it. My own commitment came when we ordered the sleeping bags. From that point on we both continued with the assumption that it would be done.

For both of us the technical aspects of planning tended to be as interesting and important as the physical and mental challenges to come later. Half of our planning dealt with scheduling and logistics, and the other half concentrated on equipment. With minor exceptions we did very little in the way of physical conditioning. Our regular activities kept us in good shape, and academic demands left little time or energy for special conditioning. Later we concluded that nothing could have prepared us for the first two weeks, and after that it made little difference.

We decided to travel from south to north. By traveling in this direction we hoped to avoid late winter storms in the North and late summer heat and overgrown trail in the South. To a considerable extent we followed moderate weather as it migrated northward. Paul prepared a list of cumulative mileage totals for each section of the trail. Based on this we could, at any place or time, calculate how far we were ahead of or behind schedule. Once on the trail we did this every evening. We prepared another list of each store or town, its distance off the trail, and the distance to the next one. Except for sections at both ends of the trail we found that we could expect to obtain food and supplies every few days from local sources. For the longer sections at each end of the trail we decided to use freeze-dried food, which we purchased before leaving for Georgia.

We selected 12 mail drops and wrote to each house or post office to insure that they would hold a package for us. By knowing fairly accurately what our schedule would have to be, we could predict within a day or two of when we could expect to arrive, when packages would have to be mailed, or where friends could meet us. Each package was made up in advance and was left with our families. Most contained standard items such as guidebook pages and maps for the next sections, diary pages, small quantities of staples, vitamins, film, a Brillo pad, and return envelopes for film, diary, and mail. In addition we left a variety of emergency, repair, and replacement items which could be sent to us if we needed them.

For us, selecting equipment was especially interesting. Our previous climbing and hiking experience gave us definite ideas about quality and the confidence to select, improvise, or modify items we would need. It was necessary for us to be self-sufficient for long periods, yet weight had to be minimal to prevent the trip from becoming a torturous ordeal. We both knew all too well what every pound would feel like after 20 miles. We continually asked ourselves if we could leave something out or substitute something better or lighter. This went as far as throwing away candy bar wrappers. We kept our pack weight down to 18 pounds with no food, and around 25 pounds with a week's food. With these loads our packs were comfortable. It was a great feeling to swing into our packs knowing our next stop for supplies was a hundred miles away.

We decided to use packframes. Though our loads could have been carried in rucksacks, we liked the load distribution of a frame with partitioned bag. In addition, we found that air circulation under a frame was important when hiking in hot, humid areas. We never begrudged the extra weight of the frame. Paul used his Kelty frame, bag, and waist belt. I built my own pack. I modified a Featherlight frame by replacing the heavy webbing with laced nylon string, designed a packbag which my mother sewed, added a light waist belt—and was quite satisfied with the result. Our only problems with the packs were with some rain leaking through seams or zippers, and in the beginning, with sores developing under pressure points. We tried using spare socks for extra padding over hip and shoulder bones but we never found a fully satisfactory solution.

We decided not to take a tent. Basically, we didn't like the idea of so much weight for a single-purpose item which would require only occasional use. We wanted our "shelter" to serve both while walking and at night. However, we never agreed on a coordinated system, so we each took our own. Paul chose Holubar's bivouac sack, and I chose a lightweight coated nylon poncho. When it rained we always found or improvised some form of relatively dry shelter. Cold was rarely a problem, and our sleeping bags were satisfactory if dry.

Rain while we were walking was another problem, since we couldn't afford the time to stop. In the beginning we tried to stay dry, but soon gave that up. A little rain was no worse than sweating under a poncho, and wind or wet brush got us wet anyway. Our eventual solution was just to keep walking. While walking we produced enough body heat to stay warm and evaporate a pretty good summer shower. If the rain increased, we simply rolled down our shirt sleeves, buttoned up, and used our bandannas to reduce heat radiation from our heads. If it was especially cold we might put on extra clothes, but we tried to save them for the evening. It was never fun to put on wet clothes the next morning, but once walking they became tolerable and dried eventually.

Our primary emphasis in clothing was flexibility and temperature control. As we became acclimatized to the trail we found that we could handle the extremes of hot humid river valleys and cold wet windy mountain peaks without excessive discomfort. In spite of previous warnings we wore Boy Scout shorts most of the way. To us the tortures of briers, nettles, and poison ivy were no worse than the sweat and confinement of long pants. Though we both carried lightweight synthetic pants, we used them only for warmth or insect protection at night, or during periods of very cold wind or rain, or while washing and drying our shorts.

We wore fishnet shirts under lightweight, long-sleeved, cotton-Orlon shirts. Paul carried a Dacron jacket, and I carried a Dacron-filled inner jacket and a hooded nylon wind shell. Later, in the North, I had a heavier Dacron jacket sent to me. The first week I carried Dacron-filled underwear pants—a heavy mistake. We ruled out down clothing, since cold usually came with rain, and rain makes down useless.

Shoes were a special consideration. Paul and I chose different boots to start with and later had other boots sent to us. We both had foot problems, but were never sure that the problems had any solution. After 20 miles our feet were simply pounded to a pulp. Due to rain, dew-wet grass, and occasional streams, our feet were often soaked, and blisters became a normal though painful routine. We used three pairs of Ward's nylon cushion-sole socks, rotating them by wearing two and washing the third. They wore well and might have lasted the entire trip if we had not received a new set in one of the mail drops. Ironically, after returning I had my feet checked by a doctor who implied that due to flat feet I could not make a long hike. Such is life.

Our sleeping bags were our most expensive and sophisticated equipment. We chose the lightest bags we could find. Trailwise Slimline bags, mummy type, no zipper, two pounds of down in chevron tubes. They were more than satisfactory. Despite their minimal weight, they were often too warm to use—even as protection against mosquitoes. One night in Maine we had snow, and with no additional shelter our bags were sufficient. Our stuff sacks were worn out by the end of the hike and gave little protection; however, my bag is still performing well. The bags were well worth their cost. We never seriously considered air mattresses due to weight, preferring to substitute extra clothing—carefully concentrated under our hips, shoulders, and ankles. This method worked quite well and was certainly the best solution as far as weight was concerned.

We decided that a gasoline stove was essential and found our tiny Borde burner to be worth every ounce of its weight. At one point we tried giving it up to save weight but found this totally unsatisfactory. By cooking only dinners (and turning the stove off!) we got over 1,400 miles per gallon of white gas. We carried only a one-quart aluminum bottle of gasoline with us. For cleanup we got a Brillo pad and paper towels in each mail drop. Our 1½- and 2½-quart nesting aluminum pots with lids worked well. We gave the pot lifter away as useless weight. We also carried a salt-and-pepper shaker, plastic bags, and a plastic squeeze tube for margarine. We gave up carrying water the first week but continued to carry an empty two-quart polyethylene bottle for use when we camped.

First-aid items we carried included paregoric, Darvon (a painkiller), aspirin, cold tablets, salt tablets, Merthiolate, and antibiotic salve. We soon gave up the salt tablets and depended on the salt we put on our food. Bandages included one roll of adhesive tape, a roll of gauze, moleskin, and assorted clothing which could be torn up in an emergency. Two elastic Ace roll bandages were essential during the first two weeks of painful body rebuilding. After that we sent one of the bandages home. Our Cutter snakebite kit was used only as a preventive charm. Along the way we found a can of bug spray that was worth its weight in gold thereafter. I had poison ivy several times, and one time it almost ended our trip. This became such a problem that I wished I had tried desensitization before the trip. One special item was Gerry's Formula A Vitamins. We were fully convinced they helped in the early weeks. We forgot to take them one morning and were positive we could tell the difference. An invisible part of our first-aid equipment was experience. We felt that we could improvise enough to get us out of any situation that might develop. Only one problem—a case of dysentery—required medicine that we didn't have with us.

The technique we developed for blisters differed from accepted practice but worked very well for us over a long period of time. Many books say never to open blisters for fear of infection. Since we knew they would eventually be torn open, we preferred to do it under reasonably clean conditions. After washing with soap and swabbing the area with Merthiolate, we would drain the blister, add a little antibiotic salve, and then put adhesive tape directly over the skin. Several days and many miles later, when the tape fell off, the blister was healed. Occasionally we added a moleskin ring or gauze pad, or reinforced an area with tape before the blister developed. We were also very careful about clean feet and clean fresh socks. Despite many blisters, we had only one tiny infection and no complications.

We carried a variety of smaller items. For route finding we carried pages from the guidebooks, the trail maps, strips of local highway maps, and a lensatic compass. Paul had a watch, which—like the compass—became less necessary as we became integrated with the environment. By knowing either the approximate direction or the time, the sun will usually supply the other. We carried a small towel, a washcloth, and Dial soap in a plastic bag; a small sewing kit with ripstop tape; nylon cord; our Swiss army knives; and a flashlight using C batteries. I took an Olympus Pen half-frame camera which slipped into my shirt or pack pocket and gave us 72 pictures per roll of color film. I also carried a small light meter until the rain made it less accurate than guessing.

We made a few token conditioning hikes, complete with gallon jugs of conditioning elixir, and Paul tried exercising with an overloaded pack. Other than that and breaking in our boots by walking to school, our final preparation consisted of staying up late studying for exams. Finally we boarded the bus for Georgia, where a cousin drove us to Springer Mountain. We climbed the Nimblewill Gap access trail in high spirits. At the top, we switched to shorts and signed the register: "June 7. Destination: Mt. Katahdin, Maine." After three miles we began following a poorly blazed forest service road that led six miles to Hawk Mountain where we picked up a well-blazed trail. Six miles later we came to a sign: "Hawk Mountain 6 miles—Springer Mountain 3 miles." Our first day on the trail and *we had circled 12 miles back to the beginning!* We hauled our mutinous bodies back to Hawk Mountain and collapsed in a quivering, aching heap.

The next week was totally exhausting. Aches and pains came and went as our bodies rebuilt and adjusted to new demands. We had started two days early and were still ahead of schedule, but at the end of the day that was little consolation. Each day did have its good points, however, and eventually we became more or less accustomed to the pace. We discovered that the key to good mileage was steady continuous progress. Every rest break was costly in terms of mileage, but it was those five-minute stops that lasted an hour that hurt. Were we stopping to adjust something, or adjusting something to stop? By strictly limiting breaks, we found we could depend on making two miles an hour, and could occasionally reach four miles an hour. We did not, however, regain our initial two-day lead until we had hiked a quarter of the trail.

An early discovery was that for us, at least, it was not necessary to carry water. It was often hot and dry, yet somewhere in the 20 daily miles we could expect to find water. In spite of the familiar warnings about cramps, whenever we found water we lay down and drank like camels. When there was no water, we simply did without —once for an entire day. Eventually the mechanics of living and traveling settled into a routine and we began to enjoy our trip.

Our day began anytime after 5:00 A.M. We got up, turned our bags inside out to dry, split a box of Kellogg's Concentrate with a quart of powdered milk, and took a vitamin capsule. After cleaning our dishes with paper towels, we would pack, burn our trash, and leave by 6:30 A.M.

Most days we would hike continuously until lunch, which might last an hour. Occasionally we experimented with in-flight refueling if we needed the mileage. Often we would stop for a second lunch several miles from where we planned to camp, or at a restaurant if it was especially tempting.

Our lunch stops were total breaks. We would stretch out with our shoes off and socks drying. Paul would mix a quart of Wyler's Lemonade and I would spread out cheese, raisins, peanuts, crackers, and two chocolate bars. While playing mix-and-match food combinations, we would study the guidebook and maps, write in the diary, or just rest. If we stopped at a store we would buy enough food to get us to the next store and then move outside for a luxurious lunch of bread, sandwich fixings, a quart or two of fresh milk, and pints of ice cream. While eating we would repack all of the food in plastic bags—thus saving up to a pound of useless packaging. When convenient we might stay at a hotel, eat at restaurants, or visit the local laundromat.

When we approached a mail drop we would calculate our mileage several days in advance and try to arrive in the evening so that we would have time to read and write letters and prepare the diary and film to be sent home. Often this meant especially long days of hiking. Once we discovered to our dismay that at our usual pace we would arrive Saturday evening after the post office had closed. Rather than risk a day's delay, we pushed on as fast as possible and arrived in time.

On a typical day we hiked between 21 and 23 trail miles, with an overall average of 21.2 miles a day. Our longest mileage was 35 miles when several springs were dry, and our shortest was 2.7 miles when I had dysentery and a doctor insisted that we rest for a few days. These were "on-trail" miles, as indicated by the guidebook figures. Extra miles walked when we lost our way or when going to town were added up separately. Our cumulative total for the trail was 1,993 miles. We walked an additional 200 miles off the trail.

We always tried to stop before dark. We stayed in the regular trail shelters about half the time. The other nights were spent in a variety of places. If things were going well, we would often pick up a few extra miles by passing a regular shelter and then simply camping in the middle of the trail. Other shelters included picnic tables, motels, homes, farmyards, porches, garages, the AMC huts in the White Mountains, and the comfort station at Clingmans Dome. We took great pleasure in asking for water and permission to camp in someone's field. This technique often resulted in an evening of hospitality and new friendships which expanded our trip from just a trip through the woods to a trip through different and interesting cultures.

When we reached a typical trail camp we quickly set about the task of making dinner. Since we were obtaining food from small local stores, dinner usually consisted of 2½ quarts of noodles or macaroni, some kind of sauce, and a can of Spam. We also prepared a quart of powdered milk, adding a little sugar for flavor, and took our vitamin capsules. By the time dinner was ready we had our sleeping bags out, and our extra clothes carefully in place for padding so we could lie down to eat. If there was enough light, Paul would total our mileage and speculate on where we might be the next day. After cleaning the pots we would pack the food away and either write in the diary or fall asleep.

Though our routine was much the same every day, each part of the country was different and each section of trail was different in varying degrees. In the South there were the massive and remote Nantahala and Great Smoky mountains, with isolated well-graded trail. In other backwoods hills of Appalachia we followed graveled roads past shanty farms, each with its dog and collection of automobile remains. Shenandoah National Park was highly developed, with a superhighway of a trail and crowded commercialized tent cities. We passed through Maryland's rolling hills and Pennsylvania's rough rocky ridges and broad farm valleys. Farther north we saw the trail's tenuous search for accommodation as it skirted the New Jersey and New York megalopolis. We passed through Connecticut, with its small ravines and cathedral-like forests, the beautiful Green Mountains of Vermont, New Hampshire's spectacular White Mountains, and the wilds of Maine. Ultimately we reached Mt. Katahdin.

We saw many animals—deer, moose, bears, raccoons, and many grouse—though at our pace we probably missed more than we saw. We saw one wild rattlesnake and two that were confined in a New York zoo. We had encounters with farm dogs and curious cows all along the way. Once in North Carolina we watched a bear from a private zoo being set free in the woods. Later, as we tried to pass, he came looking for food and gave us quite a chase back to a fire tower. If Paul had not distracted him with some hamburger, our trip might have ended right there.

And of course there were people. A few were hostile and many had put up no-trespassing signs, but most of them were friendly. Except in Maine, we never went an entire day without seeing someone—at least at a distance. Meeting people became an important part of our trip. Except when we could share an evening together, we unfortunately could never stop for long. Old friends met us at many places and sometimes hiked with us, or took our packs around to our next camp in their cars. With a few exceptions most of the hikers we passed were soon out of sight. In Pennsylvania we met Warren Mengle who was also hiking the entire trail, section by section, over a period of years. We spent a most enjoyable day hiking together. We found him to be an amazing person and he gave both Paul and me much to think about. Throughout our trip we were told of previous hikers who had passed. We began hearing that Grandma Gatewood was coming again from north to south, and we hoped we might meet, but we never did.

Doing the entire Appalachian Trail in one trip is more than just a long hike. There are the normal things that are found in any hike, but on a long hike these things are compounded and multiplied. However, there are other factors which become an integral part of the experience and demand special attention. I could never have known all of Paul's objectives and reactions; however, for me, the trip was as much a mental as a physical experience and it has had a profound effect on me since I finished it. People hike the Appalachian Trail for many reasons. Each reason has its own validity when related to the personalities and objectives of those concerned. Our trip in many respects was a challenge, and perhaps we made it especially so. We had hiked many sections of the trail previously for different reasons, but on this trip our objective was to do something big, to stretch ourselves beyond our previous limits. In many ways we discovered more about ourselves than about the trail itself.

One of the problems we faced was living continuously with another person in a high-stress situation in which we were dependent on each other and needed the other's cooperation. Previous hikers had warned us about the importance of mental conditioning and told us that petty arguments could grow irrationally and out of proportion. We discussed this ahead of time and decided that we simply would not allow it to happen. Surprisingly, our prohibition worked quite well. We occasionally had "serious discussions" but in every case one or both of us would back down short of anger. We had accepted the idea that our trip would be primary, and that nothing, including our own egos, would be allowed to jeopardize it. Another technique was to eliminate the sources of problems. Rather than argue over whose turn it was to do something, we both tended to grab the worst tasks first. We often openly joked or mock-fought about things which if left to fester might eventually have exploded in bitterness and resentment.

We found that it was also essential to recognize individual differences and, wherever possible, accept or at least respect them. We knew we could depend on each other, and yet integral to this were certain strong elements of personal self-sufficiency and independence. Many days we split up just enough so that each could hike alone— both on the same ridge, but leading separate trips. Traveling together, but going our individual way, too. By these and similar techniques, we managed to all but eliminate superficial problems. However, several problems developed out of assumptions that we would not or could not openly question. Towards the end of the trip we developed a basic difference of opinion about the pace. Paul wanted to conclude the trip in the shortest possible time. He had found a pace that he preferred and enjoyed. On the other hand, once ahead of schedule and with the end in sight, I wanted to ease off and enjoy the trip more. For me, completion of the trail within the summer was enough, and I felt that I was missing much of what the trail had to offer. I, too, had found a pace that could achieve my objective and was comfortable. Pushing faster became an ordeal which was no longer necessary.

We were moving fast and efficiently, and this gave its own satisfaction. I felt that it was not necessary to finish ahead of schedule, but I allowed myself to follow Paul to a fast finish and so the underlying conflict remained and grew deeper, in part a result of personality differences—something which we could subjugate, but not change—and perhaps by that time we didn't want to. One unspoken objective of mine had been to use the trip to tear into myself in search of identity. The process was gradual, and by the time the conflict about pace had surfaced, we both had come a very long way in the process of self-discovery.

We had recognized that it would be a long trip and had accepted that fact from the beginning. However, 2,000 miles is more than four or five million steps. Walking became as elemental as breathing, but 95 days, from sunup to sundown, hour after hour, was a long time. Much of the time there was little to do but think. The trip had a certain totality, but that totality consisted of innumerable parts. Many parts were interesting and satisfying, but many were of dubious value except in the context of totality. Some sections of the trail were interesting and enjoyable; others were not. Too often the best parts were on side trails which we rarely stopped to explore. Every day, every mile, we continued our long grind over one mountain only to reach the base of the next. Several times, high on a fire tower with mountains extending to both horizons, we could see neither where breakfast had been nor where dinner would be. Events, experiences, and obstacles passed by like mileposts in time, noted perhaps in the diary but often ignored completely. Once my pack strap tore loose as we stopped for lunch. We ignored it and ate, confident that it would be repaired—and it was. At another place, Paul's raingear was left behind. We never went back. We continued always onward, through sun and rain, exhilaration and exhaustion, day after day, mile after mile. Cool rain rinsed dust and sweat from our faces, and soaked our shoes, causing new blisters. The blisters healed, only as a prelude to the next blister. During four long days I walked 60 miles in a daze, dysentery exploding my body and mind in a silently howling rage.

We had periods of torturous frustration which at the same time gave a degree of satisfaction. We had great experiences on some days, and these made the other days worthwhile. Our satisfaction began to grow. We had said we were going to make it, and slowly, as the days passed, it became evident that we could. In spite of this realization, or possibly because of it, I began to question the meaning of the trip more deeply. At times I thought in terms of "a long green tunnel" and of a treadmill, like one I remembered from a physiology experiment back at school. Paul seemed to be enjoying the trip more than I. At our pace, could getting there be half the fun? I often thought of the effort being expended towards achieving arbitrary goals. What were we actually doing, and if trying to prove something, what, why, and to whom? What else might I or anyone else be doing that summer? Was the trip worth it? Was what worth what? And, what was *worth?* At first these questions plagued me only in the worst parts of the trip, but later they plagued me even on the best days. Still we continued. We had decided to do it, all of it, and it became impossible to stop. Sometimes I led, and sometimes I simply followed Paul's lead. It was essential to continue to the end, but I refused to stop questioning. I wanted to know, and this became part of my trip.

In Pennsylvania we passed the halfway point—five days ahead of schedule. From then on the miles, days, and states passed with increasing speed. The tremendous distances of the South were behind us, and we now seemed to be encountering more variety. Physically we were in excellent condition. As our daily mileage cut dependable slices off the remaining distance, mileage became less of a factor and we could appreciate more of the trail. We came across stores frequently, so our packs were light. Friends met us, and hiking along from point to point was often pure joy.

As we traversed New Jersey and New York we were surprised that so many remote areas could be found so close to the cities. Yet we could always feel the pressure and sadly see the litter and destructive development that spilled out from urbanity. We traversed the ridges and river valleys of the Green Mountains, with their incomparable sunsets, and ran head-on into the rugged White Mountains. It was late August and we could feel that summer was ending.

Wind and cold rain raged across the Presidential Range. On Mt. Washington we needed a map to find the Summit House, only 70 feet away. When occasionally it cleared the views were unforgettable. We entered Maine by crossing the Mahoosuc Range, a section which deserves its reputation as the most difficult part of the trail. Most of the trail in the lakes area of Maine was even more remote than the trail had been in the South. In many sections the trail was overgrown, and yet the wilderness aspect of these sections made the struggle worthwhile. Towns and people were scarce and one day we saw no one at all.

After several very fast days we arrived at Katahdin Stream Campground at noon on our ninety-fifth day. We had a quick lunch with friends. Leaving our packs with them we literally ran the last five miles to the top of Baxter Peak. Free of our packs, and in the best condition ever, it seemed as if we were floating up the trail. It was late and a storm was brewing. We met several parties on their way down. They must have thought us insane as we ran by, hopping from boulder to boulder. We came out of the forest and scrambled up the rocky ridge to the final plateau. Crossing its tundralike moss, we found a spring and drank deep from its cold clear water. As we continued our approach to the final rise, the summit sign appeared just above the clouds that were lightly touching Katahdin.

We looked out over the clouds toward the southern horizon so far away, and then down into Chimney Pond—thousands of feet below. It was late but that fact no longer mattered. There in the raging wind it was a moment to enjoy. We signed the register and sat down, shielded by a rock, to eat and rest. Mt. Katahdin was a spectacular end to a long hard trip. After a while we knew we would have to leave. The clouds were closing in, and our friends would have a hot dinner and champagne waiting. We started back down, down through the wind and rain to the world below.

Backpacking in the Good Old Days.
Photo courtesy of Appalachian Trail Conference.

Friendly Little Markers

By Chuck Ebersole

Started at SPRINGER MOUNTAIN on March 31, 1964
Finished at MT. KATAHDIN on September 17, 1964

We trudged onward through a misty forest as eerie silence surrounded us. We were more than a month out on what was to be a
2,000-mile hike along the Appalachian Trail. Springtime foliage was
luxuriant in the green hills and lofty ridges of North Carolina and
Tennessee. We were hiking North with Spring. Minute by minute,
every hour, all day long, we absorbed the beauty around us. We felt like
the luckiest trio on earth.

The trio was my oldest son Johnny, our beagle Snuffy, and myself,
Chuck Ebersole. We had thought about this trail venture for years. We
had talked about it incessantly while I was still in the navy and Johnny
was in high school. Later we found ourselves training on practice hikes
and planning the adventure, and now here we were—actually hiking
the trail of our dreams.

My birthplace is Bainbridge, Pennsylvania, a small town on the
banks of the Susquehanna River in Lancaster County. Some 30 miles
upstream, at Duncannon, the Appalachian Trail crosses the same river.
The Appalachian Trail must have exerted its woodland magic over me
even then, and the magic remained with me throughout my navy
career. Finally, on March 20, 1964, after 23 years of service, I retired
from the U.S. Navy and put the problem underfoot, so to speak; I
answered the call of the trail.

Trails always have had an air of intrigue for me. They are saturated
with mystery. Who uses them? What lies ahead? Take any trail, and
what is it? Well, I suppose one must say it is a path that leads from one
place to another. Notice the word "lead." That is how trails are to me; I
can't pass a new trail without setting foot on it to see where it goes.
First a trail draws me to it; then it leads me around the next bend, or up
a hill, or across a creek. There is enjoyment just in contemplating the

John Ebersole and Snuffy in Laurel Fork Gorge, Tennessee.
Photo by Chuck Ebersole.

"how" and "why" of the greatest of modern footpaths: the Appalachian Trail. If you let it lead you onward, it will take you through the experience of a lifetime. I was only an infant in 1921 when Benton MacKaye dreamed of such a trail. I was still a small child when the first sections of the trail were laid out in New York State in 1922 and 1923. Through my childhood and early teens several dedicated people made the trail a reality. I never knew Arthur Myron Avery personally, but eventually I read of their labors and have thanked them ever since.

My eighteenth birthday occurred in the same week that the Appalachian Trail was completed in Maine in August, 1937. Other boys from my hometown were joining the army, but not me. I joined the navy. I wasn't going to be caught with a pack on my back, traveling miles by shoe-leather express and then sleeping out at night. Ha! Little did I know the trick that fate had in store for me! In the early fifties I was based ashore temporarily and took up bow hunting. I met another bow hunter who expressed an interest in hiking on the Appalachian Trail and we promptly laid out a 100-mile hike. In May of 1956, with my friend Hugh Carty, I made my first hike on the trail. I was full of apprehension. The trail was scary and full of unknowns. Could I stand up to the physical exertion required? Would I get lost? Could I find enough water? Did I have enough food?

At that time the trail's southern terminus was on Mt. Oglethorpe, Georgia, and our trip was planned from Mt. Oglethorpe to Deep Gap, North Carolina. With our wives, we drove up from Jacksonville, Florida, to the trail's southern terminus. We all slept out on top of Mt. Oglethorpe that night. It was the first week in May but seemed like winter. It was cold. There was no foliage on the trees yet, and the wind moaned through the bare branches all night. Local people had told our wives some tall tales about the woods being "infested" with mountain lions. When I got back from checking the trail I found my wife, Brady, standing guard over our two boys with a bow and arrow! We had a hearty chuckle later, but at the time she was really scared.

Next morning, after a cold night and a fast breakfast, we packed for departure: Hugh and I on the trail and our wives back to Jacksonville. We checked everything. Did we have *this*, did we have that, canteen filled, plenty of matches? Then off they went. About two minutes later we discovered that we didn't have our carefully prepared trail maps— and we could still hear my car going down the mountain!

Maps or no maps, we went ahead. On the second day Hugh had blistered feet and was in trouble. At a mountain road he got a ride out, then caught a bus back to Jacksonville. He and his wife kept it a secret from my wife that I was now alone. Meanwhile, my wife had found the forgotten maps in our car and had kept that fact a secret from Alice. Each of them didn't want to reveal information that could be a source of worry to the other. They all came to pick me up at Deep Gap the following Sunday. Tanned and leaner, I was in great physical condition and felt that my first hike on the Appalachian Trail had been a success.

Another navy transfer in late August of 1956 took me to New Jersey. I began to look forward to more Appalachian Trail adventures. By mail Hugh and I planned another jaunt for the spring of 1957. With another friend, David Van Derzee, I drove down from New Jersey and picked up Hugh in Franklin, North Carolina. My wife was along to facilitate car-driving and trail's-end meeting. We planned to go from Deep Gap, North Carolina, to the Nantahala River crossing up-stream from Wesser, North Carolina. This was only a 50-mile excursion, but on the third day Dave was in trouble. His knee joints weren't standing up to the 40-pound pack on top of his six-foot, two-inch frame. At Wayah Gap, 29 miles from where we started, he said good-bye. Hugh and I kept going and met Brady at a campground above Wesser. We spent a rainy night there, and left for home early the next day.

Over the Fourth of July weekend, 1957, I took my son Johnny and nephew Butchy to the Appalachian Trail in Pennsylvania. We camped out, hiked a total of about nine miles, enjoyed the woods, and came home. My real purpose was to see a little more of the trail; the two boys were just an excuse for making the trip.

That fall, over the Labor Day holidays, Brady and I and our two boys drove up to Maine. I wanted to see Mt. Katahdin, northern terminus of the trail. We set up our tent in Roaring Brook Campground, went up to Chimney Pond, and from there ascended the Cathedral Trail. It was steep, rough, and rocky, but finally we were on top of Mt. Katahdin, where we signed the register in awe. The state of Maine lay below us: lakes, ponds, streams, the Knife-Edge, the Chimney and Chimney Pond, The Saddle, campgrounds, and the Appalachian Trail coming across the plateau from Thoreau Spring. I gazed southward and thought of all the wonderful green hills stretching to the horizon and beyond it all the way to Georgia.

We went down Katahdin via The Saddle Trail. Darkness was coming on, and so were clouds, thunder, lightning, and rain. Luckily I had a flashlight, for we had to walk the last mile or so in darkness, with rain pouring down and bolts of lightning stabbing the night. I made everybody hold hands, and put our two sons in the lead. This way, in the beam of my flashlight, I could see the two boys and direct our course at the same time. I held tight to Brady's hand and we went slowly and carefully. The batteries held out, we made no wrong turns, and although soaked to the skin, we made it back safely. Our tent was flat on the ground and full of water, but I set it up and used an old sweater to mop it out. I stripped and briskly rubbed down each person, the youngest first and myself last. Then I put everyone into a dry sleeping bag and got something hot for them to drink. Soon everyone was asleep. The next morning was beautiful. Well-rested, we headed for home.

I had learned the importance of having a canteen of water and a flashlight with *fresh* batteries, and I was pleased to find that I could keep my family together and bring them back safely. I had learned that you can't control the elements but that you can live with them if you are prepared and keep cool.

Each of my trips on the Appalachian Trail helped me make the next hike more efficient and whetted my appetite for more hikes. The next journey took place in May, 1958. Once more Hugh came up from Florida by bus to meet us in North Carolina. This time my 12-year-old son, Johnny, was to hike with Hugh and me. During the previous several months Johnny walked five 10-mile and one 20-mile stretch to earn his hiking merit badge in the Scouts. I had accompanied him on these hikes and felt that he was physically capable of making a longer hike.

What an introduction to the Appalachian Trail this 55-mile trip was for a youngster! We started at Wesser, North Carolina. Johnny was so scared of bears the first night that he couldn't eat all of his supper, and later upchucked what he did eat. Next day the going was easy, and Johnny got over his fright. We were comfortable that night, with a pleasant camping spot. Up until this trip I had never used a lean-to or shelter along the Appalachian Trail. I preferred to bed down on the soft leaf-carpeted floor of the forest, and I did—until the last part of this trip.

At Fontana Dam we had a giant milk shake and several candy bars apiece. As it turned out, we needed the extra energy. On the far side of the dam we headed up Shuckstack Ridge into the Great Smoky Mountains National Park. When we reached the exposed portion of Shuckstack Ridge we were hit by raging winds and rain. On the ridge the rain turned to sleet, hail, and snow. What an experience! We stayed together, ponchos whipping and flying, and made it to the top in a foggy snowy whiteout.

A fire tower and ranger's cabin were located on Shuckstack. We were wet and cold and knew we were in for a stormy night, so hoping for a pardon from the ranger we sheltered in the cabin and used some of his wood for a fire. We chased various bears off during the night. In the morning we discovered 8 to 10 inches of snow and couldn't believe our eyes. This was the tenth of May! Springtime in the Smokies wasn't supposed to be like this, but here it was, and we still had many miles to go.

The trail was difficult. The white trail markers were obliterated by the snow that was plastered on the tree trunks, and the pathway was treacherous and slippery. I led the way and Hugh brought up the rear, with Johnny between us. Bushes, shrubs, and trees bowed over the trail from the weight of the snow. Johnny continually slipped and fell. He got mad and miserable and I could see that tears of frustration were about to well up. I told him to walk alongside the trail or on the edge of it. This got him off the hard-packed center of the trail where everybody else had walked and his shoes made a notch for every step he took. That bit of know-how kept him from falling so much and getting his hands wet and cold and bruised.

On we went, pushing and plowing our way through the snow-covered growth. Rhododendron arched over the trail, making graceful tunnels or blocking the trail completely until I shouldered my way through. When the heavy wet snow was knocked off, the rhododendron sprang upright and the trail became clear for a little way.

We ate a cold lunch and went on. The wind had abated, and everything was white and quiet around us. I saw squirrel and turkey and bobcat tracks in several places. It was getting late in the afternoon and we didn't know just where we were. Then, as so often happens in the mountains, fog began to set in. After a time we came to one of the extensive balds through which the Appalachian Trail passes in the Smokies. There were no trees, stumps, bushes, or anything else to use as a reference point. We could see only 15 or 20 yards at most. We thought we knew where we were, but couldn't be sure. If we were correct, there was a shelter close-by. But where?

Fortunately, we had our maps. It appeared that up ahead there should be a trail going off to the right to a shelter, but a trail in the fog didn't show up as distinctly as it did on the map. I've been forever thankful that the guy who laid out that map had the trail correctly marked for compass direction. Being out there on top of a mountain in fog gave us a feeling of desperation, and without the compass every step could have been in the wrong direction.

Here's what we did: I stood in the grass on the open bald but in sight of where we had come out of the forest. Hugh went ahead in the compass direction we had picked, and when I could barely see him I shouted for him to stop. Johnny then went from my position to Hugh's and on past him on the same line. Hugh stopped him before he got out of sight in the fog. Then I moved forward along the same line until I was in front. This method gave us at least two reference points all the time. After about 20 minutes of this maneuvering in the windy fog we reached an Appalachian Trail sign which told us of a lean-to off to our right. We were a thankful group when we got to that shelter. It was nightfall and we were wet and shivering with cold. Johnny was suffering from chills and exhaustion. Quickly he stripped, rubbed down, got into dry clothes and then into his bag. I got a smoky fire going and made a hot supper which fixed Johnny up fine. Hugh and I also got into dry clothes and ate, and then we put out the fire and got into our sacks for a night's sleep.

Next morning it was clear and cool. We ate breakfast and stayed around the fire until midmorning when the sun came up and warmed things up fast. By dinner time half the snow had melted and was running off in every direction. The trail was almost clear of snow, but it was still soggy and wet. By late afternoon almost all the snow was gone, but the forest was still soaked, and so was the firewood. We'd had wet feet all day and were fortunate to be at a shelter again. Somehow, with wax-soaked lengths of small rope, we managed to get a fire going. Acrid, eye-burning smoke from the wet wood filled the shelter. Was it better to stand clear-eyed on the cold side of the fire, or choose the warm side and endure the foul smoke? Such is life: decisions, decisions, decisions.

By diligent effort we managed to gather firewood and get it partly dried over our meager fire. As the minutes passed both the fire and our spirits brightened considerably and we had a nice evening—a satisfying supper, a cheerful campfire, and a comfortable night of peaceful slumber.

Next morning dawned misty. It started to drizzle, and then rained intermittently for the rest of the day. All we could see as we approached Clingmans Dome were damp wisps of vapor rising from every surface. The clouds hung low and the drizzle never stopped. Hugh became somber as we waited for our ride at Clingmans Dome, and as it turned out, that was the last time he ever attempted a hike on the Appalachian Trail with me. I think it was the bad weather that turned him against any more hiking ventures.

On my first trips on the Appalachian Trail I figured how many breakfasts, dinners, and suppers I'd need. Then I made out a menu for each meal. In this way I broke the whole trip down into small units. Next, I made a list of all food items needed, the quantity of each, the weight, and the cost. When I came home from a hike I would cross off the list those items I hadn't used. Items that I needed (but which I didn't have along) were added to the list for the next trip. This same procedure was used for clothing and equipment. I kept eliminating from the list the things I found I didn't need, and adding items I wanted to try. Before long I had built a personalized list that suited my needs very well. I weighed each item separately, and then weighed my pack when I was ready to go. In this way I double-checked the weight.

What about the physical part of hiking? Well, it takes muscles to hike, and muscles have a way of getting sore. Then there are blisters. Out on the trail you want to enjoy the outdoors to the fullest, and you can't do this with blisters and sore muscles. Here's what happened to a friend and me on an Appalachian Trail venture: for several weeks before our scheduled hike I walked to and from work every day. On Saturday I put on my hiking boots and headed out on a nearby road, walking hard and fast and carrying my pack with something in it for weight. My wife would leave the house four hours later and catch me, wherever I was. We noted the mileage on the odometer, and this figure, used with the number of hours I had been walking, gave me a fair estimate of my walking speed. On Sunday I walked without a pack, at a pace that I considered to be pleasant yet didn't waste any time. Again the mileage and time provided an estimate of my walking pace. This knowledge was useful in estimating what my daily mileage on the Appalachian Trail would be, but the main thing was that my muscles were being exercised and toned up.

Meanwhile my friend stayed home and soaked his feet in various solutions to toughen them up. He'd read about this method somewhere. On one occasion he did put on his pack and hiking shoes and walked around the block. When he returned he declared himself ready for the hike.

In the afternoon of the second day on the trail my friend developed blisters. They were really painful, and with more than 80 miles to go, he decided it was too much for him. He bathed his feet in a stream while we talked. We decided to separate: I to go ahead on the trail, he to limp out to the nearest road and catch a bus home. I had sore muscles and blisters, too, but mine occurred during the practice sessions. By the time we headed out on the trail my feet had toughened up and my blisters had healed. Things just aren't the same on the trail with a heavy pack on your back as they are sitting at home dreaming about a hiking trip. For most of us, planning is essential, and adequate planning includes physical preparation.

On March 20, 1964, I retired from the navy. Johnny had completed high school at midterm in January; to do this he had attended school the previous summer. We were all set. We had food and equipment. We were physically ready—and mentally ready, too, I hoped. I had collected most of the guidebooks and maps of the trail. I took out all of the south-to-north data and made five separate books. I carried the first two, wrapped in plastic, in a pouch (actually an army canteen cover) on a web belt around my waist. In this way the maps were protected but readily available. The other guidebooks were kept by my wife and given to us as we progressed up the trail. I also carried a water canteen and cup in a similar cover on the belt. A 35-mm camera was protected by two separate plastic bags and placed in still another pouch on the belt. The web belt and canteen covers were obtained in an army-navy surplus store. A collapsible drinking cup, squeezed into any of the pouches, completed the waist-belt items when we started. When we were something like a thousand miles up the trail we each added another pouch in which we carried all kinds of goodies for our noon meal. This saved space in our packs and also saved us the time it took to dig into the packs. There was another advantage: we could eat our lunch while walking and not lose time. Later, when Brady joined us, we often carried sandwiches and even fried chicken in these pouches.

Six days after I retired from the navy, Johnny and I started for Georgia in a 1948 Plymouth Coupe that cost $75. It was a dirty brown color, and we named it the Brown Bomber. Brady and our youngest son, Michael, would meet us after Mike was out of school. In Georgia we found an old mountaineer who agreed to buy the Brown Bomber for $44 cash and take us up to Nimblewill Gap as part of the deal.

With emotions of sadness (and some apprehension) we watched the old Brown Bomber fade from sight down the winding mountain road. Our sentimental moment was soon over, and we headed up the trail. In an easy 2.3 miles we were on Springer Mountain at the southern terminus sign. We pitched our shelters under a screen of mountain laurel and by the time we built a campfire, cooked and ate supper, and had everything squared away for the night, dusk was creeping into the forest.

On the west side of Springer Mountain there is a prominent rock ledge. Johnny and I stepped out there to view the sunset. In a few minutes the sunset colors faded and darkness began to settle rapidly. Stars twinkled here and there in the clear night sky. The chilly night air bit through our clothes and we scurried for our sleeping bags. Snuffy was bedded down in a tremendous pile of leaves and was snoring away before we could get to sleep. In fact, the ability of that beagle to sleep and snore just about any place and under any conditions became one of the fun events all the way to Maine.

Next morning, March 31, 1964, dawn came with a breath of winter. Hoarfrost laced twigs and branches. Leaves on the forest floor were crunchy underfoot. When we could force ourselves out of our sleeping bags, we were like slow-moving flies stunned by the cold. We were so miserable that instead of building a fire for breakfast we packed up and got moving as quickly as we could. From Johnny's little transistor radio we learned that the temperature was 16 degrees. That was down in the valley—no telling what it had been on Springer Mountain. We learned later that this was Georgia's coldest spring in many years, and after three years in Texas these colder climes weren't exactly a picnic for us.

Many mornings that followed were similar to that first one. We put off having breakfast until we were warmed up by several hours of walking. We were absolutely miserable every morning for those first few weeks. For 17 consecutive days my diary reads: frost, freezing, snow, cold, sleet, rain, cloudy, pouring rain, freezing, and so on. Fortunately, we had planned well in the matter of clothing. We each had several pairs of socks and enough extra clothing for a complete change. Our extra clothing was kept dry in plastic bags, and we slept in it to keep warm. We were very thankful to have dry clothing as the clothes we wore while hiking usually soaking wet from rain, melting snow, or moisture-laden bushes. We hung these wet clothes in the shelter or on a tree and by morning they were usually frozen. If we wanted dry clothes to sleep in that night it was off with the nice dry warm clothes and then, stark naked and shivering, force ourselves into the frozen or clammy cold garments. We learned to grit our teeth and move fast. On many a morning we laughed at one another's antics as we went through what we dubbed our "ritual of agony."

The worst part of the morning misery came last: our shoes. They became soaking wet almost every day, and we didn't dare dry them out too fast by the campfire as everything depended on taking care of our feet and footwear. Our shoes were often frozen stiff by morning. Have you ever tried to force your feet into frozen leather? Well, besides our "ritual of agony" with clothing we also had a "shoe-leather stomp." Every morning at dawn, there in the forest, two earthlings went through a contorted dance around their campfire altar.

Sometimes in the middle of the afternoon, at some valley crossing where the sun beamed into a streamside cove, we managed a hurried bath. Furious winds and pelting rain almost blew us off the exposed ridge above Bly Gap, where we crossed the Georgia-North Carolina line. On another day, going from Deep Gap up Standing Indian, we were blanketed by thunder and lightning. Rain poured down and the trail was like a miniature creek. Once during this difficult time we talked of quitting. We came to a dirt road and from our maps we knew the road would lead us down to a valley town. For 20 or 30 minutes we stood there and talked about quitting. Then we headed up the trail and never talked about it again. Perhaps if we hadn't been father and son the outcome might have been different, but what kind of father could bring himself to back down in front of his son, and what 17-year-old would want his father to think of him as a quitter? I liked the way Johnny put it in his diary: "We came within a snap of the fingers of quitting today."

Early next morning we headed into the Great Smoky Mountains National Park. We went up Shuckstack Ridge and before midmorning we were at the tower and cabin which had been the site of our snowy adventure in May, 1958. A huge snow-covered blowdown at a trail fork caused us to take a wrong turn. It cost us three extra miles of walking in wet snow. When we discovered our mistake, we retraced our steps and found that the tree had fallen in such a way that it couldn't have concealed our trail any better if someone had planned it that way. We clambered through the blowdown and reached a shelter just at dark. A group of Scouts had a fire going. We warmed up, ate our supper, and hit the sack fast.

Next morning we were up at 2:15 and headed out on the trail by 2:40 A.M. Have you ever walked a trail at night by flashlight? Try it sometime. It's a wonderfully exciting adventure. If the weather cooperates, it's downright beautiful. We were within nine miles of the Robertses' home in Waterville, and Johnny and I wanted to be there in time for breakfast. That's why we had started so early. The night was clear and cool as well as pitch black. Stars were out, but there was no moon. Lights were visible in towns and villages that were miles away. Except for an owl hooting once in a while, the forest was silent. Resting on a ledge on the mountainside, we could hear the muted sound of mountain streams below us, and see a glow of diffused light coming from the valley that held Waterville. It was a wonderful experience to be there on that mountain at that particular moment in time.

We wanted to be sitting in the Robertses' garden outside their kitchen window when they got up. With both of us walking in the beam from one flashlight, we made good progress. The first flashlight would begin to dim after about 30 minutes and we'd use the other one. I'd keep the first flashlight in my pocket with my hand around it for warmth. In another 30 minutes, when the second flashlight was beginning to dim, the warmth had regenerated the first one. By 6:00 A.M., after walking nine miles, we reached the Robertses' garden. Ten minutes later Mitch turned on the kitchen lights. He looked out and a big grin signaled that he'd seen us.

We spent the next four days in Waterville. We rested and washed dirty clothes. Nell stuffed us at breakfast, dinner, and supper as well as in between, and gave us dessert for a nighttime snack. I had lost 16 pounds in 244 miles and 18 days on the trail. Half of that was gained back in the four days. Johnny and I went with Nell and Mitch to Newport, Tennessee, to help with their grocery shopping and do some of our own. We got haircuts, and when the barber learned that we were hiking the Appalachian Trail all the way to Maine, he called the editor of the local paper, *Plain Talk*. We were invited for a picture and an interview, and later Mr. Al Petrey, the editor, sent the news story and a copy of the photograph to us. Our hike was officially on record in the news media.

On Tuesday, April 21, we got up at 5:00 A.M. We wanted to leave quickly, with only a light breakfast. We'd learned that you don't hike your best on a full stomach. However, Nell had a breakfast banquet ready and we ate a little of everything even though we knew we shouldn't. Then after a handshake with Mitch and a hug from Nell we walked off quickly before the tears started to show our feelings.

Hot Springs, Rich Mountain, and Allen Gap followed in quick succession. At a little store in Allen Gap we filled up on peanut butter, Spam sandwiches, ice cream, and soda pop as rain clouds gathered overhead and thunder and lightning rolled and flashed. We left the store reluctantly, and after several wet and dripping miles came to a country church. Behind the church was a cabin and a barn. We stopped and talked with a woman who was chopping wood. The storm clouds were becoming thicker and more threatening, so we asked if we could sleep in her barn. Peering out from under the huge hood of her weather bonnet, the mountain lady reckoned we could do just that. But weren't we hungry?

Before we could answer, she'd laid aside her axe and was leading us toward the cabin. Talking to us all the while, Grandma Rachael Chandler, who was the 81-year-old widow of a mountaineer, made us a real hill-country supper. The menu included bacon, ham, fried eggs, cornbread, fried potatoes, beans, biscuits, milk, rhubarb, cold sour milk out of a crock, strong coffee, and home-canned peach preserves for dessert. What a bountiful and wonderful meal! It was like a special Thanksgiving dinner just for us. Grandma Chandler, who was hovering over us, refilling and replenishing, said we might just as well sleep in her back bedroom. Night had fallen and rain was splattering the cabin roof so we accepted her offer and had a wonderful night's sleep.

Bright and early next morning, with better weather, we left Grandma Chandler's haven of cheerful warmth. She had sold two dozen eggs from her small flock of chickens the day before for 50 cents, and as we departed she tried to talk us into taking the 50 cents along.

We went across more Tennessee ridges, seemingly always accompanied by mist, fog, and rain. Devil Fork Gap, Nolichucky River Gorge, and finally Erwin, Tennessee. Next morning on our way to Cherry Gap Lean-to we just about got blown up the trail. The wind blew so hard that all we had to do was raise a foot and we practically floated upward. When we topped the ridge, we had to work hard to go *downhill*. No rain, but wow, what a wind!

We climbed Roan Mountain in drizzle and rain, and then in mist and fog. We reached the top in eerie quietness. It was late April and the rhododendron bushes were fat-budded and almost ready to burst into bloom. The rain, wind, and fog increased. When we came to the campground at Carvers Gap we couldn't see where to cross the road because of the fog. We knew Grassy Ridge was over there somewhere with a shelter close-by, but daylight was beginning to wane.

A miserable night followed. For the first time on our trip we couldn't get a fire started. As the wind and rain increased we took shelter in a double-unit toilet we found in the public campground. We put Snuffy on the men's side, and we bedded down on the hard cold cement floor of the ladies' side. We had cold soup for supper, and there is nothing as unappetizing as dehydrated soup mixed with cold water. We were saved from total misery by the 10 candy bars we had bought earlier in the day at a country store.

As May approached the weather warmed up considerably. On some days it got downright hot. The trees didn't have leaves yet, so we got the full benefit of the sun when it did shine. On some afternoons, if we happened to be hiking uphill on a mountain facing south and west, the heat was exhausting. How different from the days when we were wet and cold in freezing temperatures!

Snuffy would be panting too, but he stopped to catch his breath in the shade of a tree or stump, and when they weren't convenient he'd park himself in *our* shadow. Snuffy's pack seemed to fit him well, and he appeared to adapt to it without undue discomfort. He was giving us no trouble. In almost 400 miles we'd had to help him only once. We had come to a creek where the water was high and splashing on the rocks and banks. It was after several days of freezing temperatures and all surfaces near the creek were icy. The creek was too wide for Snuffy to jump and too cold and rapid for him to swim. He couldn't leap from rock to rock as they were too far apart for his short laden frame, and were ice-covered, besides. Johnny worked his way across the creek, stopping just short of the far bank. I picked up Snuffy and gingerly worked myself part of the way across. When we were all set I tossed

Snuffy to Johnny who tossed him onto the far bank in a continuous motion. The problem was solved.

In early May we perspiringly made our way past South Pierce Lean-to, Wilbur Lake, and up the Watauga Dam Road. Our intention was to stay at the Vanderventer Lean-to. Thirsty as all get-out, and almost out of water, we approached the shelter. We were surprised to see a pile of burlap sacks, a half-bushel of potatoes and other food items, and half-emptied paper plates of pork and beans. The bountiful display of food reminded us of our own hunger. We didn't want to go seven miles to the next shelter, yet we didn't know if this shelter was big enough for us and whoever owned all of that gear. We were discussing the mystery when a lanky one-eyed character with a bulging burlap sack over his shoulder came striding into view. Howdy, he said, and that was our introduction to Noah Taylor of Stony Creek, Tennessee. A few minutes later his two teenage sons came up the trail from the other direction. They also had bulging burlap sacks slung over their shoulders. We learned that Noah and his boys were gathering moss, which they sold for 13 cents a pound to a nursery. The moss was used to protect the roots of plants when they were shipped.

A fire was built and supper prepared. Our meager meal was quickly made and just as quickly over with. Their meal was like a banquet. We were fascinated by the huge skillet Noah put on the fire, and the absolute mountain of potatoes he peeled and sliced into it. Johnny and I lived through a lifetime of hunger while watching them prepare their meal. When their plates were filled, Noah told us to help ourselves. We asked him for two potatoes to roast in the embers. Hungry or not, my upbringing wouldn't allow me to ask for more, even though I wanted to. It seemed like it took those potatoes forever to get done, and then another lifetime for them to cool enough to be eaten, but eventually they were ready, and they were the greatest!

Snuffy had never liked vegetables. It was either dog food, bones, or table scraps for him. If vegetables were included in the scraps, he'd eat around them. However, that night he ate the peelings from the potatoes Noah had prepared with apparent relish. He chewed up every last peeling, and then looked as if he wanted more.

The night held more surprises. Ominous clouds were gathering across the night sky as the fire died down and we all crawled into our sacks. Later we could hear thunder rolling in the distance. Lightning began to flash. It was soon evident that Noah didn't want to spend the night on the mountain ridge with a thunderstorm coming up. The boys weren't much for leaving, but Noah knew of an abandoned cabin down the mountain in a ravine somewhere, and in about an hour he had talked them into moving. Around midnight they all crawled out and began to pack. I've never seen so much gear in my life. It was a staggering amount. It was hard to understand how they managed to carry it all.

The generosity of these hill folk was revealed as they packed. First it was, "Hey, you fellers, here's some eggs in a sack. I'll set it up here on a ledge for you."

"Okay, Noah, thanks a lot," we replied from our sleeping bags.

A few minutes passed, and then it was, "Hey, you fellers, here's some coffee to go with your breakfast."

"Okay, Noah, thanks."

Still later it was, "Hey, you fellers, here's a couple tomatoes you can have."

"Thanks, Noah."

And for the next half hour it was, "Hey you fellers, this———," and "Hey, you fellers, that———," until he'd given us what must have been a little of everything they had to eat. In the black of night the last thing that man did was to split and stack firewood for us. "Now, thar, that ought to take care of a breakfast fire," he told us, and with that they tramped off into the darkness.

Noah's generosity may have been sparked by our look of hunger, but whatever the motivation, it was hard for us to believe that anyone would do so much for two complete strangers. A brown paper sack on a ledge over our heads contained 10 beautiful large eggs. Another bag had a hefty portion of ground coffee in it. A small jar was half full of lard. Laid out neatly on another ledge were three nice tomatoes, and beside the tomatoes were nine large potatoes. Noah had even left us some of their fresh water.

For breakfast we had two eggs each from Noah's gift, and plenty of good hot coffee. When the last of Noah's firewood had been burned and our appetites satisfied, we packed and headed out. It was a cool cloudy morning. Our plans were to go 14.5 miles to the Double Springs Gap Lean-to as quickly as possible, get a huge fire going to warm us, and gorge ourselves on Noah's food.

We got to the shelter at noon, but the place was dark and gloomy and had a foreboding atmosphere. Since the day was only half over, we decided to go another seven or eight miles to the next shelter. We would still have time for our feast. In three hours we came to the fire tower on McQueens Knob, which was about a mile before the lean-to. As we approached, a man in the tower invited us up. We tied Snuffy and clambered up to talk and see the view.

Ernest Whitehead must have put the coffee on when he saw us coming for he was pouring cups of steaming coffee with one hand as he shook ours with the other. He showed us maps of the area and pointed out the trail ahead as well as hills, ridges, and mountains we had already crossed. This was Ernest's last day in the tower, and he was getting ready to clean out his refrigerator, batten down the windows, lock the door, and go home that very night to Elizabethton, Tennessee. However, he said he would stay one more night if we wanted to spend the night there. Johnny and I looked at one another and grinned. Yes, we wanted to stay. Ernest had hamburger, cheese, and other good food in his refrigerator which he said would be thrown out if we didn't eat it. We ate hamburgers and cheese while Johnny peeled, sliced, and fried the potatoes Ernest gave us. For lunch the next day I hard-boiled six of the eggs Noah had given us. I'd carried them 21 miles and hadn't cracked one. The fried potatoes were so delicious that Johnny got out the nine large potatoes Noah had left for us and put them into the skillet, too. It was a real banquet. I thought Ernest would grin his head off at our exclamations of appreciation. We tried to stay awake and make conversation, but after 400 miles of hiking and hitting the sack early, it was no good. Full stomachs and the comfortable warmth of the cabin soon put us to sleep.

The next morning was one of the few times on the entire hike when daylight found us still asleep. When we did get up for breakfast each of us had four slices of toast, four eggs, and six slices of bacon, along with all the hot coffee we could swallow. Then with sincere thanks we bade our benefactor good-bye.

The day started out cool, drizzly, and cloudy, but it soon began to clear. About 3:00 P.M., in sunshine, we walked into the little town of Damascus, Virginia. The trail comes in one end of town and goes out the other. Appalachian Trail blazes on the trees and telephone poles lead you right up the main street.

Damascus was a friendly town. People smiled a welcome to us, or voiced a pleasant hello. We spent three sunny and mild days there. We got up every morning and went down to the Owl Drug Store and had breakfast—a stack of hotcakes, doughnuts, and coffee, all for 55 cents. Then at the grocery store we bought a large box of cereal and a half-gallon of milk for a second breakfast in our room.

We had walked in rain and through dew-laden shrubbery so much that our shoes, pack straps, jackets, and Snuffy's pack were literally coming apart at the seams. At a shoe shop we got all of these items repaired. With repairs made and food purchased, we called Texas and talked with Brady and Mike. Johnny and I would hike for another 10 days, then head for a rendezvous with the family. We had hiked faster than expected, and were already past the point we had planned to stop for the reunion—Newport, Tennessee.

The weather was better now, and we felt more enthusiastic about our hike. On many nights in Georgia and North Carolina we had lain out in the hills at night, listening to Johnny's pocket radio. It seemed that all we ever heard were predictions of more miserable weather, followed by advertisements about the new 16-ounce bottle of Pepsi-Cola which we never saw. Now we were enjoying mild nights and balmy days, and washing down ice cream with all the Pepsis we wanted. We hiked the next 10 days with exuberance. Flowers were blooming and birds were nesting. Spring foliage, clear streams, and luscious green hills beckoned us onward. We crossed a highway on Big Walker Mountain on Mother's Day and tried to call Brady from a store, but had no luck.

From a ridgetop we looked down into Sinking Creek Valley, where we would leave the trail. We saw a country store down in the valley and headed for it. A mile of dirt road and another half-mile of black-top brought us to the store. I pulled the screen door open and stepped inside. A pair of legs stuck out from under an opened newspaper. The rocker was going back and forth. You certainly wouldn't mistake this store for a city supermarket. Bib overalls, Red Man Chewing Tobacco, lanterns, seed packets, and salt blocks proclaimed this establishment to be a crossroads country store. Pictures of sea battles and large lithographs of ship scenes and naval artifacts decorated the walls. The rocker stopped and the newspaper was lowered. Retired U.S. Navy Chief Chuck Ebersole was looking into the eyes of retired U.S. Navy Chief Joe Sublett. What a time when the introductions were over! The hot coffee was in navy mugs, and the navy talk raced along at a million words a minute.

Snuffy was tied under a shed and Johnny and I ate our fill of sandwiches, fried pies, and ice cream. When Joe Sublett learned what we were doing, he jumped up and cranked an old-style telephone. About 20 minutes later a sunbonneted woman walked into the store and Joe introduced us to Lucille Price. She and her husband John lived on a farm near Joe's store. Lucille told us she and her husband would like to have us for supper, and that we were welcome to spend the night and use the bathtub. We declined this kind invitation, saying we wanted to be on our way to Newport for the family reunion.

What a fool I was, declining that hospitality! I had turned down a warm, comfortable soak in a bathtub for a shivering bath in the cold water of a little spring-fed brook. I had exchanged a satisfying country supper for the indifferent fare of a bus station cafeteria. And instead of a good night's sleep in a soft bed, we sat up half the night on hard benches. Lucille was a member of the local hiking club, and her home was a favored gathering place for hikers. Later we visited Lucille and John and enjoyed their hospitality.

Joe Sublett said he would see that Snuffy got fed, then he drove us to Newcastle where we caught a bus. After a long hard journey on several buses we arrived at Newport and weighed ourselves. My own weight was down by 32 pounds and Johnny had lost 30 pounds.

Next day we hiked to the edge of town and waited for Brady. The owner of a service station ran us off and wouldn't even let us buy cold drinks or candy bars from his vending machine. We waited across the road all afternoon in the hot sun, sharing the shade of a telephone pole. One of us would keep watch, standing in the shade of the pole, while the other tried to nap in the shade of a poncho stretched across our packs. We waited 10 hours. Just before 6:00 P.M. the cops came out and started questioning us. We were trying to explain the whole complicated business when I saw our car and trailer coming up the highway. Oh, happy day! Johnny and I rushed away from the open-mouthed cops, grabbed our packs, and ran to the car and trailer. A few minutes later we were headed for the home in Waterville.

Johnny and I had a beautiful day when we hit the trail where we had left it nine days before. Brady towed the trailer and met us on Catawba Mountain, where we had our first "family only" supper since two months before in Texas.

The trail was now a real joy. We started hiking at daylight—and by daylight I mean that time in the morning when you can just begin to see objects in the woods. For me, that's when Nature is full of excitement. Night animals are often still abroad, and the day animals are beginning to stir. As the sun climbs over the horizon, birds are announcing their territorial claims with bursts of song. Dawn in a woodland setting is Nature's golden moment.

Our well-fed condition and toned-up muscles enabled us to push the miles underfoot at a rapid pace, especially as we were carrying lighter packs. We often covered 10 or 11 miles by 8:00 A.M. We now had time to enjoy scenic viewpoints and still get our mileage completed before we were very far into the afternoon. Soon we were in the Blue Ridge Parkway area, where days and miles passed pleasantly and rapidly. The diary entries tell the story: 16.55 miles in eight hours, 20.15 miles in nine hours, 13.05 miles in five hours, 14.19 miles in five hours, 10.93 miles in four hours, 20.92 miles in nine hours, 17.7 miles in seven hours, 15.1 miles in six hours, 14.9 miles in six hours. At this pace we went through Shenandoah National Park so fast it seemed almost like a dream. The trail was as smooth as a boulevard, and on many stretches we averaged three miles an hour. We had good walking, beautiful woods, and a mixture of spring and summer weather as we approached the Virginia-Maryland line. Maryland in June with summery weather was heady trail fare indeed. More people were in the woods and on the trail, even on weekdays. The weekends made you aware that vacation time and the month of June were practically synonymous. On Saturdays and Sundays the trail was crowded. Scoutmasters had their young charges out in full force.

We walked out of Virginia, through Maryland, and into Pennsylvania in less than three days. One day, as we hiked through a pleasant woods area in Maryland, we came upon a man and woman finishing their trailside snack. As we chatted the man astonished me by asking if I was the Chuck Ebersole who was hiking the whole Appalachian Trail. I was surprised to meet a perfect stranger in the woods who knew my name.

It turned out that Sterling and Ellen Edwards were retired schoolteachers who had hiked a lot on the Appalachian Trail. That spring they had been hiking in Georgia and had met Dr. and Mrs. Molyneaux soon after Johnny and I had spent the night with the Molyneauxes at Addis Gap Lean-to. The Molyneaux family had told the Edwards family about us.

When we visited the Edwardses that night we learned that Sterling had hiked more than 1,600 miles of the Appalachian Trail in the last 15 years. He had kept meticulous notes on those portions of the trail that he had walked. He handed these notes to us that evening. It was a generous gift of information about many hundreds of trail miles we would hike. I was able to repay this generosity by supplying him with information on the sections he hadn't hiked yet, and in Maine we hiked with him across a section he had long dreaded to do on his own: the Mahoosuc Notch.

Early summer saw us walking the trail into Pennsylvania. Wild strawberries were still flourishing in hidden nooks, blackcap raspberries were ripe for trailside eating, and even black cherries and mulberries offered their luscious fruits along rural farm roads. Standing on a mountain in York County we looked down at the Susquehanna River, whose water flowed past my hometown 30 miles downstream. Upstream we could see the town of Duncannon, and we knew that once across the bridges at Duncannon we would have completed approximately one-half of our hike. I had set a tentatitve date of June 30 for crossing the Susquehanna River, and here we were, ready to cross it on June 24. We were six full days ahead of schedule. At this rate we should reach Mt.

Katahdin between the end of August and the middle of September. We were in top-notch physical condition, and with Brady playing the part of quartermaster and providing us with many home-cooked meals, I had put back 13 of the 32 pounds I had lost at one point on our hike.

All the way from Georgia through Pennsylvania people had been warning us about snakes. It was always the *next* mountain. We were never warned about the mountain we had just come over. Sometimes we were warned about rattlers lying in wait along the trail, sometimes we were told that a whole mountain was infested with them. Marshes and swampy places were pictured as being the gloomy haunts of other "pizenous sarpints." At first we worried some, but soon the warnings lost their power. I've never been afraid of snakes. I treat poisonous snakes with respect, but find them objects of curiosity rather than of fear. I have lain belly down at snake-eye level to take pictures of approaching snakes. Once as I lay in a bed of leaves taking a nap on a balmy spring day a slight rustling sound awoke me. There, close to my face, a blacksnake was looking me over. He was using his brown-red forked tongue to taste my odor in the air. When he had flicked his tongue into the air for sample collection, he withdrew it and quickly inserted it into a pocket in the roof of his mouth. This pocket is another sensing mechanism known as the Jacobson's organ. It was fascinating to watch this blacksnake taste me, so to speak, then lower his head and glide off.

Near the Clarks Ferry Bridge over the Susquehanna River we were met by a reporter and photographer from the *Harrisburg Telegraph*, a newspaper I had delivered as a boy 30 years earlier. A photograph and story about our hike appeared on the front page of the *Telegraph* the next day.

We were up at 3:30 the next morning, had a bowl of cereal, and were on the trail at 4:07. We did 9.3 miles in 2 hours and 55 minutes, then met Brady. The reason for the speed was that I wanted to visit my hometown without losing a day's hiking. We were in Bainbridge by 9:00 A.M. Since I had been away for many years and now had a beard, I was able to walk around town and get a look at other folks before they recognized me. You've heard about cousins by the dozen; I got to see many of my cousins that day, and favorite aunts stuffed me at every stop.

In Pennsylvania the hot July weather started to bear down on us. We tried to get the day's mileage in early so we could nap and swim, but the hot weather got to us on many days, nevertheless. One day stands out: it dawned clear but warm and muggy. The heat and humidity combined to give us a lazy feeling. The trail was rough and rocky and we sweated as the sun bore down. It got hotter and we took off our shirts. We had three long ascents, and much of the trail was on ridges exposed to the sun. We had started at 4:20 A.M. after eating only a bowl of cereal for breakfast, and we completed 20.44 miles in a little less than seven hours. The day's trek ended in a grove of trees behind Ansbach's Motel on U.S. Route 309. We were nearly prostrated by the heat. We each drank a king-size Pepsi, then Brady arrived with more Pepsis. It was like putting fluid on a dry sponge. My diary noted that I had walked 20 miles on a bowl of cereal and then consumed 76 ounces of cola.

More days and miles, more summer heat and perspiration, then New York was behind us and we were walking in Connecticut where we ran into a deerfly and mosquito problem. The deerflies made an absolute nuisance of themselves in our hair. The mosquitoes always got me around the ears and temple as well as on the back of my neck. Johnny and Mike (who was now hiking with us) were having just as much trouble as I was. Only Snuffy seemed to escape the onslaught. Johnny and Mike laughed at my habit of fastening a handkerchief over my head with a loose-fitting rubber band to thwart the deerflies and mosquitoes, but when they saw how well the idea worked they took up their dad's funny-looking headgear.

Coming down off a granite ledge on Jug End in Massachusetts, Snuffy slipped and fell. He landed heavily at the bottom of the ledge. For several days he didn't want to eat. We took a day off so Snuffy could rest—we could use the rest ourselves, too. Snuffy regained his appetite somewhat, but he had cut his right front foot when he fell, and for the next two weeks he limped. He would start out on three feet in the morning, shift to occasional use of the sore foot, and finally use the hurt foot as much as the others. We cut down on our daily mileage until he recuperated.

We were in Vermont by the end of July. Every time we topped a high ridge or climbed to a mountain peak we could see the rugged terrain that was waiting for us ahead. From pay binoculars on Bromley Mountain we had a look at the Presidential Range in the White Mountain National Forest. Even though we had completed more than 1,500 miles of trail, that massive outline of rock had us worried.

Johnny's eighteenth birthday came on the trail in Vermont. Three days later I had my forty-fifth birthday. We climbed Mt. Moosilauke in fog, clouds, drizzle, and a stiff breeze. We were wet, cold, and shivering, and went into the winter cabin on Mt. Moosilauke to get warm and rest. We found bologna, cheese, and bread on a shelf and made sandwiches. Thus fortified we headed down to Kinsman Notch. It was a steep wet rough rocky descent but we made it with the help of the cables and ladders.

The first 10 days in New Hampshire prepared us for what lay ahead. Smarts Mountain and Mt. Cube built up to Mt. Moosilauke, Mt. Wolf, and the Kinsmans, South and North. Overgrown trails gave us a lot of trouble over Mt. Wolf. We got lost going up South Kinsman and became thoroughly tangled in the old blowdowns through which new conifers had been growing for perhaps 10 or 15 years. We found ourselves walking on the blowdowns, trying to force a way between and through the thick growth of young trees. The map showed that the trail cut across the top of South Kinsman, and since we were already a long way past the shelter at Eliza Brook and didn't want to go back through the tangled mess, we headed straight for the mountaintop. In about 30 minutes we came to a trail, and it proved to be the Appalachian Trail! Talk about friendly little markers!

We came to Franconia Notch and started our assault on the Presidential Range. We crossed Mts. Liberty, Lincoln, Lafayette, and Garfield and arrived at Galehead Hut, where we stayed for the night. Those hut boys are really something! They are the chief cooks and bottle washers, friends, and dispensers of warmth and good cheer on the mountaintops. They backpack all food from the valley roads below. A set of scales and a record sheet on the hut porch show how keenly they compete to see who can tote the most supplies in the shortest time.

South Twin Mountain and Mt. Guyot went by quickly the next day. Michael, who was not quite 13 1/2 years of age, had rather stumbly feet, and as a consequence he took many falls. As we descended the granite ledges on the steep Zealand Mountain, Mike was in the lead. Suddenly he stumbled and disappeared over a granite ledge! I heard a dull thud, then silence. I hurried to the edge and looked over. Mike lay on his back about 20 feet below. He was looking up and grinning. He had landed on his back on a granite boulder but the pack had cushioned his head and broke his fall. He stood up, tested his muscles and appendages, and declared himself OK. In a few minutes we were on our way again, but what a scare! From then on, I noticed that Mike placed his feet a bit more carefully.

From Crawford Notch we were on the Webster Cliffs in 50 minutes, wondering where the tough trail was that everybody kept talking about. The explanation probably was that our tough trails were 1,600 miles behind us. We went on past the site where Mizpah Hut was being built. It was a beautiful day, with wonderful views of Washing-

ton. We had an easy trail from the summit of Mt. Webster all the way
to Lake-of-the-Clouds Hut.

Lakes-of-the-Clouds Hut proved to be a special place for our whole
family. Brady came up on the Cog Railway to the summit of Mt.
Washington and then walked down to the hut. What a marvelous time
we had! The afternoon sunlight was great for pictures, and we climbed
several slopes and enjoyed views of the surrounding country. When
suppertime came the guests sat on long benches while the hut boys
served steaming dishes family style on the varnished surfaces of the
wooden tables. Grace was said, and then amid laughter and chatter,
everyone enjoyed the tasty meal. While the hut boys cleared things
away, hiking groups recited poems or sang songs. Darkness settled in,
and then the real fun began. Hiking musicians arrived with an accor-
dion, two guitars, a banjo, and an enormous bull fiddle. When the
kitchen chores were finished those instruments were tuned up and put
to work. All kinds of songs were played, with everyone singing. The
hut boys made another huge pot of hot chocolate and served it with
cookies. The singing lasted for several hours. One song which tugged
at my heart was *This Land Is Your Land*. A song like that always brings
tears to my eyes. I love the green hills, the blue sky, the clean streams,
and the good soil of Mother Earth, and that song exemplified what I
was trying to find and enjoy by hiking the Appalachian Trail.

The next morning we got up late, 6:30 instead of the usual 4:00 A.M.
We hit the trail a little after 7:00 and it took us 8½ hours to put Mts.
Washington, Clay, Jefferson, Sam Adams, Adams, and Madison behind
us and get down to Pinkham Notch. We were sore and tired. The day's
mileage had been only 14.5 miles, but most of it was across rugged terrain. Brady had taken the Cog Railway down and was waiting for us
with a note from the Sterling Edwardses. They were in Gorham, New
Hampshire, a few miles away, and had invited us for supper.

We took the next day off, but were back on the trail the following
day. We went from Pinkham Notch to Carter Notch, up past Carter
Dome and Imp Shelter, then down along Rattle River. We took an
invigorating swim in a deep pool at Rattle River Shelter, then went on
to U.S. Route 2 for a total of over 20 miles for the day. We had planned
to take two days for this stretch of trail (the guidebook recommends
three) but wanted to make up for the day we had lost.

We were approaching the big one: Mahoosuc Notch. If everything
went as planned, Sterling Edwards would be waiting on the trail before
we came to Mr. Big Place. Sure enough, where a trail came up from
Success Pond we saw a figure hunched under a poncho, reading a book.
On the damp mossy forest floor we sneaked up behind him. When we

were in position, we burst forth singing "Good morning to you" to the tune of the *Happy Birthday Song*. This brought a big grin. Sterling had a candy bar for each of us, so we munched away as we discussed what lay ahead.

Mahoosuc Notch is indeed unique. There is nothing on the trail to compare with it. Imagine two tremendous mountains with faces steeply inclined, coming together at a sharp angle where they meet at the bottom. Imagine this sharp angle stretched out for almost a mile. Imagine house-sized boulders tumbling down those mountain-sides to lodge at the bottom in a jumbled mass, alongside and atop of each other. At some places the narrow notch at the bottom was completely filled with boulders, but there were huge cracks and crevices and niches existing as spaces. This jumbled and confused mess is Mahoosuc Notch. The familiar white blazes, augmented by painted arrows, point out the tortuous pathway. The trail leads around, between, behind, in and out, through, over, and under these mammoth boulders. You can't get lost. You are hemmed in by the steep-faced mountains on either side. You can only go forward or backward. In the notch you are never out of sight of either blazes or directional arrows. Most places in the notch can be walked through, but boulder clambering is necessary in several instances and passage through the cavelike places is possible by sometimes crouching, sometimes crawling on hands and knees. At other places it is necessary to take your pack off and either push it ahead of you or drag it after you, as the passage is too small for you and your pack at the same time.

It was misty on our day in Mahoosuc Notch. Everything was moist and the rocks and trees glistened with wetness. Moss grew everywhere it could attach itself and lichens crowded one another on exposed surfaces. Our apprehension turned to wonder and awe as we gazed at the scene. Our sense of satisfaction as we worked our way through the notch changed to a feeling of delight when we realized that we had finally conquered the much-talked-about Mahoosuc Notch. Mr. Edwards scrambled his 65-year-old figure through like an enthusiastic teenager. As for Snuffy, he either scrambled up the rocks or meandered through the tunnels in great style.

Then the tough part came: going up Mahoosuc Arm. Sterling Edwards and I thought we'd never make it. We stopped to rest often, eating from the tremendous crop of wild blueberries growing everywhere. Eventually we achieved the summit and headed for Speck Pond, where a trail led back to Success Pond. Mr. Edwards took this trail, and Johnny, Mike, and I continued on toward Old Speck Mountain. We went up and over a ridge and down to a warden's cabin. From that point, for over an hour, hurrying all the way, we slipped and skidded down to Grafton Notch. Old Speck's flank was black dirt turned to mud from several days of rain. Never have I been so tired of going downhill. We couldn't use the trail as it was too slippery. Instead, we stayed in the timber and paralleled the trail, using trees to cling to as we went down. We finally got down safely despite many falls. When we reached the trailer we were practically encased in mud, and laughed at the spectacle we presented.

It was time for Mike to go back to school. Good friends near Denver, Colorado, had agreed to keep him for a while. On August we went to Lewiston, had a last family supper in a Chinese restaurant, and put Mike on the bus for Denver.

Next day Johnny and I were back on the trail with about 270 miles to go. On the second day out we must have lost and found the trail 20 times in 13 miles, and after a noontime snack at Squirrel Rock Lean-to we really did get lost. We hunted left and right, then made circles over an ever-increasing area, but had no luck in finding the trail. We did find an old woods road that went in a general north direction. It also led toward the distant sound of chain saws, and in a couple of miles we came upon a timber crew at work in the woods.

One by one every man in the whole crew stopped work. The roar of chain saws was quieted and the ringing sound of axe work stopped. The burly fellow we spoke to hollered to the others and they all gathered round us. There were friendly smiles, broad grins, extended arms, pointing fingers, and men scratching lines and drawing maps on the ground, but to no avail. They were French-Canadians, and not a man in the whole crew spoke a word of English!

We stayed on the old tote road and eventually came out on a black-top road. We sat down and waited and in about an hour a man came along in a pickup truck and we learned that the Appalachian Trail was miles to our left. When we were back on the trail the time and miles passed quickly. Places like Elephant Mountain, Sabbath Day Pond, Rangeley, Saddleback Mountain, and Orbeton Stream were passed; others such as Spaulding Mountain, Mt. Sugarloaf, and Avery Peak on Mt. Bigelow followed in quick succession.

Lots of hikers see bears in the but we had passed through the Smokies before the bears came out of hibernation. We saw bear sign for almost 1,500 miles before we sighted our first bruin. It was an early misty morning in Vermont, at the edge of a fern forest. We watched the bear as he vigorously broke a tree apart to get at the black ants inside. When he scented us he quickly disappeared. We let Snuffy smell around the tree, and took a picture as he wagged his tail in excitement.

We encountered our first moose near Rangeley, and soon after that watched three more moose feeding in a pond. It was early September, and geese and ducks were plentiful. We began to encounter more bears, too, but unlike the protected bears in the national parks, the bears in Maine are hunted. As a consequence, one whiff of man is enough to send them running. We saw marten as they hunted in the early morning hours. Many times we saw buck deer munching away on some favorite browse, their antlers still in velvet. They stood and looked at us in an unconcerned manner, but when hunting season came I'm sure that attitude would change drastically.

The meeting with Brady after Mt. Bigelow was an important one. She had purchased some special equipment for us—nails. There was a handful of nails approximately four inches in length, and about 25 eight-inch spikes. When we had planned the hike we knew there were rivers to cross, but we assumed there was a bridge of some kind at each crossing. As we approached Maine we learned that there was no bridge where the trail crossed the Kennebec River. After walking all the way from Georgia it seemed a shame not to cross the Kennebec under our own power, so we decided to build a raft. We had swim trunks and several plastic bags. We would put our clothes and the camera, wrapped in plastic, in our packs. Both packs, and Snuffy, would be placed on the raft.

We met Brady, traded dirty clothes for clean, got the nails and spikes, and picked up fresh rations. Early morning found us on our way through a stretch of absolutely miserable storm-twisted and tangled blowdowns, followed by an extensive area where logging operations had obliterated the trail markings. Eventually, however, we stood on the bank of the Kennebec River, looking across the dark blue water. It was two o'clock in the afternoon and not a cloud marred the clear blue sky. The sun shone brightly, no breeze stirred, and the day was mild and warm. The current of the river wasn't what I'd call sluggish, but I didn't think it was dangerously swift, either. I figured we could navigate it by building our raft well upstream and letting the current carry us across on a diagonal slant. The distance straight across seemed to be at least 100 yards, and perhaps more.

Across the river we could see an occasional car traveling on U.S. Route 201. As we stood looking over the river Brady arrived and parked to watch the proceedings through a pair of binoculars. There was also another lady sitting on the far shore. We didn't know who she was.

We changed to swim trunks and went upstream to find wood for our raft. As we scouted the river bank we saw short logs of every dimension strewn up and down the shore. At the time we didn't realize these were pulpwood logs destined for a paper mill downstream. Three of the largest logs were laid side by side and the nails and spikes were used to fasten smaller pieces of wood at right angles. We finished the raft by making a sturdy handrail on two sides. We planned to hold on to these rails as we navigated the raft by swimming alongside.

When the raft was finished we pulled it into the water and placed both packs on it. While Johnny held the raft, I carried Snuffy out and put him on top of the packs. Snuffy was as nonchalant as if he rode a raft across a swift river every day.

We were out in waist-deep water when I glanced at the shore. Something didn't look quite right. I couldn't see the rocks on which we had assembled our raft. Then I noticed that the logs along the shore were afloat. Suddenly I knew why the rocks were covered and the logs were floating. The river was rising—fast! I looked upstream. What a sight! I saw a surging crest of water bearing down on us. Hurtling along with the water were hundreds of pulp logs. We were now deep in the water and hanging onto the raft's handrails. Holy smokes, I thought, now we're really in for it!

However, it wasn't as bad as my frantic imagination pictured it. It was scary, but our raft was steady as it floated through the surge of onrushing water. To have become panic-stricken and fought the water would have been our undoing, so we just went along with it. As a log came at us, we gripped the rail with one hand and pushed off the approaching log with the other. It seemed like it took forever to cross that river. We went sweeping past our intended landing place, but made a landing farther downstream in fine style. We pulled our raft ashore and Snuffy hopped off. Brady ran down and hugged us. The packs were dry and everything was in good shape. Neither Johnny nor I got a scratch while crossing the river, but my feet got bruised as I tried to stop the raft as we approached the shore.

I guess Brady and I were the only ones who were scared. Johnny's youthful exuberance blinded him to any danger at the time. Looking back now, he views the event with a little more awe. I don't mind admitting that my heart was pretty far up in my throat from the time I first sighted those logs bearing down on us until we stood on shore. As for Snuffy, I've never seen such an unruffled dog. He must have had plenty of confidence in us.

The lady who had observed our crossing snapped a picture of Johnny and me standing by the raft, then introduced herself. She was

Mrs. Eva Batchelder, a reporter for the Waterville, Maine, newspaper. The next day the picture appeared on the front page, along with a story of our hike.

It wasn't until we saw Katahdin from the lookout tower on White Cap that I believed our hike would be successful. For some reason I had felt that something would keep us from reaching our goal, but now I felt optimistic. We said good-bye to Brady, shouldered our heavy packs, and headed out in beautiful weather. In three hours, over easy terrain, we came to Cooper Brook Falls. What a peaceful place! A stream fed into a quiet pool upon whose mirror surface floated colored leaves. Reds and golds predominated, but more subtle tones were represented in various yellows, creams, tans, and browns. We sat down to let this loveliness soak in.

After a midmorning snack we reluctantly headed for Potaywadjo Spring. The day was beautifully clear and crisply invigorating. We saw a pair of martens investigating the possibilities of a squirrel dinner. We passed within 15 yards of an eight-point buck. With a small pair of binoculars, I watched a three-toed black-backed woodpecker, and in the same vicinity I saw two yellow-bellied sapsuckers and a family of flickers. Because of all this, the five miles to Lower Joe Mary Lake took longer than usual, and hurrying to make up for lost time almost proved my undoing. Summer plants were hip-high and their foliage obscured the trail. Suddenly I found myself on the ground, as though I'd been knocked down. My upper right leg was throbbing with excruciating pain.

With Johnny's help I finally managed to stand. The source of the pain was the large muscle midway between knee and hip. I leaned on Johnny and checked for broken bones and everything to be normal despite the pain. I limped a few tentative steps. As soon as I could put more of my weight on the injured leg we looked for the cause of the accident. We found a huge log laying parallel to the trail, held off the ground by its own branches. At the level of my mid-thigh the thick stub of a broken limb stuck out into the trailway. The bushes had concealed this stub and almost caused us to have a serious accident. Gritting my teeth, I helped Johnny heave that hiker's trap away from the trail.

It was about three miles to Potaywadjo Spring Lean-to. We went slow and easy all the way. The lean-to was nice enough, but a heavy canopy of trees made the area dark and gloomy. We went on to Antler Camps so I could lay in the sun and warm my leg. I'm convinced that the miles of hiking had strengthened my leg muscles and saved me from serious injury. Proceeding at a little faster pace, we came to

Pemadumcook Lake. Across the lake, in brilliant sunshine, we could see Mt. Katahdin. What a glorious sight!

On the shoreline of Pemadumcook Lake lay several acres of driftwood—all the firewood we could want. Thick luxuriant grass grew between the forest and the lake. We decided to make our camp there, as the thick grass would make a good bed. Before the sun faded that evening, trumpeter swans cruised slowly by, just beyond the driftwood. From across the lake came the haunting cry of loons. Mt. Katahdin faded to a silhouette. We stacked driftwood within reach of our sleeping bags so that all through the night we had only to reach out to replenish the fire.

Frost-beaded grass surrounded us at daylight, and mist hung over the lake. Going to the beach for more driftwood I saw a beaver swimming toward me. He had a stick in his mouth. He approached to within a few yards and climbed up on a small rock. He proceeded to gnaw breakfast off the stick. For several minutes the only sounds I could hear were the lap-lap-lap of tiny wavelets on the shore and the beaver's teeth as he ate his vegetarian fare. A loon's piercing call shattered the stillness. In instant reaction the beaver left his rock, slapped his tail on the water, and disappeared beneath its surface. My little private drama had ended.

My leg was stiff and painful. We went slowly at first, but the farther we went the more limber my leg muscles became. Soon we were able to maintain a near-normal pace. We came to the privately owned Nahmakanta Lake Camps and met an elderly gentleman out clearing the trail. Miss Jean Stephenson was with him, painting new blaze marks. Like all hikers, I owed this lady a great debt of thanks for her numerous contributions to the Appalachian Trail. We chatted awhile and then Johnny and I went on.

The day had started off clear and frosty, then clouds moved in, and as evening came on it was getting damper and colder. It was dusk when we reached the Rainbow Lake Lean-to, where we found a huge stack of dry firewood and a three-pound box of milk powder, which we needed. There were also two iron-framed bunks. With a cheery fire, a warm supper, and good bunks, we were enjoying real trail luxury. We had hiked 20 miles that day, and sleep came early and easy.

We planned a leisurely breakfast as we had only 12 miles to go, but habits are hard to break and we found ourselves leaving the lean-to at 7:30 A.M. Every view was gorgeous in the beautiful fall weather. Blueberries were abundant. In Pennsylvania, where strawberries, blackcap raspberries, and cherries were ripe, we had fed Snuffy some of whatever we picked. Later, we held his nose to the strawberries and he learned to glean them for himself. When he had learned on strawberries, it was an easy step for him to learn to pick low-hanging raspberries. We had to hold him up to a cherry tree, of course. He'd much rather have us pick the berries and feed them to him, but we would jokingly shove him aside and tell him to go pick his own, and he learned to do just that. He would pull his lips back and delicately strip fruit off the bush. On such things as huckleberries and lowbush blueberries his tongue would do most of the work. He learned to treat raspberry and blackberry briers with a certain respect. He also learned to stand on his hind legs to reach higher bushes, and even to use a forepaw in pulling branches closer.

Next day was the easiest day we had on the whole trail—we hiked only a little over nine miles. On this day, since we would walk past our trailer, Johnny and I didn't carry packs. Only Snuffy had his pack, with one day's ration in it. We wanted to be able to say that he had made the whole trail carrying his own food. Fall colors greeted us everywhere as we walked at a leisurely pace. In fact, we used six hours to do the nine miles, and took three swims along the way. When we reached Katahdin Stream Campground, Brady and the trailer were waiting for us. We planned to sleep on Mt. Katahdin on our last night on the trail and as Baxter Peak lies above timberline we decided to take a two-man tent and a small stove as survival insurance in case of bad weather.

That evening there was a knock on the trailer door. It was a young park ranger, and he told us that dogs were not allowed in Baxter State Park, not even on a leash. Brady's reaction was open-mouthed consternation. Johnny's eyes reflected anger. I didn't think I had heard correctly, but the young man repeated his message. It meant that after 2,000 miles on the Appalachian Trail, Snuffy couldn't finish it. I thought it was worth a try to get this rule suspended in Snuffy's case. Johnny and I went back to the ranger's quarters and he got in touch with Park Superintendent Helon Taylor on his shortwave radio. As a result of our conversation, Superintendent Taylor was kind enough to allow Snuffy to complete the hike upon our promise to keep him on a leash while in Baxter State Park. (As a matter of fact, I agree that dogs and cats and other pets don't belong in parks. In addition to the problem of excrement, no owner can be sure his pet won't obey his hunting instinct.)

September 17, 1964, dawned misty and cloudy. We were up at and had a hearty breakfast. Without too much effort we were soon at timberline, then the going became somewhat rougher as the trail went up over huge granite rocks. It was during the climb over these huge granite boulders that Snuffy had to be helped for the third and last time.

There were steel rods placed in the granite as handholds to assist the hiker, but of course Snuffy couldn't cope with these handholds. We gave him a boost over one granite ledge, but otherwise he made it on his own.

Climbing at a steady leisurely pace we soon gained the plateau. This was the last mile of our journey. For 2,000 miles Johnny, Snuffy, and I had shared a common goal and a special companionship. Our goal was now in sight, but it also represented the end of our adventure together.

In a few moments we were standing on Baxter Peak. Clouds had closed over us in a solid mass. We snapped several pictures as we signed the register. Now the hike was officially completed. The last ascent of the last mountain over the last mile was done. As was our habit, we set up our tent and hit the sack early.

Next morning was cold, frosty, and misty. We packed and took The Saddle Trail down. Brady was waiting on us at the campground. We stopped to thank Park Superintendent Helon Taylor for letting Snuffy complete the hike. Superintendent Taylor looked our canine hiker over, examined his pack, and then presented Snuffy with a Mt. Katahdin patch. We tried to get a picture of Mr. Taylor presenting the emblem, but Snuffy's reaction was to try to bite the hand of the man who bad been kind enough to let him finish his hike. Some dogs just don't have any gratitude.

Before starting our hike I had collected the names dresses of relatives, close friends, and acquaintances—a total of 68 names. Along the trail we had met many people who befriended us, and they had wanted to know when we finished our hike. These folks added 84 more names to the list. So, there at the foot of Mt. Katahdin, I sent out 152 postcards and short letters.

During those two days of writing cards and letters, Johnny and I kept looking at Mt. Katahdin. I think we had the same thought. Finally, on the third morning, I said, "Johnny, let's hike Mt. Katahdin again." His grin was an answer. We grabbed canteens, waist belts, food, and ponchos. Brady couldn't see the sense of our big idea, but said she'd meet us at Roaring Brook Campground at the designated time. We left at 7:15 A.M. on a beautiful day and were on top of our favorite mountain at 10:30. At timberline we caught up with another through hiker, Ray Baker of New Jersey. We stopped and talked awhile, and then moved on. I certainly didn't want to intrude on his big day. We waited at Baxter Peak and soon Ray Baker came across the plateau to complete his hike. We offered him our congratulations, and at that moment there were three end-to-enders standing on Mt. Katahdin.

Following the Appalachian Trail; or Don't Spare the White Paint

By Jim Shattuck

Started at MT. KATAHDIN on August 24, 1966
Arrived at SPRINGER MOUNTAIN on May 23, 1967

"Lord, help me! Help me! I need Your help!"

In the early morning of March 1, 1967, this cry emanated from behind a slant rock outcropping and mingled with the sound of wind and drifting snow atop Sinking Creek Mountain. Yes, and I'm not ashamed to say that it was I who was doing the yelling. Fortunately, I did not know that an unofficial temperature reading of twenty-seven degrees below zero was being registered at nearby Mountain Lake. All I knew was that the cold in these southwest Virginia mountains had a peculiar penetrating effect. My numbed hands and fingers were behaving like uncoordinated, unfeeling claws as I tried without success to lace my boots; the rawhide would mash up against the grommet holes, or if it did poke through I seemed unable to grasp the end and pull the lacing tight. All my blasphemy was exhausted; I had run through my limited vocabulary of meaningless oaths several times. It was only when I began to call on The Great Master for help that I made any progress in the simple, yet incredibly difficult, task of lacing my boots. I turned next to what, in that temperature, was equally hard—stuffing my sleeping bag in its carrying sack and strapping it onto the packframe. Then came the snowshoes; the straps were ice-coated and as stiff as iron. They had to be blown on and limbered long enough to secure the snowshoes to my boots. Each step of each operation was accompanied by the same urgent appeal for help. When I was finally on the trail that morning I had the feeling that I was not walking alone and that perhaps the Lord still had a job for me when I was through. Certainly I had an obligation to seek it.

This one incident impressed me more than any other adventure during my trek from Maine to Georgia on the Appalachian Trail.[1] In a sense it culminated a series of events that for me revealed a presence more powerful than anything human, and yet it was peculiarly human. It was as if some kindly, knowing person had stepped in, time and time again, to compensate for my ignorance, bullheadedness, and lack of skill. These repeated intercessions gave me another chance and taught me lessons without inflicting serious injury.

One lesson, which was repeated several times, aimed to make me almost ridiculously cautious when on rough footway. I remember getting my foot caught in the loop of a fallen communications wire while descending a mountain in Maine. The resultant spill brought my eye to within an inch of the sharp end of a sapling that had broken off close to the ground. Another time, while slabbing a Georgia hillside on a wet day, my left foot came down on a slippery, leaf-covered pole. My foot shot out from under me and I fell forward completely out of control. I remember thinking that the science of judo could not have done a better job on me. When I hit the ground I felt something snug against my right side between hip and rib. This turned out to be the broken trunk of a sapling. I could almost feel its spikelike tip penetrating my vitals. However, I had been spared, and once again was reminded to take it easy over the rough stuff.

I know there are those who welcome rough footway as a challenge and like to see how fast they can go while picking their way from rock to rock. At the moment I am not in their ranks and, being a newcomer to hiking at the age of 51, I expect to continue to resist this temptation.

As I gained more experience, I found that it was folly to try to enjoy the scenery while actually walking; this luxury required a full stop. Intermittent, quick glances were permitted, even mandatory, to pick up signs, trail markings, and changes in terrain. But, just as when driving a car, you really have to keep your eye on the road. To me this meant concentration on the twenty-one square feet of constantly changing footway which lay immediately ahead. Believe me, there is a remarkable similarity in this limited vista all the way from Maine to Georgia.

The unique landscape characteristics along the trail are borne in on one during pauses that allow contemplative viewing. It is during such pauses that the names of the various ranges of the Appalachians suggest themselves. Without realizing it you would probably come up with the

---

[1] This account covers the complete journey afoot during the period mentioned on the preceding page. The detours mentioned in the text were made up in 1968. Hence 1968 is the official year of completion.—ED.

same handles or ones that would mean the same thing. For example, the "White" Mountains of New Hampshire were snow-covered when I first saw them in September from the summit of Old Speck in Maine. The utter lack of foliage above the tree line emphasized starkness and whiteness when seen from that distance. Later, when I crossed the Connecticut River to Vermont, the "Green" Mountains were green and parklike; in many places en route to Sherburne Pass the landscape would be the envy of any city park commissioner. The summits and ridges in Virginia loom up as blue silhouettes of various shades depending on distance; "Blue Ridge" could not have been more appropriate. Farther south the summits of the "Great Smokies" of North Carolina and Tennessee are nearly always rising midst a gray cloudy mist that looks like smoke.

There are a hundred memories from a trip like this which crowd in for expression, particularly if this is one's first hike and every experience is new. In my case, my only previous brush with wilderness travel had been as a youngster on a guided three-day canoe trip. It was rugged in spots, but hardly preparation for backpacking 2,000 miles in the Appalachian Mountains.[2]

Maine

I first set foot on the Appalachian Trail in Maine in the late afternoon of August 24, 1966, after a climb from Roaring Brook to Katahdin's Baxter Peak, the northern terminus of the Appalachian Trail.

---

[2] Why did Jim Shattuck make his hike in wintertime, when the weather made every part of the trip much more difficult? The answer is that this was a point in his life when he had the time, which is the limiting factor for most people who want to hike the entire trail. In Jim's case, the time happened to come partly in winter. When queried on his motive for walking the Appalachian Trail, Jim replied: "I can only say that the idea had intrigued me ever since I heard there was such a trail. When I left my job at Yale University I figured I would take a couple of months off and walk it. My wife gave the project her blessing and that was that. The estimate of 'a couple of months' proved to be a measure of my inexperience and my inability to prophesy accurately how long it would take me to walk anywhere in the wilderness. I will say that the people I met at the Appalachian Trail Conference office in Washington accepted me and my plans with a straight face. They were very helpful and suggested that I might better plan on a little more time, say three months. If I ever go again I feel that five months would be a reasonable target for me. So, you might say, I started off with absolutely no idea of the hazards or strains to be encountered. It was an unfolding adventure which, like a good book, I just couldn't put down. During my Christmas break I was offered a job as director of personnel at the University of New Haven (then called New Haven College). I accepted, with the understanding that I could finish the trail before starting to work. I figured that, once employed, I could never put the trail ahead of the job. What a feeling of emancipation to have been able to do it just once!"—ED.

Jim Shattuck demonstrating his equipment for friends. Photo by John Green.

The climb to this eminence proved to be a two-day effort for me, with an interim stop at Chimney Pond. Like a typical neophyte, I was carrying too much. I labored under a pack that weighed sixty-two pounds. Hence at 7:00 P.M., Chimney Pond with its cabins, lean-tos, and ranger substation was a most welcome sight. I gratefully shed my burden and spent the night in a lean-to.

Next morning I saw my first moose, a big fan-horned bull, who was wandering sociably among sleeping campers during the predawn hours.

As the camp began to waken, word came from the ranger station that adverse weather conditions at the summit required closing all but the Saddle Trail. This, of course, was fine with me because I would now have company on the easiest, most sheltered route. I reported to the ranger, as required, that I intended to take off on the Appalachian Trail when I reached Baxter Peak. He, in turn, relayed this information by phone to his colleague on the other side of the mountain at Katahdin Stream Campground. He told the other ranger to be on the lookout for me some time that evening.

As it turned out, my pace was such that my expected company began to drift ahead of me, around me, and all but over me as I struggled with my excessively heavy pack. In the afternoon I met the same faces as they repassed me on their return to Chimney Pond.

I asked one acquaintance to report to the ranger that I would not be getting to Katahdin Stream Campground that night, but not to be concerned because I was well equipped and would spend the night at the top.

All I could do when I finally reached the crest of Katahdin's saddle was to drop my pack behind a rock and continue in a forty-mile-an-hour gale to Baxter Peak. There, midst the fog, mist, and wind, I noted Old Glory snapping straight out from its pole and a sign marking the start of the Appalachian Trail to Georgia. The first white trail blaze was barely visible in the fog and already I had just about had it. I made my way back to my pack after scratching my name and the date on the door of the cabinet which was supposed to house a logbook and pencil, but didn't.

The night of August 24 is one I shall always remember as my first, and I hope last, sojourn on the crest of Mt. Katahdin after dark. It was cold even on this summer night. The wind was hungry and aggressive and grabbed anything that wasn't weighted down. Fortunately, my only loss was a foam rubber pillow. This was snapped up and whisked away the instant I raised my head in the act of grabbing at a far corner of my ground cloth. Even with the cloth wrapped completely around me I still got plenty of air as it whistled through the stitching along the seams.

August 25 dawned clear, bright, and warm. The view from my lofty perch was positively overwhelming. The tiny lookingglass ponds and lakes scattered over an undulating green carpet of covered hills were in peaceful contrast to the travail of the preceding night.

Descending to Katahdin Stream was almost as difficult for me as climbing. It took me all day. Parents and their children, Boy Scouts, and other assorted hikers met me on their way up in the morning, then repassed me on their return in the afternoon. One young girl was climbing barefoot because it was "more of a challenge."

If I hadn't been so new at the game I would have been demoralized by this show of prowess on the part of others. As it was, I knew I could only improve. One party of men gave me a lift with my pack and without their help I never would have made Katahdin Stream Campground that night. On arrival I was good only for a drink of water and a supine position.

A change was in order, and I did lighten my pack somewhat. However, my cautious purging of material was nothing compared to what happened nineteen days later at the little town of Caratunk on the Kennebec River. It was here that Sig Wojcik and Joe Thompson overtook me. They had started independently from Katahdin and had met when Joe overtook Sig. Both men were extremely weight conscious. Sig had drilled seven holes in his toothbrush handle to lighten his load; in all he was carrying only twenty pounds on his back.

I let them go to work on my pack and they cut it down by at least twenty pounds. They sliced off my pants at boot-top level, and lectured me on the sins of carrying too much.

Needless to say, life on the trail became much more tolerable after that. The first nineteen days, however, are a blur of confused striving in the lonely deserted wilderness that the southbound hiker encounters when he leaves the Katahdin area. Looking back on this period, I can divide it into "Hell," "Heaven," and "Purgatory."

"Hell" included (1) mile-long ascents with no letup, (2) breaking through a rotted log in the bed of an old tote road and sinking hip-deep in black muck, (3) tripping and stumbling along a strewn trail, (4) trying to keep warm on a cold night either in or out of a lean-to, (5) trying to get hips comfortable on a lean-to floor, (6) in the still of the night hearing the snap of a fallen branch followed by a heavy step and the sound of sniffing outside the lean-to, (7) getting tangled in a communications wire while making a steep mountainous descent, (8) looking a bear in the eye at Mahar's Landing before he decided to turn and run (I was absolutely riveted to the ground), (9) being thirsty and having no water, (10) the last mile or so before sighting a lean-to, (11) hiking in the rain, and (12) losing the trail.

"Heaven" included (1) the sight, the sound, and the taste of a mountain brook or stream, (2) the glorious panoramic view from the tops of mountains—made more glorious by the fact that you have climbed there yourself, not come in a car, (3) the first sight of the bright corrugated roof (or other evidence) of a lean-to after an arduous day on the trail, (4) the first moments of utter relaxation and the sensation of floating on air after shedding the pack, (5) the taste of wild mountain blueberries, (6) sardines, crackers, and canned apricots found in a deserted sporting camp, (7) the peace and stillness of an isolated lakeshore, (8) a well-shaded, smooth, slightly downhill woods road and a plainly visible trail marker, (9) a cold beer at Abol Bridge and again at a lean-to near a sporting camp—the gifts of weekend mountain climbers and fishermen, respectively, (10) taking a bath after a week or ten days on the trail, (11) the hushed, high-pitched serene sound that the wind makes at the top of a mountain, and (12) the sight of another person when you think you are lost. I became a proud dues-paying member of the Maine Appalachian Trail Club on August 30 when I met Mr. and Mrs. Steve Clark, two of its officers. They were putting up much-needed signs and markers.

"Purgatory" included just two items: (1) climbing on hands and knees up steep ascents or descending via the seat of the pants, and (2) the pull and tug of the pack when one needed assurance that his house is on his back.

During this early period (September 2 to be exact), I came across three northbound hikers: Chuck Ebersole, his son Mike, and their dog Snuffy. They were en route to Katahdin from Georgia. They had just emerged from a dip in the lake at Antlers Camps, a deserted lumbering headquarters. Chuck remained modestly behind a tree until I assured him that I had no women with me. In Chuck's party there were no freeloaders—even Snuffy had a backpack containing his food.

Getting back to Caratunk and the surgery Joe Thompson and Sig Wojcik performed on my pack and trousers, I can say that Caratunk marked the start of a new era in my hiking career. After shedding twenty pounds the contrasts between "Hell" and "Heaven" were no longer pronounced. The only thing I really missed was the sensation of floating on air after removing my pack.

Sig said that people he met at Katahdin Stream had described me as "a man in his late thirties, carrying an eighty-eight pound pack, utterly exhausted, and staggering." The ranger, Sig said, had urged him to have me lighten my pack if he caught up with me.

Sig, Joe, and I were ferried by canoe across the Kennebec River, a broad, fast-moving avenue for floating logs. We spent the night on the opposite bank and decided to continue as independent units, each at his own pace. As it turned out, however, we stayed together for the next two months, largely because we were hiking from lean-to to lean-to. Our respective paces had us separated by not much more than a mile toward the end of any given day.

I usually arrived in camp after Sig and Joe were settled in and had a fire going. My contribution was building the fire the next morning, aided, of course, by much helpful advice from the two occupied sleeping bags.

Joe Thompson, a June graduate of Duke University, was by all odds the speed demon in our triumvirate. He was from Raleigh, North Carolina, and was expecting to meet his draft board around each bend in the trail.

Sig Wojcik, a forty-two year old amateur biologist, was getting material for a book on the uses of plants along the Appalachian Trail. He kept us well supplied with mushrooms and other supplements to our diet which I never would have assayed on my own. Traveling with Sig was assurance against starvation if not hunger.

Sig's propensity for snoring had its advantages. One night at East Carry Pond Lean-to I lost my bearings during a nocturnal rendezvous with nature, but those somnolent sonorous blasts guided me back unerringly.

On September 16, Sig and Joe got off to an early start and I fully expected to see them that night at Avery Memorial Lean-to on top of Big Bigelow Mountain. However, I proceeded to lose my way three times and finally became benighted at the foot of Little Bigelow Mountain. I camped in the woods near a lake—I even built a fire in hopes that some warden would spot it and appear to arrest me. What puzzled me was that white trail markings led right down to the water's edge.

Backtracking next morning I found where a bear had completely destroyed a sign that would have guided me left and up the slopes of Big Bigelow. At the summit I was hailed by the fire warden, Bill Connors, who seemed to be expecting me. I ascended his lofty perch and met this most intelligent, articulate gentleman. Bill was a college professor during the academic year and said that his two occupations meshed nicely. He told me that Sig and Joe had spent the preceding night with him.

It was from Mr. Connors that I heard another of the many tales about Emma Gatewood, the elderly hiker who walked the trail three times and is a tradition along its every mile. He said that one foggy morning he looked out to see a lone figure approaching from the southwest. As this hiker neared the base of his tower he could see it was a woman dressed in a long black skirt (a real maxi, reaching almost to her ankles). Her hat was a broad-brimmed affair and her footgear consisted of a pair of light sneakers. Over one shoulder she carried a sack which contained all seventeen pounds of her camping equipment, and in her hand was a six-foot staff.

He said she was not to be kidded about her costume. His attempted levity concerning her sneakers received a chilly response. But she stayed long enough for him to bake her a cake and they parted good friends. He said she expressed as much admiration for his domestic prowess as he did for her stamina in hiking from Georgia.

On September 19, I finally caught up to Sig and Joe at Piazza Rock Lean-to after a sixteen-mile trek in rain and fog from Mt. Sugarloaf Lean-to. The route was over Saddleback Mountain where Alan Scanlon, the fire warden at the summit, gave me coffee and reported that Sig and Joe had passed through a few hours earlier. This news, as well as the coffee, helped overcome the temptation to stop as darkness approached.

I remember thinking that I would never see Sig and Joe again and that I had never really expressed anything but skepticism at the way they had pared down my pack at Caratunk. If possible, I wanted to thank them for this act of mercy before their faster pace carried them completely out of my orbit. So when the smell of their campfire reached me high up on the mountain, my progress became a race against night. My arrival in camp was like a class reunion. Sig and Joe said they had heard me wheezing and blowing as I clambered down the last quarter mile of mountainous trail.

Next morning, with supplies running low, we decided to surface midst civilization in the town of Rangeley, Maine. Rangeley was only a few miles north of the trail and could be reached by highway at the next trail crossing. My particular route to the highway proved memorable in that I encountered a beaver dam that had backed up water in a low swampy area and completely flooded the trail. There was no way to avoid wading knee-deep for some fifty yards. Sig and Joe, who started later, found a cutoff to the highway which missed this mess.

In town we found a laundromat which promptly became headquarters. Sig and I dried everything, including our boots, in one of the dryers. Drying boots in this manner is not recommended, inasmuch as it has a delayed but disastrous effect on their longevity. It also is quite disturbing to other customers who are used to a quiet hum as opposed to a muffled clippety-clop during the drying operation.

From Speck Pond Shelter we had just ten more miles to go in Maine, but those ten miles were to prove more than a single day's hike. The first leg of the journey, 4.8 miles to Full Goose Shelter, led through that obstacle course called the Mahoosuc Notch. This trip, which looks ridiculously short on the map, took us more than eight hours. The trail markers along it are plainly visible, but they seem to dare you to come rather than to beckon.

We found ourselves crawling through tunnels and caves, clambering over huge boulders, and wedging through narrow rocky passages. My pack took a terrific beating. For the most part I could not wear it, but had to push it, pull it, heft it, or drop it, depending on the situation. A little of this goes a long way, but we were at a point of no return and had to continue through "Lena's Den" as we termed this memorable section of trail.

Our last stop in Maine was at Carlo Col Shelter, a picturesque mountain haven, after another rough day. A great deal of rain had fallen, and this made the journey from Speck Pond a very slippery one, whether climbing or descending. I probably made more three-point landings here than in any other stretch of similar length.

In looking over my diary notes, I find this quote: "The Maine terrain is tough but the people are wonderful." Maine in many ways is the most picturesque section of the trail. Its seclusion and wildness cannot be matched by any of the other thirteen states through which the trail passes. Maine also presents the toughest going—at least that is my impression. Granted, I was in better condition as the trip progressed; but I recall that in Maine I had a constant backache which did not reappear until the strenuous twenty-three mile section south of Wesser, North Carolina. This barometer of pain has, I think, some significance.

New Hampshire

Crossing the state line into New Hampshire called for a celebration. In our case this took the form of a dip in the icy waters of isolated Gentian Pond on the evening of September 29. Maine was behind us and we looked forward to manicured parklike travel from here on!

Although this idyllic condition was not to be, I never had cause to complain. By comparison, all other difficult terrain came in acceptable and manageable quantities.

Our first stop in the White Mountain National Forest was at Rattle River Lean-to, just a short distance from Gorham, on October 1. Next day we again strung out on the trail, with Sig and Joe homing in on Imp Shelter. I, head down, passed the turnoff sign and continued until night caught me at Zeta Pass. While this made for a shelterless night on the ground, it did put me ahead of Sig and Joe for the first time since Caratunk, Maine. When this lead held up the rest of the way to Pinkham Notch my morale improved no end.

At Pinkham Notch we spent the night of October 3 at the Appalachian Mountain Club headquarters hut; hot showers, warm bed, dinner, and breakfast with all you could eat for only eight dollars. It is surprising how these simple creature comforts loom in importance out of all proportion to their place in the normal, civilized, workaday world.

But even more important for us, we learned of the dangers to be encountered in the Presidential Range, notably around Mt. Washington. We bought maps that showed the maze of trails as well as the location of refuge huts. For the first time since Mt. Katahdin, the Appalachian Trail was facing real competition and was losing its single identity. This of course made trail junctions, signs, and maps all-important.

Next morning, Joe as usual was off and flying. Sig and I stayed together in the climb up Mt. Madison. Just below tree line we passed large yellow-and-black signs that warned of the most dangerous weather conditions in the country; the signs suggested that hikers turn back immediately if there was evidence of a storm brewing. Fortunately, all was well and we spent the night of October 4 in the deserted Madison Hut.

The concealing power and danger of fog were borne in on Sig and me before we had gone a hundred yards from Madison Hut. We glanced back from a slight elevation and saw a fog bank rolling in. Within seconds it enveloped and completely concealed the hut and its adjacent refuge shelter.

We made our way to Gray Knob through a gathering snowstorm. This cabin, which is maintained by interested citizens of Randolph, New Hampshire, is located at about tree line. As we approached it we passed through a winter wonderland with snow building up on the branches of the tiny evergreen trees bordering the trail.

We found Joe in the warm, cozy confines of the hut. He was feeling no pangs of hunger midst all the leftover food supplies. He said his companions on the previous night had been Dan Cole and a well-armed young man carrying a rifle and a revolver. The latter told him that he worked as a short-order cook when not tramping the mountains. He then proceeded to demonstrate his culinary prowess by cooking a delicious apple dumpling from the supplies at hand.

The snow continued all night and built up to several inches. Consequently, we maintained our Gray Knob headquarters for two more days until the sun began to shine again on October 8. Four MIT students arrived on our last night, having made their way with the aid of flashlights.

Joe and I had tested the footway on the seventh when we made a round trip to the impressive lone peak of Mt. Adams, which affords a magnificent view in all directions. Next day our route to Mt. Washington took us over Mt. Jefferson. The latter had at least three high points, which looked of equal height, and I couldn't help but contrast it with the single unmistakable peak of Mt. Adams—so like the two characters themselves. Adams was one who took a stand and would not budge from it, while Jefferson was a man of compromise.

We spent the night of October 9 at the House on Washington. Weekend crowds arrived by car and the Cog Railway and provided a carnival atmosphere. This was a bit of a shock if one was used to loneliness in high places.

The weather station on Mt. Washington was of great interest. There we learned that a wind velocity of 231 miles an hour had been registered in 1934. Evidence of the power of wind was apparent during the night. Its incessant howling was positively inspiring. At one point I looked out the window expecting to see gutters breaking loose and all sorts of debris flying around. Instead, the moonlight revealed a scene of perfect stillness and peace. Everything that was going to blow away had long since blown.

October 9 was a perfect summer day. All evidence of snow was gone and we went on to Mizpah Spring Hut, another AMC establishment. As we were leaving the vicinity of the Summit House we saw, scarcely two hundred yards distant, a large cross implanted in the ground. It marked the spot where a man and his son were found dead of exposure. Remembering the concealing power of the fog on Mt. Madison I could well imagine how a person might give up without realizing the proximity of shelter.

At Mizpah Spring we found the hut still in operation. We also found a custom of celebrating the birthdays of anyone who had achieved fame or near fame. The night of October 9 was the Queen of England's turn. As no women were present, the hut master had to do the honors as queen. This he did with appropriate and telling references to the king.

Our next stop of note was the refuge room at the Hut on Garfield Ridge. Like so many of the huts at this time of year, it was closed for the season but maintained a room for hikers like ourselves. Our arrival was accompanied by another snowstorm, which made for an extended stay of two days.

It was at Galehead that we were able to use our ropes for the first and only time—rappelling from the rafters of the refuge room.

It was also here that Sig stoked up the oil-drum boiler of a make-shift sauna that he discovered a short distance from the hut. This had been constructed of a double layer of polyethylene and retained heat up to temperatures of 130° F. He insisted that Joe and I join him in a communal sweat followed by a roll in the snow. I am sure that if there had been witnesses to this episode they would have rushed for the nearest net. However, I have never felt cleaner than after that hot-cold treatment high in the White Mountains.

In contrast to this wintry desert world in which we were cavorting was the indescribable New Hampshire foliage at lower altitudes and in the valleys. Looking down, one saw a carpet of red, gold, orange, and green as Nature touched the leaves with her autumn brush.

October 14 dawned clear, bright, and warm. We traversed the 11.5 miles to the Liberty Spring Shelter. This memorable journey led over Mt. Garfield, Mt. Lafayette, Mt. Lincoln, and Little Haystack. Mt. Lafayette particularly impressed me with its snow-covered ridge along which the trail runs between lines of small trees. A new-comer to the White Mountains should not miss it.

Sig's shoes and mine began to show signs of the torture we had subjected them to in the laundromat dryer in Rangeley. His soles were shot and the stitching in mine began to come loose. When we reached Franconia Notch, Joe continued on to Mt. Moosilauke and the Dartmouth Outing Club Winter Cabin located there while Sig and I got a ride into the nearby town of Lincoln.

We found a cobbler, Ivone Cloutier, who gave us immediate attention. In fact, his whole family cooperated to make this a unique experience. Mrs. Cloutier gave us coffee while his sons and daughters showed us their litter of puppies, half-boxer and half-water spaniel. The only trick these cute little creatures had learned was to squeal when placed on their backs.

When we returned to the woods, Sig and I promptly lost the trail and had to bushwhack our respective ways to the summit of Moosilauke. There we found winter conditions with hoarfrost so thick it looked like snow. The wind was very strong and it was bitterly cold.

The DOC cabin where we found Joe was in an area above the tree line. Being so exposed, it was held to the ground by giant cables that crisscrossed the roof and were anchored to concrete footings. As the wind increased in velocity and the temperature dropped to 26° F. we had proof of the need for this shelter and its strained bindings.

As I approached the Quinttown area I noticed a few old weathered barns and houses, unoccupied but still rather neat, with surrounding land that looked almost as if it had been recently tended.

In search of a place to lay my sleeping bag, I climbed a fence and started for the nearest barn. As I came over a slight rise I noticed a small cabin about two hundred yards back from the road. Smoke was pouring from its tubular metal chimney.

Curiosity aroused, I approached and knocked on the door. There was no answer so I went around to the side where a window revealed the profile of a little old man with an enormous beard. He was slightly bent over and intent on some kind of close work.

I tapped on the window and he glanced up, then turned to open the door. I shall never forget the look of warm welcome that lit up his eyes when he saw me, a bearded, bedraggled stranger sporting a black eye. It was the only time I was really thankful for my beard.

He invited me in and introduced himself as Bill Brown, sole resident of Quinttown. He said that doctors had given him up for dead years ago, so he had moved to this little cabin and doctored himself.

Inside this one-room haven was a stove, easy chair, couch, and a couple of wooden chairs. The ceiling was used as storage for drying apples, and every inch of wall space was taken up with dangling straps, harnesses, coats, caps, boots, and belts.

Bill was very deaf, but when it registered that I was looking for a place to spend the night he offered me the couch. I finally convinced him that a spot on the floor next to the stove would do very nicely.

I "helped" Bill with his evening chores, which meant mainly accompanying him to the barn and watching him milk his cow, brush his horse, clean the stalls of two young bulls and a calf, and tend to his one chicken. It was during the milking operation that Bill gave me my first delicious taste of warm cow's milk. In return I was able to lend some muscle in grinding the corn.

Bill's boon companion was a beagle pup called Little Dog. As far as I know, this bouncy youngster had no other name. Bill shared his meals with Little Dog, and unreserved affection seemed to flow between them.

During the night Bill slept in the armchair because of a rheumatic condition. Every two hours or so he would get up, add a log to the fire, and call off the time as the face of the clock gleamed in the flare of the freshly stoked blaze.

In the morning I offered to pay for my night's lodging, but Bill didn't want money. He did, however, receive with gratitude a can of beef stew I had found in the Mt. Cube shelter. He also accepted my sixty feet of rope; doubtless it since has been put to some use other than rappelling from the ceiling of a mountain refuge.

Because of their scarcity along the trail, I think that the people one meets tend to stand out and punctuate the wilderness experience. Certainly Bill Brown with his animal kingdom at Quinttown was the most unforgettable character I met. If one word could be used to describe him, Little Dog, the horse, cow, bulls, and chicken—that word would be "gentle."

In Hanover, the Appalachian Trail runs right down Wheelock Street, past Dartmouth College and the main intersection of town. I homed in on a laundromat, and found I had enough money to do my washing, get a meal in a restaurant, and see a movie. However, that cut into my finances considerably and I had to find some place to spend a couple of nights. Fifty dollars was waiting for me in general delivery, but the post office would not be open until Monday.

Fortunately, Hanover firemen and police take kindly to hikers. The firemen offered me a spot on the engine house floor. The one caution was that I move quickly in case of an alarm. Later, however, the night duty police officer offered me the use of an upstairs cell complete with cot and plumbing. According to regulations he had to lock me in, but before doing so asked what time I wished to be called in the morning!

This was service beyond my wildest dreams, and when the morning call was accompanied by an invitation to coffee my gratitude for official Hanoverian hospitality knew no bounds.

On Monday I made a round trip to White River Junction and found that I could average about four miles an hour when unencumbered and with no mountainous obstacles to contend with. The Hanover Post Office was open when I returned and my good wife had sent the much-needed cash. There was also a note from Sig and Joe, who I later met on the corner of Main and Wheelock streets.

Joe's draft board had finally caught up with him; his general delivery mail included "greetings" from the commander in chief. The army, however, was to allow him time to almost complete the trail in Vermont before claiming him for their own and shearing off his luxuriant beard. No scissors or razor had touched or defiled that massive growth for nearly a year.

There followed an interlude of one week. Sig and I went to New Haven while Joe visited his sister in Rhode Island. During this time Joe made his peace with his draft board and was allowed to continue hiking until November 12.

Vermont

It was on the fifty-mile jaunt to Sherburne that the unique beauty of the Green Mountains impressed me most. The mountaintops and broad-limbed trees lend a sensation of disciplined wildness. Many big-city parks strive for this effect, yet never quite achieve it. It requires a depth of vista, which the Green Mountains have in abundance.

At Sherburne Pass I found Joe and Sig in a gift shop. They had just consumed breakfast in the little restaurant next door. Although Sig had put away five dollars worth of food, he presently returned to this gastronomic emporium and ordered a complete steak dinner. I had long since ceased trying to keep up with him either on the trail or at the table.

The trail at Sherburne turns sharply south onto the Long Trail. At that time, the old Long Trail Lodge was still standing near the trail junction, though of course closed for the season. We spent the night of November 5 in the cabin on Pico Peak.

From here my diary takes on a rather frantic, almost panicky, note as winter began to show its signs. For example, we only made about seven miles on November 6, stopping at the Governor Clement Shelter south of Killington Peak. There was much slipping and sliding in the new-fallen snow. I complicated my journey by detouring on the seat of my pants down a Killington ski trail in three inches of snow. I was motivated by thoughts of a good breakfast at the ski lodge, but found it closed except for coffee and doughnuts. Meals would be served starting the next day when the skiing season officially opened.

This last bit of news motivated me back up the mountain on hands and knees in the gathering snow and fog. I missed the trail intersection and went all the way to Killington's 4,241-foot peak. There I found the fire warden's hut and met the chief fire warden, a fine young man who was packing to break camp.

Since this was the last day of the season for him he gladly loaded me up with canned goods, margarine, and bread. It was a tremendous windfall which more than made up for my disappointment at the ski lodge. He even sold me his Long Trail guidebook, a priceless acquisition, for only fifty cents.

My pack was again almost as heavy as in the pre-Caratunk days in Maine, and the footing on snow-covered leaves and rocks was extremely slippery. I fell many times and could see where Sig and Joe had done the same. When I finally found them at the shelter they were talking about calling it quits. It had been a frustrating day. I had spent a lot of time going laterally and vertically in useless detours. I felt that if I could only "put it all together" and expend all that energy straight out on the trail I would begin to log some respectable mileage.

Fortunately, we were still independent units and could make our own decisions, a method of travel that had caused us to meet and separate all the way from Caratunk, Maine. It's a delightful way to travel and a good way to maintain friendships.

In spite of my admonishment to make speed to the state border, Sig and Joe could not resist the lure of Sunny Side Health Camp, a sanatorium off the trail. There they hoped to find more hot showers and a good meal.

As a result of their decision to wander, I became the pacemaker in our trio and didn't see them again until the late afternoon of November 11.

On November 10 I stopped for a bite to eat at Swezey Camp, a small shack containing a stove and space for about six people to sleep. I was contentedly munching my pemmican, using my jackknife for cutlery, when I heard a car drive up and stop. Because it is considered common courtesy to welcome strangers, I got up and prepared to do the honors for Swezey Camp. When I opened the door the two teenage boys standing there suddenly took on looks of absolute terror. They leaped backwards, falling and scrambling in an attempt to get back to their jeep where a cohort was revving up the motor for a quick takeoff.

I managed to get a few words in edgewise to the nearest boy and he was reassured. He called to his mates that all was well, whereupon they came in for a visit. It seemed that they had been unnerved by both my appearance (gray stubble, dirty clothes) and because I carried an open jackknife in my right hand—not exactly a vision of welcome.

I managed a total of sixteen miles on November 10, which was far from earthshaking, but I felt I was beginning to move. That night was spent at a lovely secluded spot on the east shore of Stratton Pond. There, in a shack similar to the one at Swezey Camp, I managed to stoke up a fire and heat a can of beef stew that had been weighting my pack; it was absolute ambrosia!

During the night there was a good deal of rain and wind, which tapered off to a clear but chilly morning on November 11. Around 2:00 P.M. I stopped at Story Spring Shelter for lunch and was surprised when I heard my name called. Then through the woods came Sig and Joe.

Our reunion was cut short by the increasing chill in the air and the chance to get to another shanty before dark. My Long Trail guidebook stated that such a haven of refuge awaited us at the top of Glastenbury Mountain nearly eight miles distant and involving total climbing of about fourteen hundred feet.

Fear lent wings to my feet and I sailed past Sig and, to my amazement, passed Joe as well. I remember thinking, as I saw him ahead of me, that he must be a fourth traveler out on this godforsaken afternoon.

When Joe got over his surprise, his North Carolina blood answered the challenge and he managed to win a footrace to the summit of Glastenbury Mountain. In the process we cut a good ninety minutes off the guidebook's recommended time allowance for the trip from Story Spring Shelter. After all that exertion we discovered only the charred remains of the promised shelter.

Sig arrived very shortly and we did our best to make things livable at a three-sided lean-to. The night was wet and cold, but Sig managed to "will" a fire into existence while Joe acted as a human bellows. My contribution was all the birch bark and twigs I could gather.

At this point the safety of the Massachusetts state line lay 20.4 miles to the south. The word "safety" is used advisedly because the Vermont deer-hunting season was due to open the next day.

The shooting started early and shots rang out on all sides of us as we warily made our way on November 12. Sig and Joe carried whistles, which they blew periodically. I draped a bright orange vest over my pack. Fortuitously, I had found this garment hanging from the branch of a tree.

As we covered the seven miles to Vermont Highway 9 we never knew when we would come face to face with a silent and disapproving red-clad hunter. Like sentinels, these fellows would stand on the top of a hill, rifle at the ready and loaded with live ammunition. When added to the background of intermittent firing, such sights add a thrill to the rigors of walking the trail.

Massachusetts

Sig's hometown of Amsterdam, New York, lay just to the west of Williamstown. The call of the New York hunting season was strong, and the soles of his shoes were again in need of gluing. All things considered; he decided to pack it in for the winter and come back next summer.

I was sorry to part with Sig; he had taught me all that I knew about hiking and wilderness survival. His practical approach to the problems and hardships would be inspiring even for an experienced person. In the days to come I would recall many a cold bleak morning at open trail shelters when Sig's strident voice would dispel the surrounding gloom with "Breakfast now being served in the main dining hall!" This cheerful blast helped us choke down the cups of cold gruel that comprised breakfast on the trail.

I now knew that I was free of a serious threat of snow. The going in the south of was not difficult, and my daily mileage responded accordingly.

However, I was reminded often that I was on no manicured path. My lack of experience in wilderness travel will become evident when I admit to nursing a feeling of indignation that the great state of Massachusetts would allow its section of the Appalachian Trail to be so rough underfoot. That sort of thing was OK in Maine and Vermont, but in these smaller mountains I felt I had a right to expect almost paved conditions.

My pique reached its peak during the seventeen-mile pull from Dalton to the Massachusetts Turnpike. Thereafter I began to realize that trail conditions were trail conditions regardless of a state's reputation for culture and refinement.

New York-New Jersey

In this area I had a problem similar to one I had found in Maine. This was the occasional absolute disappearance of trail markings. The cause: lumbering in Maine and highway construction in New York. Both activities play havoc with the Appalachian Trail. However, one tends to forgive Maine. At least the big paper companies have a stated policy of trying to spare those trees on which key trail blazes have been painted. Maine also makes a big thing out of the Appalachian Trail at every highway crossing. The impressive signs which herald the Maine-to-Georgia footway cause motorists to sit up and take notice. It's a form of red-carpet treatment for weary hikers.

New York, on the other hand, seems barely to tolerate the trail. The gleeful arrogance with which the road-building equipment muscles in and the utter lack of recognition at points where the trail crossed a highway all helped to make me feel unwanted in this part of the Empire State.

December 10 was marked by dense pea-soup fog as I followed the trail over Bear Mountain Bridge and the Hudson River. Pedestrian toll on the bridge had been set at five cents back in 1924 and I found it was still being religiously collected on this December day in 1966. My only complaint is that on the day I crossed, the view was visible only on a ten-cent postcard at Bear Mountain Inn. On a clear day the toll would have been a bargain.

With Christmas coming up I left the trail at Bear Mountain for a shopping trip in nearby New York City. All I had to wear were my hiking clothes, but I found the youthful revolt against conventional dress had softened the citizenry, and I was accepted in Tiffany's and at the theatre without encountering so much as a raised eyebrow.

The Appalachian Trail south from Bear Mountain runs into terrific competition. The local trails in both Bear Mountain and Harriman State Parks were confusing in their multiplicity. Along the same pathway I encountered the white Appalachian Trail markers interspersed in haphazard fashion with white blazes with red dots, white blazes with blue dots, and other blazes colored orange or red or blue. These side trails fed into and away from the main line in such a way that the overall result was chaos. In my case I got so fouled up after two days of striving that I found myself emerging from Harriman State Park at Sloatsburg, so far south it wasn't even on the section trail map.

On to Unionville, New York, after a brief dip into New Jersey and more trouble with nonexistent trail markers. Repeated difficulties led to the thought that a suitable title for an account of my trip would be "Don't Spare the White Paint!"

For two dollars I spent the night of December 15 at a small family-run hotel in Unionville. These establishments are like autumn leaves that hang on after their days of blooming are through. Only a winter hiker can fully appreciate their worth. Across the street from the hotel was another family-run establishment that specialized in fine baking. I gratefully had meals there and bought a loaf of bread to take along.

On December 17 I set out at dawn for Delaware Water Gap, determined not to lose the trail again. Then, at an intersection a mile or so west of Unionville, I ran into another case of indifferent marking. The result was that I trudged the roads from High Point, New Jersey, to Delaware Water Gap, Pennsylvania. It was too cold to play hide-and-seek with trail markers. On Memorial Day weekend, 1968, I returned to walk the actual route of the trail.

Continuing on through Warwick, New Jersey, where I spent the night, I arrived December 18 on the east bank of the Delaware River. In the darkness I rolled out my sleeping bag at a point opposite the town of Delaware Water Gap.

Next morning the temperature was in the low teens, and I was thankful for my insulated boots and mittens. The trail and I crossed the Delaware on the modern Delaware Water Gap Bridge where, unlike the Bear Mountain Bridge, pedestrians pass toll-free. I couldn't help but think of George Washington and his Continental troops who crossed the same stream 190 years before, almost to the day. Their method was different, and it must have been a chilling experience.

Pennsylvania

After a break for Christmas at home I returned to Delaware Water Gap on January 8,1967. The interim had been spent in reading about Peary's North Pole expeditions and survival in cold climates. I read that discomfort could not be alleviated, that there was no magic formula except an enclosed shelter and a fire.

While at home I purchased a pair of snowshoes about four feet in length including the trailing tails. A Christmas Eve snowstorm had deposited some eighteen inches of snow in the Pennsylvania mountains, so the snowshoes were put to immediate use.

January 8, 1967, marked the start of the truly winter phase of my hike, complete with deep snow on the trail. My costume consisted of long flannel underwear drawers cut off above the knee, long-sleeved cotton jersey shirt, heavy woolen shirt tucked into a pair of medium-weight wool slacks, three pairs of heavy wool socks, nine-inch insulated Canadian walking boots, wool cap with visor and ear flaps, lightweight shell windbreaker with hood, and sheepskin mittens.

In my pack for nightwear was a wool stocking cap which could be pulled down over my face, and a suit of three-ounce insulated underwear which I pulled on over my clothes. If I did the trail again in winter I would use five-ounce-weight underwear. I also had my trusty $4^{1}/_{2}$-pound down mummy sleeping bag, a small foam rubber square for a pillow, a full-length, half-inch-thick foam sleeping pad, and a light-weight ground cloth. The only apparel removed at night was my boots, which I stuffed into a large plastic bag and took to bed with me; this was a sure way to keep them soft and pliable. The snowshoes, of course, had to take their chances out in the chill night air; often the straps would be stiff in the morning, but this was not catastrophic.

My food could be anything desired. Nothing spoiled in the low tem-peratures. So, in addition to the staple dehydrated milk, wheat germ, high-protein (soybean) baby cereal, brown sugar, raisins, peanuts, onions, and vinegar, I carried liverwurst, cheese, bread, doughnuts, and vitamin pills.

I started from Delaware Water Gap about 8:45 A.M. and rounded the crest of Mt. Minsi, which with Mt. Tammany on the Jersey side forms the gap. The view is dramatic, especially as a stark winter scene. The fjordlike slopes of Tammany and Minsi formed a high narrow gateway through which the dark waters of the Delaware flowed between snow-covered banks; it was a striking contrast in colors.

The temperature on this January morning was barely freezing and the snow was a bit tacky underfoot. I began the rather painful process of getting acquainted with my snowshoes. My only previous experience with them had been a half-hour trial run at Christmas. I was soon to learn that climbing and keeping track of trail markings added interest-ing ingredients to the basic problem of progress.

For example, I lost my balance on a slope while pausing to get my bearings. Normally recovery would have been a mere matter of step-ping back with my downhill foot. In this case, however, the edge of my uphill snowshoe was firmly pinning the edge of the other and the result was inevitable: I fell with a crash. Being encumbered with a thirty-five pound pack, I found that getting back to my feet was almost as difficult as arising after a skiing fall. I managed also to strain a groin muscle in my right thigh, which helped lower my advance that first day to only seven miles.

The use of the Appalachian Trail by other than hiking enthusiasts is very apparent in winter. In places the trail had the look of a traveled city sidewalk. The footprints were not those of human beings, but of deer, wildcats, wild dogs, and other forest animals. Sometimes the tracks would branch off at abrupt angles, leaving the trail trackless for a mile or so. The tracks often returned just as abruptly. I imagine these diversions led to water.

At one point the snow revealed evidence of a woodland encounter. A set of bloodstained tracks led to an off-trail arena where two animals had obviously had it out over a prize caught by one of them. There was fresh blood on the snow and feathers were scattered all around.

As darkness approached along about 4:30 P.M., I climbed to the crest of a ridge in search of a flat surface for my sleeping bag. To my right I saw the lights of what turned out to be Kirkridge Retreat House. No one was present so I bivouacked on the porch, using my ground cloth as shelter against a developing cold drizzle.

Suddenly the whole scene was illuminated by the glare of approaching headlights. I emerged from my sleeping bag to be welcomed with open arms by John Oliver Nelson, former Yale Divinity School professor, and board member of the New Haven YMCA. John was a man of many interests, among which was the Kirkridge Retreat House. He took me in and gave me the run of the place: hot water, stove, bunk bed, and modern plumbing! This bit of good fortune was enhanced by a visit to his home, where Mrs. Nelson served hot tea and I met some of John's Kirkridge friends. They were making plans for starting a prep school in that mountain setting.

The night view from the retreat house's picture windows revealed both sides of Mt. Minsi. In the valleys to the right and left were shining the lights of Stroudsburg and Bangor, while in the gap straight ahead were the six homes of Kirkridge which I had just visited. The brilliance of this distant twinkling illumination gave the effect of a lighted Christmas tree with Kirkridge at its peak.

Next morning I lingered by the picture windows, which enclose the southern extremity of the main assembly room. My excuse was to catch up on my diary. My reason was to savor the scene from this lofty and comfortable perch. To the east all evidence of the city of Bangor had vanished in the bright light of day; Stroudsburg to the west and Kirkridge to the south could still be seen in the distance.

Back on the trail my right thigh was joined by my left knee in the common bond of pain. My method of snowshoeing was obviously using, or abusing, muscles that had hitherto been dormant.

My progress on January 9 was again leisurely. I had some apprehension about Wolf Rocks, which the guidebook stated were "very difficult in wintertime." However, I found the dangerous crevices filled with snow and I was able to paddle across on my snowshoes with no difficulty at all. The only problem was that deer were using the footway as a thoroughfare and their hooves had trampled a shaped depression into which the tails of my snowshoes kept sliding. In all other respects, however, I can recommend the Pennsylvania stretch of the Appalachian Trail as ideal for the snowshoe novice, at least under conditions similar to those I encountered. The mountains in Pennsylvania provide one continuous skyline trail at an elevation of about twelve hundred feet. There is very little change in elevation for distances of up to thirty-seven miles. The trail is narrow and you know when you are off it if, as sometimes happened to me, the white markers of the state game lands' perimeters are mistaken for trail markers. When these began to lead me down the side of the mountain I knew it was time to backtrack.

On clear cold nights I spread my ground cloth and pad on the snow and crawled into the sleeping bag where I would eat my cold supper. This was not so much because of hunger as from the knowledge that the human machine needed fuel. On these occasions I never ate much, but I did keep the sack of peanuts and raisins near my head to provide a quick midnight snack to quiet a churning stomach.

It is simply amazing how the body can take in frigid food and turn it into heat. I could put my canteen of water and bottle of honey inside my shirt and this human furnace would keep the contents pourable. It also served to keep my boots pliable and proved to be a very useful piece of equipment all around! It, along with my windbreaker, cap, belt, and boots, were the only pieces of original equipment remaining from that August day in 1966 when I started the trail at Katahdin. Everything else, including sleeping bag, pack, and clothes, had long since been replaced.

The snowshoes had begun to feel natural and I found that I was moving painlessly over difficult terrain. Climbing in snow became a genuine pleasure when I remembered my floundering on the slopes of Killington back in Vermont.

A word of advice for the snowshoe hiker would be to carry an extra pair of shoelaces. If necessary, they can be used as heel strap slings by anchoring them through the top grommets of the boots. Without this device my snowshoes kept coming off as the heel straps would slip down and under my boots during an extended climb.

The Blue Mountain Motel at the trail crossing of U.S. Route 309 became my resting place on the night of January 14. It was here that Emma had arrived on one of her jaunts from Georgia. The owner said she emerged from the woods having walked right through her sneakers and socks. He took her to town for an interview and picture for the newspaper, as well as to get reshod.

My diary for January 18 starts: "Still bitter cold; this type of cold is the worst enemy of the hiker. The simplest tasks become incredibly difficult; putting on socks and lacing boots, drinking, and eating—you do the latter without real appetite and only because you know your body needs nourishment. The all-pervading sting is the cold."

I will say, however, that cold weather makes for progress on the trail. In motion there is warmth, and cold is a strict taskmaster. Its counterpart in summer would be the flies and the mosquitoes that badger the resting hiker unmercifully.

Another night out on a frozen tree-studded mountaintop, and another lesson learned—always tuck in your shirttail firmly before retiring. (I tried sleepily to do this all night from a prone position.) And still another lesson: read the trail map intelligently. Had I done so I might have spent the night in a cabin belonging to a young man I had met at a road-building site in New York.

The halfway point on the trail was reached January 21 on Peters Mountain. I came to the sign announcing the fact just as the noon siren sounded in distant Duncannon. The siren was like a welcoming brass band as I gazed at the large engraving marked with a small home-made HOORAY! painted on it.

The snowshoes were put to use in negotiating a snow-covered fire lane, and then on a precipitous descent to the Penn Central Railroad tracks and the Susquehanna River. In the first case they operated as footgear, in the second as crutches, although the latter descent was negotiated mostly on the seat of my pants.

I spent Sunday, January 22, in Duncannon, the town of churches, where I attended a Baptist service. This peaceful community on the south shore of the Susquehanna seemed content to let the world go by. The trains of the Penn Central clattered past the boarded-up station; from the distance came a steady hum of traffic on the Pennsylvania Turnpike; overhead sailed the most modern commercial planes. Duncannon seemed to doze in memories of a less hurried past.

I have lost my diary for the period from late January to February, but I vividly remember the thaw when the thermometer hit 71° F in the Cumberland Valley. Farmers were out doing their spring plowing as I walked by with snowshoes strapped to my pack. The incongruity of the situation finally got to me and I mailed my snowshoes ahead to Harpers Ferry, West Virginia.

West Virginia-Virginia

At Harpers Ferry, where the Potomac and Shenandoah rivers meet, history was again to delay me for a day. It was also at Harpers Ferry that I made a miscalculation in weather. I had not been seriously threatened by snow since crossing the Susquehanna River. The incident north of Boonsboro was fleeting, and another snow had amounted to no more than an inch or two. I felt that I really had it made now that I was south of the Mason-Dixon line. With this happy thought in mind, I mailed my snowshoes ahead to Waynesboro, Virginia, from Harpers Ferry.

I set out from Harpers Ferry in the crisp, snowless afternoon air with no qualms. My thoughts were on the Civil War as I left the town and climbed to Loudoun Heights. From here Walker's Confederate battery of six rifled guns had virtually bombed its target across the Shenandoah River. Far below me Harpers Ferry presented itself like a map.

All along the trail to Keys Gap were additional reminders of the nameless battles and skirmishes that had filled the voids between the Antietams, Chancellorsvilles, Gettysburgs, and Cold Harbors. Stone walls, waist-high, enclosed infantry defense areas on both sides of the trail. These structures, which appear at irregular intervals, are sometimes no more than fifteen feet on a side; others look almost like small pastures. I remember digging unsuccessfully along some of these walls in hopes of finding a uniform button or cartridge.

And so it was that, gripped by a fascination that only a Civil War buff could experience, I covered the eight miles to Keys Gap. Here, about 250 yards south of the crossing of the Charles Town Road, I found the Keys Gap Shelter and put up for the night. So immersed was I in the lore of yesteryear that I was totally unprepared for what was about to befall me.

During the night it began to snow, reaching blizzard proportions before morning. All the next day and the following night I remained in the lean-to while the storm raged in white fury. From time to time I heard snowplows at work along the highway.

At dawn of the second morning, February 10, the elements were again at peace and the Appalachian Trail lay patiently beneath some twenty inches of snow. After a few experimental steps, I turned back to Keys Gap and Charles Town Road. Much as I disliked leaving the trail, my one purpose now was to get to Waynesboro, Virginia, pick up my snowshoes, and never let them out of my sight.

I had resolved never to ask for a ride under any circumstances, but in order to reunited with my snowshoes I decided to accept any and all offers. My first lift, southern style, about three miles south of Charles Town. A young man hailed me from his car and asked if I wanted a ride. True to my lowered code of ethics, I accepted.

He introduced himself as Sydney Culver of White Post, Virginia. He was dressed in a wrangler's outfit, complete with cowboy boots and hat. After helping me stow my pack, we drove to his farm on the

Shenandoah River where I met his wife and tiny daughter Virginia Lee, who was just learning to walk.

Sydney's neighbors were other farmers who, like himself, bred and raised racehorses. There were plenty of wide open spaces. One neighbor owned over three thousand acres. Sydney said that their community of interest made it possible to hold far-ranging fox hunts, English style with all the trimmings—red coats, fast horses, hounds, trumpets, the works.

After a very substantial lunch, Sydney packed his family in the car and we drove to Front Royal where I was dropped off a good thirty miles closer to Waynesboro.

On February 14, reunited with my snowshoes, I headed south on the trail at Rockfish Gap.

The rain and consequent melting of the snow made snowshoes unnecessary the next day. I still managed to exhaust myself on three slopes beyond Reeds Gap. The three-thousand-foot descent to the Tye River was a welcome contrast. It also brought me to Mr. Station's pigsty, and that kind gentleman gave me permission to sleep in it. The sty looked so dry and secure, when compared with my previous two bedrooms, that I actually preferred it to anything under a domestic roof. I don't doubt that my appearance and odor suited the sty to perfection.

During the night I was awakened by the muffled straining of a snowplow. Wisps of snow were blowing in through the many horizontal cracks in the board sides of the sty. As morning broke on February 17, I looked out on a raging blizzard.

The trail led up the four-thousand-foot mountain called The Priest, and I wanted an early start to allow for slow going. A drifting blanket of snow whirled about my knees as I struggled out to the plowed road that led to the southbound turnoff of the trail.

As it turned out, the snowshoes made the climb less difficult than expected and I negotiated the ridge of The Priest and what seemed to be innumerable succeeding peaks before darkness began to fall. It was still snowing hard and I wouldn't have minded crawling into a rotting log or fallen tree trunk. I envied the small forest animals who could call these snug places home. No hollow log presented itself but I finally came to a formation of rocks. By careful maneuvering it was possible to crawl into my sleeping bag at the entrance to this natural refuge. The snow was blowing and drifting a few inches away, but the overhang provided shelter. My feet were slightly higher than my head and my shoulders were pinned; it was impossible to turn. Extricating myself was almost as difficult as escaping from a wrestling hold. From time to time I heard a rustling movement in the recesses of the rocks, and I knew that I was not alone in the haven. The creature—was it a fox or a bobcat or a raccoon or something else?—did not reveal itself.

By morning the snowfall had stopped and the sun rose on a pristine mountain setting, the likes of which I have never seen before or since. Not a track showed on the glossy white blanket of snow, not a sound split the air. The leafless trees lent an effect of fine white lace as one looked through their snow-covered twigs and branches to the brilliant blue sky and the blue and white mountains.

For several miles south of the James River the trail closely parallels the scenic Blue Ridge Parkway. At one point I found I was just below this deserted thoroughfare, but not getting any views because of the brush and trees. Climbing up on the highway gave me an entirely different vista. The road was open for ranger traffic only and I enjoyed an exclusive stroll on this twenty-foot-wide plowed "sidewalk" all the way to Black Horse Gap. Then it was back to the snowshoes as the trail took off to the southwest. It occurred to me that the forest service would do well to close this road to motor vehicles periodically during the summer months. Then, as pedestrians, the American public could really enjoy the scenic overlooks with their magnificent views. The frequent descriptive signs, which point out features of the landscape and give bits of history, could all be taken in stride, so to speak; stopping to get out of the car, no missing a good spot because of oncoming traffic. This was the only mountaintop stretch where I could both walk and look out at the same time. On the wilderness trail it was either stop and look, or walk-look-trip-fall.

I came to Wilson Creek Lean-to about 5:00 P.M. and called it a day. It was much too cold to enjoy eating a great deal, so I put a small sack of peanuts and raisins near the head of my sleeping bag to allay any hunger pangs during the night.

It was not long before I realized I was sharing the lean-to with a young skunk. When this little rascal approached sack of peanuts and raisins reaction was violent, but instead of scurrying away he simply moved off with dignity to reconnoiter for another attack. After his second attempt he jumped off the lean-to platform onto the ground and ran out into the moonlight where he became silhouetted against a background of snow.

Meanwhile, I reached for a rake hanging on the lean-to wall. When my young friend returned, I took a "sound shot." There was an immediate hissing like air being let out of a tire, and the atmosphere became heavy with the odor of Chanel No. 5. The youngster fired blind, however, and his perfume did not have all the mature stink of older members of his clan.

As the night wore on he returned to the platform several times; at other times he was scurrying around on the ground floor. However, he did show respect for the rake; one or two rattles of this weapon would quiet him for a half hour or so. Thus I spent the night in catnaps, which was better than no rest at all.

My diary for February 24 reads: "Very cold—couldn't seem to warm up. The going on the north ridges very lonely and wild. Deep snow, but surface frozen hard. Very slippery in spots where path was obliterated by banks of snow. Had to dig heels in hard on descents. Finally emerged on top of Fullhardt Knob and everything was sunny and downhill from there—snow virtually disappeared from southern slope. Sound of distant traffic and eventual view of Interstate Highway 81 was a great relief."

It was during the cross-country portion of this trip that my new boots began to assert their respective personalities. I spent the day of February 25 trying to reconcile them. I found the left boot had to be laced loosely, with two pairs of grommet holes at the instep being bypassed completely. The right boot had to be laced tightly through all holes. Any other combination would cause excruciating pain, particularly in the lower part of the left leg.

With my boots finally speaking to each other again I took off on the twenty-mile stretch to Catawba Mountain. The guidebook stated that "only experienced hikers with light packs" should attempt this in a single day. Here was a chance to find out if (a) I was "experienced" and (b) if my pack (thirty-seven pounds including snowshoes) was light enough. I discovered the answers on both counts to be "just barely" as I arrived at L. P. Doyle's restaurant on Catawba Mountain after dark.

It was not long before I hit snowshoe country, and from there on these extensions to my boots became as valuable as a lifeboat on an open sea. In fact, at the crest and along the ridge of Sinking Creek Mountain the drifted snow looked like five-foot waves that had congealed. This effect was caused by wind action through the bare hardwood trees, which seem to predominate in the southern mountains.

As I rocked along on these snowy waves my progress was slow. It became even slower when I hit what could best be described as a smooth rock field set at a thirty-five-degree angle. There must have been acres of this slippery rock, with nothing to grab for support. The person who planned the trail here would have had a fight on his hands if he had showed up. However, to be fair, these rock-field sections might have been fun in summer when the traction was better.

As the afternoon wore on, the wind and cold intensified. Normally the motion of walking will keep me warm. But for some reason this wasn't working out today. About 5:30 P.M. I spotted a slanted rock outcropping that protruded from the snow just off the trail to the west. It looked exactly like a lean-to roof. Closer inspection revealed a bare spot of ground under it big enough for my sleeping bag.

This being the only sign of shelter, I prepared for the night. It meant planning each step of the procedure to avoid undue exposure to the cold. Even with all the planning my left hand kept cramping up and had to be straightened periodically so I could use it.

My boots began to freeze and stiffen the instant I removed them. I had never before witnessed such speedy congealing. Previous experience had long since taught me to make bedfellows of my boots if they were to be pliable by morning.

As I lay there encased in insulated underwear, sleeping bag, and ground cloth it was borne in on me that the overhead rock was not a shelter so much as a wind baffle. Far from shielding the ground from snow it had merely guided the wind in a scooping action that cleared the narrow space where I lay. My weight alone prevented me from being scooped in similar fashion.

I could hear and feel my heart pounding like a trip-hammer. I had read about people suffering heart attacks when caught in blizzards and I could now appreciate the added strain this causes. I shivered in violent spasms even though I was wearing every article of clothing I had, including insulated underwear and three pairs of wool socks on my hands and feet.

My feet suffered most as moisture from melted snow froze enough to make the outside layer of socks stiff, hard, and of course cold. Body heat simply would not penetrate to this outer surface. Therefore, as you can well imagine, my rest that night was accompanied by much pounding and rubbing of hands and feet, and it could best be classified as an endurance contest.

The morning of March 1 found me in the situation described at the beginning of this account. There is no need to repeat it here except to say that all persons have moments that are sacred to them, and this, without question, was such a moment for me.

Five miles of snowshoeing brought me to the descent off Sinking Creek Mountain down to Highway 42. There, at a small country store, I returned to the world of the living. As Mrs. Minnie Duncan provided me with honey buns, corned beef, frozen milk, and peanuts, one of the customers informed me that the unofficial temperature reading was twenty-seven degrees below zero at Mountain Lake, six miles south of the trail.

Miraculously, on March 2 the temperature leaped to about 50° F. The change came suddenly as I was climbing Salt Pond Mountain. With the sun out and the snow melting I stopped at noon at the War Branch Lean-to. The sudden freedom from bitter cold and the unexpected appearance of the primitive shelter can best be appreciated by one who has steeled himself for another freezing night on an open mountain ridge.

All the little things that a summer hiker takes for granted were the height of luxury for me as I aired my sleeping bag, bathed in the stream, did some washing, built a fire, cooked soup and bacon, wrote in my diary, and finally turned in under a roof!

On March 4, I climbed White Rock Mountain and descended not only to civilization, but from the winter phase of my hike. I left the trail for a month and visited my parents and family before resuming operations in Pearisburg on April 8.

My logistics for this last springtime stretch of trail varied somewhat from the winter going. I was unwilling at first to let my snow-shoes get too far out of reach and so mailed them ahead to Damascus, Virginia, about one hundred miles south. My underwear consisted of a pair of swimming trunks and a short-sleeved cotton knit T-shirt *with pocket*; this, along with a newly-acquired cotton visor cap, became an acceptable hiking outfit in its own right. The rest of my clothing was just as it had been during the severest winter going—heavy wool shirt, windbreaker shell with hood, wool slacks of medium weight, heavy wool socks (two changes), and army jungle boots. The extra socks would double as mittens when and if the need arose.

I covered the hundred miles to Damascus in just over six days, averaging 16.5 miles per day. The warmer weather made for a relaxed journey and more voluminous diary notes. A hiker is faced with a variety of impressions as he meets people and situations in an intimate yet inconclusive and transient way. Because of this I feel that quotes from my diary would best bring this part of the trip alive:

"APRIL 8. Up over Pearis Mountain, past Angels Rest, over Dismal Mountain, down to Dismal Creek. Mountain section of trail quite rocky. Twisted right ankle, which slowed me somewhat. With exception of crocuses and daisies, mountain foliage still the same—trees completely bare. But beautiful sunny weather is in contrast to the icy blasts of February.

"APRIL 9. Beautiful day. Hiked in T-shirt and swimming trunks. Right ankle still giving pain.

"APRIL 10. This is the day Sig starts from Springer Mountain; wonder if I will see him or if he will beat me to the spot in Tennessee from where he started last summer. I am barely making fifteen miles a day because of sore right ankle and rocky terrain.

"It began raining about 9:30 A.M. and became quite chilly. I am testing Sig's theories on wet wool. I only wish I had kept my wool cap with ear flaps. There is a lot of comfort in this material.

"Dismal is the word for the outlook today. Rain and cold take all the pleasure out of hiking and make it an endurance contest. You can't stop, you can't build a fire, you can't get dry. As I sit here now on the lean-to platform I can look out through the leafless branches of trees in the foreground and barely see the irregular contour of a distant mountain. It is blue-gray in the mist with no contrasting lights and shades. If it weren't for the definite profile along its summit the mountain would blend right into the gray and cheerless sky.

"APRIL 11. The dismal aspect gives way suddenly to verdant growth and lush surroundings as the trail goes from dry waterless mountain ridges to a rhododendron corridor. Bushes (I believe they are mountain laurel) are beginning to come out with small white blossoms. They form patches of white on the mountainside.

"I passed a couple of farms. The outbuildings interest me; I can recognize the privy, the barn, and a storage unit, but then there is another building that is usually near a stream. Could this be the still?

"APRIL 12. In field at foot of Glade Mountain. Awoke about six to find ice chunks in my drinking water and frost on the grass. It is so much pleasanter than February that I scarcely notice the chill.

"Approach to Glade Mountain is another gem with laurel and rhododendron on both sides of the trail. Got lost in abandoned manganese diggings, a red rolling desert. Had to turn on 'fear-of-benightment' speed to reach summit of High Point before dark. Windy. Tent blew down three times.

"APRIL 14. "Got into Damascus about 10:00 A.M. A delightful little town smelling of lilac and other spring foliage. Weather so warm that a summer vacation atmosphere pervades."

The basics of living are food, clothing, and shelter. Long-distance hiking is unusual in that these basics are woven into the sport itself and assume an importance out of all proportion to their place in most other activities. The hiker's idea is to be as independent as possible, yet I found the prospect of a good meal or a place to sleep in "civilization" would often determine my pace.

My food and clothing were fairly well under control before I reached Damascus. It was here that the third basic, shelter, finally fell into place. It took the form of a lightweight one-man tent ordered from Holubar of Boulder, Colorado, and which now awaited me in general delivery. This small tapered tent had a waterproof floor, water-repellent sides, and a zippered entrance panel backed by a panel of mosquito netting. Aluminum poles, which made for a quick setup independent of trees, collapsed for storage. My canvas pup tent and my trusty snowshoes were retired by mail to New Haven, Connecticut.

Tennessee-North Carolina

On April 18 I got to Hampton, Tennessee. In my diary I see the statement: "Where the terrain is tough, the people are nice." This was certainly the case in the Hampton grocery store where I stopped for supplies. Ken, Henry, Frank, and Jack, the clerks, greeted me warmly, gave me coffee, told me what they knew of the trail south, and presented me to the owner, Mr. Brown, whom they introduced as "another Yankee," he being from Pennsylvania.

On the morning of April 19 the abundance of fresh spring flowers along White Rocks Mountain was a tremendous diversion. I seemed to be walking on a carpet of green and lavender, green and yellow, or green and white, depending on the color of the little ground flowers that were blooming by the millions.

In Hot Springs I was no more than thirty miles by trail from the Great Smoky Mountains National Park. Only one other area, the Presidential Range in New Hampshire, had created the same degree of anticipation as I approached it. Both places had been schoolroom words since early childhood, yet I was about to see them intimately for the first time. Also, both places held an added ingredient of danger: in the Presidential Range it had been the weather above tree line; here it was the prospect of meeting and dealing with wild bear.

I asked a ranger what to do in case a bear got overly curious. He said, "Grab a club and hit him over the nose. As a last resort, climb a tree." In retrospect, this sequence seems logical, though at the time the second option alone seemed attractive.

On April 30, near Max Patch Mountain, I was treated to a rare sight as a deer leaped across the trail just ahead of me. It was a magnificent sight in true picture-postcard style: tail flying, feet barely touching the ground, giant leaps through the trees and underbrush.

My camp that night was on the east bank of the Big Pigeon River. There, beyond Davenport Gap, the Great Smoky Mountains National Park was at last within easy reach. Two things were immediately apparent in the park: first, the absence of white trail markings, making it necessary to watch for signs at trail junctions; and second, the altitude.

The graded climb to the summit of Mt. Cammerer was over five miles in length and was relentless. However, instead of people passing me as was the case at Mt. Katahdin in Maine, I found myself overtaking and passing others on the trail. Nothing is better for the morale.

Of the entire sixty-eight miles of Appalachian Trail in the park, the first five, which led to Mt. Cammerer's 5,025-foot summit, were the most taxing for me. Once at that level, I enjoyed the great variety of views as I worked my way up to approximately 6,000 feet where the trail followed the central ridge of the Great Smokies. The views into North Carolina and Tennessee are excellent in clear weather because the route coincides with the line between the two states. On Old Black Mountain (6,395 feet) I thought for a moment that I could see all the way to the Mississippi River.

Time began to run out on me as I passed over Mt. Guyot (6,621 feet) and a level spot of ground for my tent became more important than a view. This I found on the ridge that connects Guyot with Mt. Chapman (6,430 feet). At that lonesome elevation, and with nothing more aromatic than a can of peas and my special gruel, I dined and slept without attracting the attention of Bruin.

Next day I was greeted by dense fog and a drizzle turning to rain. As I neared Newfound Gap there seemed no chance of viewing anything but the twenty-one square feet of ground at my feet. Therefore, with supplies running low, I made for Gatlinburg, Tennessee, when I reached the highway at the gap.

For a hiker in my bedraggled condition, a driblet or two of burg would have been sufficient. But here I was suddenly wallowing in it. I thanked my Good Samaritans for the ride and had no difficulty finding shelter for the night.

Back at Newfound Gap the rain and fog looked very familiar as I took off through the western half of the park. The rain turned to snow in Clingmans Dome (6,643 feet), the highest point on the Appalachian Trail. The wind was so strong it drove the snow against the tree trunks, where it covered the familiar vertical white stripes. The buildup of snow on the ground was not serious and I soon reentered the rainy area which prevailed at about the 6,000-foot level and below.

As I started out that morning (May 5) the sun was out and I was treated to a view from Silers Bald that made all the fog, rain, and cold of the previous day seem unreal. From that altitude (5,620 feet) I looked down on an ocean of gleaming, motionless white clouds. The mountain ridges above them gave the effect of huge rocks against which waves were breaking and spray flying in a painted seascape. It was truly a breathtaking sight from the unimpeded grassy slope where I stood.

The journey to Fontana Dam on May 6 was barely thirty minutes old when a wild crashing to the right of the trail revealed four startled black boar. They were in sudden flight parallel to the trail, and perhaps fifteen feet away from it. Their long grotesque snouts, and large heads and forequarters with tapered bodies set them apart from the usual barnyard hog. They sounded like bear as they charged single file through all obstacles. Scarcely had the four disappeared when three tiny reddish-brown piglets followed in their wake. The adults didn't seem to give a damn about the youngsters. In the light of hindsight, though, the adults may have been breaking a trail for the piglets. I was glad to see the last of these unpredictable beasts as they disappeared ahead of me.

The road across Fontana Dam affords magnificent contrasting views. On the one side is Fontana Lake just below road level. It looks like a normal body of water with peaceful boating and fishing. On the other side one stares down some five hundred feet to the TVA power plant at the foot of the massive curving concrete structure. The narrow winding bed of the Little Tennessee River continues among the hills beyond.

On May 15, with wind and rain developing, I made my way to Albert Mountain where I found a defunct fire tower and a shed, which contained a folding bed. The shed seemed safer than my tent because the crash of falling trees could be heard every few minutes as the wind increased.

During the night the wind in the trees sounded like the roar of opposing crowds at a football game: it would rise up on one side of the shed, then on the other. Intermingled was the noise of old tree trunks creaking, cracking, and thudding to the ground to join the thousands of blowdowns that abound in a wilderness forest. It was all on a very grand scale and served to cover the delighted twitters of the mice who were eating my peanut butter. If they had only nibbled I wouldn't have minded; I had learned to live with rodents and skunks with no ill effects. But this time there was evidence of the complete alimentary process. Next morning I discarded the precious peanut butter, can and all.

Georgia

Sometime during the morning of May 17 I crossed the state line into Georgia. The crossing was confirmed at Blue Ridge Gap by a sign that indicated this all-important landmark to be three miles behind me. So, in Georgia at last, and unaccountably sporting a headache, I proceeded to Dicks Creek Gap where I was fortunate in hitching a ride into Clayton. In Clayton I took a day off and stoked up for the final sixty-nine miles to Springer Mountain.

Doc Gibson of Clayton gave me a ride back to Dicks Creek Gap on May 19. As I climbed up Kelly Knob I was treated to one of the loveliest of wilderness sights when I startled three deer. They practically flew through the woods, bounding along, picking their way so they made scarcely more than a rustle of the underbrush and a light tapping sound as their hooves touched the ground. This is so different from the bear and wild boar, who sometime make terrific noises as they crash through the brush. Often you hear this racket without ever seeing the bear, especially if the bear is at a lower level on the mountain than you are.

On May 20, en route to Tesnatee Gap, I again was treated to one of nature's gems. While slabbing a hillside I noticed three deer below and upwind of me. They were walking single file slowly through the trees in my direction. I waited motionless and as they got to within about thirty yards of me the lead deer stopped. He looked me in the eye for several seconds. Then he turned, and in a single bound was off in the opposite direction. The others, although they had not been looking at me, followed their leader with no questions asked.

At Walasiyi Inn the proprietress asked me to write a couple of pages on my trip for the local newspaper. This was a strange experience because when I touched on the winter events in the Blue Ridge Mountains of southwest Virginia the tears welled up uncontrollably. I couldn't even write about those hours without crying.

The rains came about 8:30 P.M. and continued throughout May 22. It was cold and wet and I encountered some very uneven terrain. Black Mountain, Tritt Gap, Mountain, Jacks Gap, Liss Gap, Gooch Gap, Gooch Mountain, Justus Mountain, Cooper Gap, Sassafras Mountain, Horse Gap, and so it went up and down until I finally called it a day at Big Stamp Gap Lean-to, less than two miles short of the Springer Mountain terminus.

The big memory of this day, however, is not the gear-shifting climbs, which required a slowing of pace, but rather a brush with the U.S. Army Rangers on Sassafras Mountain.

The first inkling I had that things were not quite normal on this mountain was when I found what looked like a trail shelter, except that the roof and walls were sandbagged. There were sandbagged foxholes on either side of the trail.

As I continued on I noticed a bunker and was going to speak the soldier at the entrance but he quietly disappeared inside. I assumed he had orders not to converse with strangers.

On the crest of the mountain I found another manned bunker where the occupants initiated the conversation. In fact, I was taken "prisoner" by six armed men and an officer who blocked my path and conducted an interrogation as to where I had come from, where I was going, and if I had seen "the enemy."

The soldiers were dressed in bright green fatigues and said "the enemy" had similar uniforms, but of a darker hue. As we talked, the interrogation deteriorated into a discussion of the Appalachian Trail and the outdoor life in general. One of the men expressed a wish that the army would issue Kelty packs.

When the grub truck drove by at noontime I was invited to have "a sandwich." This so-called "sandwich" turned out to be a plate of mashed potatoes, hot corned beef, bacon, string beans, soup, coffee, and cake. It was my first real meal in twenty hours. When my captors "released me I felt literally jet-propelled. What a difference a good meal makes! I had been literally dragging; now I practically ran the next ten miles.

It wasn't until I had negotiated Hawk Mountain and was descending through a rhododendron grove that I finally met members of the infiltrating force.

Two soldiers stood athwart the trail with guns at the ready. They were as wet, cold, and miserable as I had been before my "capture." I greeted them with undue joviality and told of having had lunch with their "buddies" back on Sassafras Mountain. Their interest pricked up immediately at this bit of information.

One of them pulled out a map and tried to pinpoint the location of my repast. As he did so I noticed his fingers had a pulpy parboiled appearance because of the constant downpour that kept his gloves saturated. I did my best to help these poor guys, then assured them they would never get there before the so-called "games" were due to end.

That night at Big Stamp Lean-to the sounds of battle on Sassafras Mountain could be heard until about 10:00 P.M. This was several hours beyond the scheduled break-off. My two infiltrating acquaintances would certainly have had time to find their way to defense headquarters. On my next trip over Sassafras I resolved to give only name, rank, and serial number.

Next morning, April 23, 1967, it was only a matter of minutes until I reached the broad summit of Springer Mountain and signed the register at 8:00 A.M. The rain had stopped after some thirty-three hours of constant downpour but it was still overcast and foggy. The view was limited to the trees and saplings in the immediate vicinity.

Although technically at the end of the trail there were still two more mountains and some thirty miles between me and the nearest bus stop.

This was not an unwelcome prospect because it meant living the nomadic life just a bit longer. I was like a deep-sea diver who must come up in stages.

A Final Incident

On the access trail leading from Springer Mountain to Amicalola Falls State Park, I encountered something that aroused my deepest compassion. As I descended Black Mountain to the Frosty Mountain Fire Road a bright red knapsack loomed up through the haze and fog as it rested against a tree alongside the trail. Nearby was what looked like a covered corpse on a stretcher.

I approached the latter and very gingerly raised the corner of what proved to be a ground cloth. The first thing to catch my eye was a pillow in a lace-embroidered case. The remaining revelation was more camplike, consisting of a wool blanket and inflated air mattress. The human body as well as the human spirit had fled this apparent "corpse."

When I told the custodian at Amicalola Falls State Park of my find, he was very interested in the "X" that marked this particular spot. He said that a young co-ed from Florida had been given a ride to the Black Mountain trail crossing the previous afternoon. Her intent had been to start on the Appalachian Trail at Springer Mountain. However, about ten o'clock that night she was back in the park, a wetter and a wiser girl. The custodian and his wife had taken the girl to the bus stop and told her they would try to find her camping equipment and mail it to her.

Besides the bedding material already mentioned, her equipment included changes of clothing, food, shoes, college textbooks, notebooks with reams of paper, and a large, stuffed, rather waterlogged dolly-dog with floppy ears. The young lady was trying to carry perhaps sixty pounds; no wonder she gave up and went home. I could only hark back to my struggle with overburdening nonessentials on Mt. Katahdin in Maine.

In Conclusion

One can't walk the Appalachian Trail without feeling gratitude for the many hours of nonwalking activity that others have spent to make it possible. The diplomacy, tact, strategy, and interest exercised in securing a right-of-way are obvious when one faces signs reading PRIVATE PROPERTY, KEEP OUT! OR TRESPASSERS WILL BE PROSECUTED TO THE FULL EXTENT OF THE LAW. Yet just beyond these signs will appear the small white Appalachian Trail markers. Without using words, these silent symbols say, in effect, "It's OK. We've fixed everything up with the owners and as long as you behave yourself you can walk on their property."

Less obvious, of course, is the legislative fight to secure and protect public wilderness areas. This vital activity on the part of the Appalachian Trail Conference should certainly get its share of credit for creating the current ecological awakening.

My sincere thanks go to all who have made such a journey as mine possible. The planning, the laying out, and the maintaining of this wilderness footway was originally a labor of love and still remains so to a large extent. Therein, I believe, lies its unique quality and variety.

Journey of a Lifetime

By Everett W. and Nell Skinner

Started at SPRINGER MOUNTAIN on April 1, 1968
Finished at MT. KATAHDIN on October 26, 1968

From *Appalachia* for June, 1970

I follow the silver spears flung from the hand of dawn,
Through silence, through singing stars,
I journey on and on.

—E. Carbery

Thinking,

Here we are, stepping along the flank of Mount Washington. We stare at its eternal peak, New England's highest mountain. There she lies, open and bare, with her scattered buildings, the rooftops flashing in the warm sunlight. We are exultant! This is a milestone that has been coveted long before we reached New England soil.

Our first taste of the White Mountains came on the summit of Mount Moosilauke where, in the Dartmouth Outing Club's refuge cabin, we were forced to remain for two days and three nights, socked in by wild weather. It sleeted, snowed, rained, thundered, and flashed lightning intermittently. How grateful we were for the cabin which we reached before the fury of the storm broke!

During these two days, Dartmouth freshmen climbed their mountain and filled the two rooms with their presence and animated talk about this preschool week of outdoor living and exciting adventures. It was fun to be in the midst of it, unofficially acting as host and hostess.

Now looking at Mt. Washington signifies, according to our guidebook, that we are only 322 miles from lofty, mile-high Katahdin and

the Appalachian sign reading NORTHERN TERMINUS OF THE APPALACH-
IAN TRAIL. Hallelujah!

It seemed long, long ago that we had stood on Clingmans Dome,
in the Great Smokies, the highest point on the Appalachian Trail.
Then our journey had barely begun. Clingmans' observation tower
had also glinted in the sun but, unlike Washington's exposed rock,
was clothed in balsam firs. That day—May 2, 1968—the sign read
1,800 miles to Baxter Peak, Maine. . . . Whew!

But we took it in stride and strode on.

Now our pace quickens as we revel in this open, above-tree-line
traverse of the Presidentials. The previous night was spent in the new
Mizpah Spring Hut, where it was balm to body and spirit to relax on
comfortable bunks and devour plentiful gourmet fare. A jolly group
of folks gathered around the breakfast table, including a blushing
bride and bashful groom who had climbed into the clouds to celebrate
their honeymoon! That morning, September 21, we left Mizpah reluctantly, as we always did from these restful havens. It was a lovely,
fresh morning, the air warm and the sun radiant—a day to remember.
A supreme day to cross the beckoning peaks. We rejoiced in the good
weather as notices posted at tree line had warned, TURN BACK NOW
IF THE WEATHER IS BAD. Friends told us later that this was the hottest
September 21 on record.

Edmands Col was reached at eventide and camp was made with
young lads from Roxbury Latin School. The warm day turned chilly
and the wind whistled through the pass. Sure enough, by morning
heavy fog and real cold had settled in.

All of us plowed through the fog and wind to Madison Huts. Later
the sun came out, but the strong wind continued. It literally blew us
off the peaks into Pinkham Notch Camp.

From then on, with a few exceptions, the days were magnificent.
All this should mean for us, weather-wise, a glorious finish on Baxter
Peak, but no one can anticipate shifts in the weather. These good days
were appreciated when we recalled the start of our trek April 1, 1968,
at Springer Mountain, Georgia, the southern terminus of the Appalachian Trail.

It was cold and wet, half-snow and half-rain on Springer's 3,782-
foot summit. The chill factor was intense. Though dressed warmly,
we shivered. The day before the thermometer had registered 90 degrees in Gainesville, Georgia! But it was a gay, happy moment, and
exciting to think of the 2,000-mile trail and high adventure that lay
ahead. Hastily, our freezing fingers signed the hiker's register and we

stepped along. Day after day it rained, yet there were moments of humor.

U.S. Army soldiers on ranger training maneuvers in the Chattahoochee National Forest gave us a lively time! Nell tripped on a vine, and as she went sprawling several soldiers in a concealed bunker let their rifles go . . . rrrrr . . . rrrrr . . . rrrrr. . . . Later, our Shetland sheepdog Dolly tripped a practice mine—a sharp report and a blinding flash . . . was she surprised! And placed along the trail were suspicious looking things like a new shoelace, a bent pipe, and so on, which we carefully avoided because they might be booby traps.

One evening we reached the crest of Sassafras Mountain and decided during a lull in the rain to make early camp. The wind began to whistle strongly and it seemed that, maybe, this blow would clear the air and pleasant weather would come in. Quickly our two-man tent was put up. In went the gear and the two shelties, Dolly and Traily. Gratefully we crawled in and zipped up the opening. The dogs found their niches. To our consternation puddles were beginning to form on the floor, but fatigue got the best of us and we snuggled into our 2¾-pound down bags. Soon we woke up soaking wet—a pond had formed in the tent. The rain had resumed its steady, hissing beat and drove through the untreated walls of the nylon tent. It was black as pitch and the storm raged on. Now the only thing to do was to remain in one position as any movement made us more miserable. Dawn seemed millions of hours away. It was the worst night either of us had ever spent in our lives. Everett was 65, newly retired from Burlington Mills where he had been a textile designer; Nell, 57, was a housewife.

On, on. We were "marching through Georgia." Traily didn't come back from one of his runs into the woods. Now our spirits were indeed low, and made worse by the wet and the heavy packs.

Many times on the trip we met wonderful, concerned, and helpful friends. We had our first such contact with a young man who lived near Gooch Gap. He drove us to nearby Suches, where we resupplied and mailed back home all the items we could do without, including our tent. We knew it couldn't take it. We replaced the tent with a 10′ x 10′ plastic tarp. This kept us dry even in the heaviest storms.

The postmaster said that invariably the through traveler would drop by to send things home in order to lighten his pack. Furthermore, said the postmaster, most of the hikers who started out to do the trail quit when they got into Virginia or even before. They usually dropped him a card regretting they couldn't make it.

Our new friend told us to go back to where we thought Traily had left the path and that he'd most likely be waiting. He was there! What blissful barks and glad reunion after a night and a day of separation. Once more our spirits were gay and we marched off.

Our packs were Keltys. When used with rain covers our gear and supplies were always dry. We wore Russell boots, and never had so much as a blister. There were days of walking in the rain and sloshing through puddles and turbulent brooks. Boots make interesting sounds when they are wet . . . *slug, slug,* and when soaked and full of water . . . *slug, glub, slug, glub.*

Nell wore Norm Thompson Sportsman Support Socks. They help to prevent foot and leg fatigue and keep feet warm and comfortable. They never seem to wear out.

Weight is ounces! The less ounces the better! It *is* surprising how well one can live with bare essentials. Food supplies were not a problem. Everett would get a ride at a road crossing to some nearby village and resupply. Generally people will give you a ride if you are wearing a backpack. Probably having a woman along helps, too. These resupply stops were gala affairs and happened about every four or five days.

Eat, eat. Yes, raven all kinds of goodies right on the spot before moving on. The mountain stores are like oases even though variety is limited. Everything seems delicious! Our staple supplies were dry milk, oatmeal, chipped beef, sugar, margarine, Creamora, cheese, bread, cookies, freeze-dried coffee, and tea. We carried dry dog food and when we couldn't get this the shelties joined us in the oatmeal course—which they loved best!

We drank quantities of presweetened Kool-Aid during the hot summer days.

Everett's pack weighed 40 pounds—comme ci comme ça—and Nell's 20 pounds . . . and each day between supply points as we ate, the packs lightened.

It was great to eat all you wanted with no need to think of those horrid calories. To have strength for the strenuous and often arduous climbs (and every day on the Appalachian Trail one does climb a mountain or perhaps several mountains) one must eat a lot. It is a wonderful way to reduce . . . eat all you can! Everett lost 35 pounds and Nell 20 pounds.

We did not carry water, nor did we have a problem in this respect. The springs and brooks may get low or dry up in summer, but with two exceptions there was always water enough for our needs.

Almost everyone we met shared their food with us, whether it was the house by the side of the road, Boy Scouts, Girl Scouts, Campfire

Girls, church groups, Boys Club of America, private summer camp folks, or innkeepers. It was thankfully received, and helped to maintain energy and ease the strain of backpacking.

In the early days we used a Borde gasoline stove, but when the needle jammed we decided to use open fires. Small fires are very adequate and quickly cook a meal. We carried dry twigs in our pack, so regardless of weather we were always prepared.

The open fires were for us periods of rest and relaxation that contributed to the enjoyment of the trip. Indeed, they were an integral part of a nomadic experience such as ours.

Camping and walking had been our forte for many years. This trek, our dream, had been thought of, discussed, and equipment experimented with for several years. Previously we had hiked 700 miles of the Appalachian Trail in a piecemeal fashion and we are "end-to-enders" on Vermont's Long Trail.

One difficulty which faced us when at last the dream became reality was leaving the everyday world. This meant finding the right person to handle our affairs for the time we would be gone. Luckily, a most conscientious and competent friend agreed to undertake this responsibility for us and finally we were off!

Our journey was full to the brim with the joys of nature. There were breathtaking views from the crests of mountains. At times we gazed upon peaks in a 360-degree sweep . . . inspiring, yet awesome! There are vast oak forests high on the ridges in the South; day after day we shuffled through thick drifts of rustling leaves.

Having lived in the Northeast we found the balds of the southern Appalachians to be an interesting phenomenon. They are high, perhaps 5,000 to 6,000 feet in elevation, and without trees. Their covering is meadow grass and, at the most, low shrubs. The balds gave us a feeling of isolation and pleasurable loneliness. At night, gazing into the starry vault from these open spaces, one can't help but think of his Creator.

On a few nights we were awakened by the baying of coon dogs on distant hilltops. It was exciting to hear as it took on all the qualities of a chorus. The wild, ringing cries would come nearer and nearer and then fade away as we drifted back to sleep.

There was a lovely sight in the Shenandoah National Park . . . canaries were dipping and fluttering about the spring near the shelter as the last rays of the sun glinted and outlined their golden bodies, making a picture of sheer ecstasy. Savoring of Nature's pageantry often slackened our pace. It was hard to push along; there was so much at which to marvel. There were waterfalls sliding down sheer cliffs, bubbling springs, sparkling lakes, and scented forests. The acres of wild flowers on the ridges were intoxicating—violets of every hue and color, trillium dressed in shades of red, white, and pink, and bluets everywhere.

We were fascinated with the varied growth formations of the interrupted fern that grew in the trail. Tiny lavender butterflies floated about. Bumblebees hovered industriously over blossoms. The trail was edged with dwarf iris. Sometimes on high mountaintops it seemed as if we were walking through beautiful parks and gardens. A foot traveler has the advantage in that he sees so many more things of beauty and interest.

The shelters and their locations fitted into the landscape with a charm of their own. We delighted in their singular, picturesque, and primitive settings.

The slopes and summits of some mountains were thronged with berry plants. Strawberry, blueberry, and blackberry bushes were heavy with fruit. Seldom could we take time to pick, but we did let our eyes feast on them.

We battled and endured the heat, cold, rain, snow, hail, and electrical storms, all of which go to make up Nature's moods in the wilderness. Definite adjustment to these moods is necessary, but once it is made—and in time it is—all may be taken in stride.

During the summer months we often had the feeling that we were the only two souls encamped on a mountain with its thousands of acres. Upon resuming our walk in the morning, however, the woods would come alive with hikers of all sorts, in pairs and groups, and perhaps a lone school teacher or doctor.

With the great expenditure of time and effort, as well as money, on the part of many to build and maintain the Appalachian Trail, it is gratifying to know that it is being so heavily used, especially by our youth.

Why do you do it? This question pursued us from Georgia to Maine. We pondered it all the way. We knew we loved this primitive and basic way of life, good for mind, body, and spirit; the exhilaration of gaining strength and being physically in top condition; the feel of the good earth as the feet rhythmically strike the path; the oneness with Nature. Nothing very tangible, but these are some of the answers to the "whys."

There was another favorite question asked along the way, "Seen any snakes?" If we said no or that we saw a few harmless snakes the inevitable reply was, "You will. The mountain ahead is loaded with rattlers." Invariably this "mountain ahead" would be where we were planning to lay our heads for the night! What a send-off! We did carry a snakebite kit, but we think our shelties kept the snakes and other animals away from us.

These miniature collies have no great hunting instinct but are a working breed with strong herding traits. They are wonderful companions and full of larks, but at the same time watchful for our safety. They are fearless little creatures, not afraid to send an animal, big or small, on its way. We leashed them through game lands, wildlife areas, and pastures. Dolly was a good mountain climber. She would arch her back and dig in with her claws. But Traily would look for an easier way and on a few occasions needed a boost. Dolly would scramble up a cliff and then watch anxiously to see if we were making it. How she frolicked as we reached the final ledge!

When on a continuous trip over the Appalachian Trail it is fun to walk into the occasional small town along its path. After being in the wilderness for weeks a town takes on the proportions of a large and busy metropolis. By way of contrast, the solitude, such as one finds on the trail in Maine, is again a very welcome experience.

There were the usual trail problems: getting a bath, laundering clothes, haircuts, replacing worn-out clothing, receiving and picking up mail, and repairing equipment, to name a few.

After living outdoors and sleeping on the earth or on the boards of a lean-to we discovered that we could not enjoy the luxury of a soft bed. We first found this out in a motel room in Hot Springs, North Carolina. We could not sleep on the soft, downy bed. Nell moved to the couch, but that was no better, and she finally ended up on the hard floor where she did get some rest. We would have a closed-in feeling, as though we were suffocating, and just have to wait patiently for morning to get back to the woods for a good night's sleep.

Pearisburg, Virginia, borders the trail and is a good place to resupply. As we walked along the street, people came out of stores and buildings to stare and ask questions of the two hikers who so obviously showed the wear and tear of the trail. It was here that we saw the American flag at half-mast in front of the post office and learned the sad news that Senator Robert Kennedy had been assassinated. Previously, when on Blood Mountain, Georgia, we had been told by a fellow hiker that Martin Luther King had been murdered. Tragic news follows one even into the wilderness.

As we entered the great Shenandoah National Park we were introduced to the awesome experience of a furious storm on a bald mountain. A dense mist pushed rapidly over the bald. It completely enveloped us. With hurricane force the wind began to drive the heavy rain horizontally across the open expanse. The day turned black and there was nothing to do but stop. In the lee of a lone small thorn tree we managed to open up our tarp; we weighted it down foot by foot with heavy stones and secured one corner to a branch of the thorn tree. Then off with our drenched clothing and into dry sleeping bags. We curled between the rocks and what a delicious night's sleep we had while the storm raged. In the morning the sun shone brightly and we knew all was right again with the world.

It was a journey fragrant with friendships and rich in human kindness. It might even be called a journey in human relationships and fantastic hospitality, with walking secondary.

The folks we met along the way boosted our morale. Their faith in us, that we would achieve our goal, and their help in making it possible could not have been greater. In this day of hate and violence it is refreshing to meet human beings who exemplify love for their fellowman.

There were many instances when people who lived along the trail would invite us into their homes for a rest, a meal, and a chance to clean up. The facilities of the bath were invariably the first thing offered. For some reason they always knew we needed a bath! These homes ranged from mansions on large estates to humble farmhouses. We felt these folks experienced the joys and hardships of our wilderness trip through sympathetic participation.

We had escaped from the straitjacket of today's living in which so many of the satisfactions and contentments are missing. All of us become creatures of habit and custom in our living patterns. The trail gave us the opportunity to live for an extended period in a more simple and down-to-earth manner. So, sharing some of our adventures, our newfound acquaintances could live our journey vicariously.

At one point in New York the Appalachian Trail passes the farm of former Governor Thomas E. Dewey. As we went by a car swung out of the barnyard lane and turned into the drive leading to the house. We shouted, "Hi, Governor! All the way from Georgia to Maine!" Back came the reply, in his typical booming voice, as he leaned far out of the car window, "Mighty long trek!"

One morning as we searched for a place to make breakfast we came to the Sakajawea Girl Scout Camp in Wingdale, New York. We turned into the camp to ask if we might use one of their outdoor fireplaces. The girls displayed instant hospitality—they hustled us into the dining room and served us juice, French toast, and coffee. The charming director said, "We have a group of girls going on a trip to the Adirondacks. Will you give them a talk on backpacking?" Then, jokingly,

"This way you can pay for your breakfast!" After our talk, it was the girls' turn to pay us back. This they did by heaping upon us cans of freeze-dried foods. These are light in weight but expensive and not easily obtained along the way. For the rest of the trip we carried and treasured them as survival food. Fortunately, they were not needed.

The Appalachian Trail goes by the Bear Mountain Inn at Bear Mountain State Park in New York. The manager had heard of our Georgia-to-Maine journey and came out to greet us as we passed the door. He graciously invited us in to dinner. Smelly as we were, he took us into the sumptuous, air-cooled dining room and gave us carte blanche—wow! And the offer of a room for the night!

Chicken . . . canned chicken, given to us by a Boy Scout troop camping in October Mountain State Forest, Massachusetts. We treasured it and days later decided the right time had come for our special treat. (Everett did all the cooking and dishwashing for the entire trip.) Nell mixed powdered milk with water for the creamed chicken dish. At last the delectable fare was ready. We took one mouthful, made faces, and spat it out. It tasted awful! What was wrong? Checking, we discovered that the powdered milk had been put into the soap bag!

The climb of Wildcat Mountain and her Kittens in New Hampshire was very difficult because there were no places to dig toes into and nothing to grab hold of to pull oneself up the ledges. Finally we made the top and were moving along when a group from the Randolph Mountain Club caught up. They were interested in the fact that we were doing all of the trail that season and wanted to help. Supplies were needed and it was arranged that when we came out near Gorham we would be picked up, spend the night with them, and shop the next day. Our hostess entertained us in her spacious country home, which had a large picture window facing Mt. Madison. It was a festive occasion: hors d'oeuvres, then dinner in a beautifully appointed dining room with an exquisite china and crystal service. The steaks were thick, the salad delectable. It was a gay party and we wished it could go on forever.

In New England we enjoyed the beautiful fall weather, the red and gold colorings, and the smoke of a campfire rising lazily in the air with its fragrance that is so tantalizing to the senses. The dying embers call to mind the many wilderness fires of the past which served to climax our daily adventures on the trail.

Now, as the days grow shorter, we are still 200 miles from Katahdin. We have been getting up by candlelight these mornings in Maine. The bird songs are fewer. One sparkling afternoon, reaching the open summit of a mountain, we heard a great honking noise. Overhead a large flock of geese hurtled southward in their usual wavering V-formation. Almost as soon as they appeared they faded into the blue.

We must push ever harder to our goal. Mother Nature has given us one of her most positive warnings of the approaching change in weather. Late one day it started to rain and continued all night and into the next day. We climbed Saddleback Mountain and as we approached the open and bare crest, the rain turned to snow and the wind blew harder. The ledges and small vegetation were icing over. Happily, the fire ranger had not left for the season and so we spent the night in his cozy cabin. Next morning the sun shone and the sky was bright blue, but the temperature was 26 degrees. We put on every stitch of clothing we carried and moved on.

A few days later rain pelted us again, first a drizzle and then a downpour. We were climbing Sugarloaf, and when we passed over the peak it was a white world with the wind fierce and cold.

Our soaked clothing became sheets of ice. Again we were blessed. The door to the upper ski station was unlocked. Inside we found that the ladies' toilet was heated and so we made it our room for the night. Oh, how thankful we were for this place of refuge. Everett tells everyone that it was probably the nicest ladies' toilet he was ever in!

After descending Sugarloaf we purchased two-piece rainsuits in the town of Stratton. Previous to this we had ordered by phone Bean's Maine Hunting Shoes and picked them up at the Rangeley Post Office. These shoes combine rubber bottoms with leather uppers and we found them helpful in keeping our feet dry while crossing Maine's many streams, beaver flowages, and bogs.

Now we are getting glimpses of Katahdin; its peaks appear to be covered with snow! The difficulty and uncertainty of making the climb of Katahdin to Baxter Peak so late in the year was overcome by arranging to have George Smith, personnel director of the Maine State Highway Commission, and Dr. Larry Nolin, a cardiologist from Waterville, Maine, make the ascent with us. They are proficient and qualified mountaineers who know that monadnock perhaps better than any of the many who have climbed it.

When we were at Pinkham Notch Camp in New Hampshire, Bob Marvel, the assistant manager of the Appalachian Mountain Club's chain of huts for hikers and climbers in the White Mountains, had put us in touch with George Smith, who followed our progress the whole 280 miles in Maine.

October 26, 1968—six months and twenty-six days—in 5.2 miles our trip will be over. Would it be so? The morning was lowery and the air seemed warm. Our mountaineer friends were not quite ready to leave Katahdin Stream Campground, so we went on ahead. We pulled rapidly up the mountain, enjoying our last climb. When we came out above timberline we were amazed to see the change in the weather. The sky was dark, the wind was blowing hard, and pellets of ice stung our cheeks.

We steadily continued the steep ascent of the Hunt Spur over enormous and tumbled boulders. When we reached a point known as The Gateway, the storm had worsened and our better judgment said "turn back." Where were our mountaineer friends? Just then two happy faces peered over a boulder. We were relieved; we knew now that our goal would be accomplished. We reached Baxter Peak at noon. It was freezing, the wind was blowing hard, and the chill factor was low. It was gloomy on the mountaintop, but it seemed bright to us—a moment of glory.

The prize remark of the day was made by our friend George as we completed the descent of the mountain: "Now you have covered the first 5.2 miles of your trip south from Katahdin to Springer!"

The real heroes of the Appalachian Trail—volunteer trail workers.
Photo courtesy of Appalachian Trail Conference.

A Mountain Every Morning: Margaret and Bump Smith's Hike

By Margaret Smith and Wilma Servisky

Started at MT. KATAHDIN on June 13, 1970
Finished at SPRINGER MOUNTAIN on November 9, 1970

You're out of your minds!
You tried it once and couldn't do it.
Bump with a serious back problem—Margaret, high blood pressure and one kidney. *Insanity!*
You'll be back in a week.
Over 40 and quitting your job? You'll never get another one.
You'll never make it!
On June 13, 1970, as my husband and I stood on the summit of Mt. Katahdin, some of the gloom-and-doom prophecies that met our decision to walk the Appalachian Trail came back to me. Our climb to Baxter Peak, the official starting point, seemed a quarter of an inch compared to our 2,000-mile goal. However, the prophecy most vivid in my mind was my husband's cockeyed grin and flat statement, "Hell with 'em. We can do it." He stood now, looking first at me and then at the box that should have contained a registry sheet but was empty. Crazy? Maybe, but happy because we were doing it, at last. After all the planning and preparation, after the unsuccessful attempt two years before that had ended only a hundred miles down the trail in Monson, after the waiting and saving and dreaming—this time we were going all the way.

Our 19-year-old son, Steve, and his girl friend, Cathie, had come up over the Chimney Trail and across the Knife-Edge to meet us on Baxter Peak. The four of us went down the mountain together and made camp in a lean-to at Katahdin Stream Campground. It was a beautiful place with the stream clear and talkative and the air tingly cold on the thirteenth of June.

145

Margaret and Bump Smith starting their hike.
Photo courtesy of Margaret Smith.

We had hiked perhaps 10 miles, considerably less than the daily mileage necessary to reach Georgia before winter. However, tomorrow would be different. Today was a holiday, an excitement to be shared with Cathie and Steve, for after the next morning we didn't expect to see them for at least four months. Tomorrow and the days to come would belong to Bump and me and the trail. Warmed by the fire, filled with beef stew and biscuits and coffee, it was easy to discount our first ill-fated try at walking the Appalachian Trail. Steve, who had been hiking with us on that first attempt, jokingly began to talk about my arthritic knee. "This time I'm not praying for rain to drown the mosquitoes," I told him. "If I keep dry, I'll be all right."

"All the same, I hope you have lots of fly dope in those packs." That would be the extent to which Steve would voice his concern. He was eager for us to make the journey, having been directly responsible for our "walking" lifestyle which at this point encompassed three years of hiking on Jacob Buck Mountain near our home, exploring the woods for many miles around us, and walking often to our jobs in the neighboring town. His concern for us would not be voluble, but it was there.

"Those packs have everything, boy," Bump told him. "From fly dope to high bloodpressure pills to feather beds. And speaking of beds—" He yawned loudly.

I couldn't sleep. Long after the others had succumbed to the combination of clean crisp air and full stomachs and warm sleeping bags, I listened to the small animal noises that came softly out of the night. The embers of the fire spit and crackled. By the flickering light I made a final entry in my log: *We've begun. This time we're going all the way.*

Morning in Baxter State Park was incredibly beautiful. The sharp sense of beginning, plus Cathie and Steve's leave-taking and the glory of the Sunday morning made an ache in my heart. We sat at the foot of Katahdin, eating and talking, our voices hushed. The feeling was almost one of reverence. I knew that for me there never would be a church or a sacrament that could evoke what I felt here, in open air near the stream and the surrounding woods, in the presence of this mountain. I could only guess at the others' feelings. We weren't an articulate family when it came to our emotions. Finally the time for good-byes approached. The weight of all the things we would leave unsaid was heavy. We cleared the planked table in busy silence and stowed the utensils in our packs.

"Cathie, you keep Steve out of trouble while we're gone," Bump said. "You'll be at the university, too, so keep his nose to the grindstone!"

They raised hands in half-salute, and were gone, and we put on our packs. Across the Nesowadnehunk Road, a few yards into the woods, I reached for the camera slung over my shoulder. A great bull moose, his antlers bigger than any we had ever seen, stood just a few feet off the trail. I got one shot and was making adjustments for a second when Bump prodded my elbow. "Better move before he gets wind of us." I hung back, watching. For all his seeming ungainliness, the moose was handsome. He had stopped feeding when we approached and now began slowly moving his head from side to side.

"Look," I whispered. "Isn't he something!"

Bump turned, scowling. "You'll think so if he starts after you with his head down."

"Okay, okay. I'm coming."

Along Little Niagara Falls in Nesowadnehunk Stream the nip of early morning into noonday heat. Little Niagara gradually matured to become Big Niagara and we felt the purity and peace of the sun-splotched water and trees. We hiked at a steady pace for nearly 14 miles. The air grew hotter, and thicker with and mosquitoes. The fly dope helped, but not enough. When we hit Abol Bridge Campsite we were ready for a break. Off came our new boots and socks. We sat on the riverbank with our tired feet in the water, watching the pulpwood float down the Penobscot toward the Great Northern Paper Mill. Lunch was what it would often be: peanut butter and jam carried in plastic tubes, bread when we were close enough to civilization to buy it, biscuits made in a frying pan when we weren't, and water.

Out of Abol the trail took us a quarter of a mile along the highway, then back into woods where we had hiked on other occasions. Moving through them produced the same ease I felt among good friends. Having learned to pace ourselves on other hikes, we walked steadily and spoke little. Six miles farther along we came to Hurd Brook Lean-to, our home for the night. As soon as we stopped hiking we suffered from relentless mosquito raids. Burrowing into my sleeping bag, I managed to keep out the sound of their endless buzzing, but I still heard Bump's grumbling and swatting. On the heels of one particularly vehement growl and whack Bump said, "Margaret, here's company."

I saw two boys, probably 15 years old, standing uneasily by the lean-to's open face. "Hi. We're Scouts," one of them offered. "Been cleaning up this section of the trail."

"Great. Bunk in when you're ready," Bump said, waving to the vacant floor space. "Just don't bring any mosquitoes with you."

"We can take care of the mosquitoes," the second boy answered, and in moments they had a smudge pot going in a bucket they had found. "Hot coals smothered with ferns. Green leaves will work, but ferns are better. We'll set it on tinfoil," one of the boys explained. So the problem of bedding down with mosquitoes was alleviated. However, sleeping with a smudge pot burning had its side effects. In the morning our eyes felt as if someone had buttoned them shut.

After a companionable breakfast with the Scouts, we left them. A few miles of walking through fierce flies and heat brought us to the fishing lodge on Rainbow Lake. Sweaty and thirsty, we gratefully slid out of our packs and sank to the ground. The lake was spread before us like a fluffed blue blanket. Its softwood edging was mostly spruce and fir, shafts of green splitting blue water and blue sky.

I shook my head. "We'll never see anything more beautiful."

"Maybe not," Bump said, "but we're prejudiced."

Agreed. To be Mainiac by birth and by confirmation presupposed bias, yet I honestly could not imagine anything to surpass this magnificence.

Bump got to his feet. "Boy, I'm dry." We weren't carrying water on the Maine stretch. We depended on the lakes and streams, but there hadn't been a trickle of water all the way from Hurd Brook. A man emerged from the lodge and started toward us. "How would you like a good cold bottle of pop?" I could have hugged him!

The man, a guide, told us that the next lean-to was in poor condition from rough usage, and when we arrived we understood what he meant. The area was crowded with tents and boisterous fishermen. They shouted greetings and insisted that there was "always room for a coupla more," but we declined. The liquor-laden plank between two trees suggested a late and rowdy evening, and we needed rest.

The Nahmakanta Lake Camps were four or five miles farther along. We hiked on through mosquitoes, blackflies, deerflies, and heat, only to find the camps filled. Now what? Tramp miles to the next lean-to? We were hungry and tired. Throw a tarp over a tree limb? The couple operating the camps ended our indecision by offering us all they had— an old icehouse. It had an open front and a sawdust floor but to us it looked good and we were grateful. No fires were allowed so we ate freeze-dried bacon and instant chocolate pudding, and then collapsed into our sleeping bags. Even the mosquitoes left us for dead.

At 5:30 we were up and on the move, going without breakfast until we could build a fire. By 10:30 we had hiked up hill and down for 3.5 miles while rounding Wadleigh Mountain, slogged knee-deep through a brook with icy water, and stumbled onto another lean-to, also occupied by fishermen. As they headed out for the day's fishing, they offered us the use of their stove. "Help yourselves—anything at all!" We promised we would, and I, with my eye on their apple turnovers, meant every word of it. The sticky heat, our swelling hands, the bugs, the soggy boots and jeans—all of this was forgotten during a hot breakfast that was topped off with the turnovers. With a last hungry glance at the fishermen's food, we hauled on our packs. We had gone only a few steps when I turned and dashed back to the lean-to, then ran to catch up with Bump with a can of tomato soup in each hand. "They *wanted* us to help ourselves," I told him, a little sheepishly.

Eight miles brought us to a shelter at the south end of Lake, occupied by two more fishermen. Hot! And we would need a smudge, for the air was filled with mosquitoes. The midges (no-see-ums) weren't doing badly either. The two men were preparing supper. Their supplies were ample and fresh, and we needed no urging to join them. They served us fried potatoes, onions, hot dogs, and cold lemonade. What a treat! As we ate I marveled at the willingness of everyone we had met to share what they had with us. At the same time I couldn't help wondering how we would be received as we moved farther and farther away from our home territory.

From Nahmakanta Lake to Antlers to Joe Mary Lake to Cooper Brook was 18 miles. We felt every one of them. Much of the land was flat and swampy, the heat intense, and the blackflies and mosquitoes nearly unbearable. At Antlers Camps we ate the tomato soup with gusto. Some yards beyond I photographed a moose wallowing in swamp muck. With so many insects around, the idea of a mud bath was appealing. Farther along the trail we stopped to rest by one of the Joe Mary lakes. We were sitting in a thick stand of poplar enjoying the leaf-riffling breeze when it began to rain, or so we thought at first. Then we realized the plopping noises were being made by falling caterpillars. They fell like fat green raindrops, and it was a phenomenon I neither understood nor appreciated. At Cooper Brook we found the two fishing rods and four cans of baked beans we had cached last summer. The cans had frozen and bulged completely out of shape so we dared not eat the contents. The fishing rods, however, with grubs for bait, provided a few trout for supper. The day's heat still festered, heavy now with an impending thunderstorm. We cleaned our few dishes and holed up for the night. Eighteen miles of trail was a long haul.

The storm that crackled and thundered throughout the night had spent itself and there were only spasmodic grumbles and splatters of rain by morning. At the end of a 10-mile walk to the East Tote Road Lean-to we were cooler than we had been for days, and with our $15 Sears Roebuck rain suits already ripped and useless we were also considerably wetter. In order to dry our clothing and cook we needed a fire. With the woods drenched and the fireplace torn down by bear, building a fire became quite a challenge. We managed to fix the fireplace and cut green poles for a grate. Eventually, after a good deal of searching for dry wood, and using toilet tissue for kindling, we managed to start a fire. Dry and fed at last, we were relaxing when three fishermen stopped by the lean-to. After swapping stories with Bump, they gave him a can of worms and headed on down the brook. Bump, worms, and fishing rod disappeared into the drizzle. An hour later he returned with 13 rainbow trout. Thirteen! My insatiable appetite took command and when we had finished picking the bones and licking our fingers, Bump made a tally. He had eaten three of the trout. I had eaten ten! Upon leaving next morning, exclaiming once more at the good fortune of having had worms for bait, we walked smack into a sign that commanded: FLY FISHING ONLY! I'm sure my face was properly contrite, but my stomach was smiling from ear to ear.

The terrain began to grow hilly. The sky remained overcast, the weather damp. We felt the eight miles to White Cap Mountain Lean-to had earned us lunch and a rest. While our boots dried, I prepared macaroni, freeze-dried meatballs, and instant beef gravy mix. Our utensils were limited. We had one kettle and used its cover as a frying pan, one 2-cup measuring cup, one plastic bowl, one tin measuring cup and one teaspoon apiece, one large community fork and one large community spoon. Meal preparation required a little juggling and a lot of patience. I finally slopped the whole mess together and filled Bump's bowl. "There. Spaghetti and meatballs to rival the finest Italian restaurant!" He lifted his skeptic's eyebrow. "If you say so." Then he tasted. "Well! Not bad." From him, this was real praise, and he was right—it wasn't bad.

White Cap Mountain, with an elevation of 3,707 feet, was steep, strewn with blowdowns, and fingered with narrow icy streams. What a climb! It was six o'clock when we came down the mountainside to White Brook. We looked back to see vapor rising from the streams like white smoke. The exhilaration of the climb and the wild beauty all around us seemed like confirmation of the rightness of our decision to take to the trail.

We were just settling in at White Brook Lean-to when someone shouted, "Hello!" It was a young man and woman from Tennessee, hiking part of the Maine trail. They were packing a tent and when it was up we all sat around the fire drinking coffee. The woman had been severely bitten by blackflies. Ugly swellings showed the poisonous effect the tiny insects have on some people. She said nothing she had used had relieved the itching and burning caused by the bites. Bump dug into our first-aid kit and offered her a small can of salve. "Try this." She began smoothing it on her face and arms and legs. "What is it?"

"Bag balm."

She stopped rubbing. "*Bag* balm. What's that?"

"It's used on cows' udders," Bump replied.

I didn't know whether she was going to laugh or cry! "We use it a lot," I said reassuringly. "It's the most healing thing there is."

"Sure," Bump chuckled. "Wouldn't be without it."

"*Bag* balm," she exclaimed, laughing now, and repeating in her easy Southern way, "*Bag* balm! Of all things!"

When her husband finally stopped laughing he gave us a few tips. He said wood was scarce through the Smokies. We should carry a stove. In hiking some sections of the Appalachian Trail beyond Maine and New Hampshire, he and his wife had found springs to be as much as a mile off the trail. We would need a canteen. Before we slept, we had shared many experiences. They were fine people. I wondered later if they were as intrigued with our Maine dialect as we were with their Southern one.

That night another storm thrashed about us. There was lightning, and split seconds later, jolting crashes of thunder. Wind and rain lashed the lean-to. I lay quietly in my sleeping bag, remembering other nights at home when I would wake abruptly, my mind unwilling to let go of a moment and a place like this one, held over from some vivid dream I had been having about the Appalachian Trail. How badly we had wanted it! Now we were here. I remained still, ostensibly asleep, listening to the roar of White Brook. Because of the sensitivity born of years of marriage and a common bed, I wasn't surprised when Bump spoke. "Storm keeping you awake?"

"No. Just thinking."

"Worried?"

"No. It's just that it's difficult to realize we're here, really doing it. Can you think of any place you'd rather be right now?"

"Yes. In that sleeping bag with you. I'm cold."

"That isn't what I meant," I said, laughing.

"I'm exactly where I've wanted to be for the past four years. Now go to sleep, Maggie. You and I have a mountain to climb in the morning."

After breakfast we said good-bye to the couple from Tennessee and faced the West Branch of the Pleasant River. It was almost 100 feet wide, swift running, high and icy with melted snow from mountain streams. I knelt by the water's edge and dipped my fingers. *Cold!* Bump looked back at me, grinning. "You coming?" Cringing, I waded in behind him. Halfway across, waist-deep, I muttered, "Pleasant indeed!" Soaked to the waist and squishing with each step we kept going and crossed without mishap. The air was warm and we dried as we walked, like clothes hung on a line. After a time even our boots lost their sogginess.

We met a lone fisherman, rod on his shoulder, a dog at his heels. After opening howdyes came the usual exchange about the variety and ferocity of the insects. This man said he had them whipped, and introduced us to a small plastic bottle of Repel. "Made right here in Maine in the university laboratory," he said, letting us try it. We thanked him and moved on, soon discovering that he was right. It was better than anything we had tried, discouraging all the pests save an occasional deerfly.

The trail was green with fern and spruce and fir and pine. The stillness of the sun-splashed shade was broken only by the rushing brooks and chittering squirrels and the birds. God's country. At noon we came to the first Chairback. We began the climb in weather that was perfect for walking. Part way up we came upon a huge moose. He was standing on a bank near the trail, munching on the fir. His stance was as majestic as the mountainside itself. I grabbed my camera and a flashbulb! I hoped for one good shot, but he swung his head and Bump bellowed, "He's coming! Give him the right-of-way!" I did—quickly. The moose galloped up the trail, his great strides taking the steepness easily. "I wish I could have ridden up on his back," I said.

"Just be glad you didn't ride on his antlers," Bump retorted. We went up and up and up and finally, at the top of a last 150 feet of sheer ledge, we came to a lean-to. Weak-kneed and thirsty, the first thing we saw was a sign: SPRING—150 FEET. The arrow pointed straight down! I groaned. "We must have come right past it!"

"Okay," Bump said, sliding to the ground, "what do you want to die of—thirst or exhaustion?" That did it. We broke up in laughter and then fetched water and made ready for the night. Perched on top of the bluff, the lean-to was raked mercilessly by the wind. The only tree cover was short stubby spruce. Firewood was scarce. Our space blanket, and indispensible 40-by-60-inch sheet of tinfoil and insulation, was used as a windbreak across the open front of the lean-to. Bump chinked many of the holes between the logs with moss. There was a register, and I wondered if the scarcity of names was testimony to Chairback's ruggedness.

A jeep road led through the woods to Little Wilson Campsite, and here we took a break. People were camping in the area and within moments of our arrival we were having coffee with a family from Bangor, a city not 20 miles from where we lived. It would have been a most pleasant interval had it not been for the little girl with the chocolate-covered cherries. A whole box! She played happily about, popping one chocolate after another into her mouth. My salivary glands began to work overtime, and I made a concerted effort to keep my eyes away from the child and her treasure until we left.

Just past the campsite there was a deep shady brook. We crossed it slowly, jumping from rock to rock, trying to keep our feet dry. I was poised in midstream, waiting for Bump to make his next move, when he said, "I saw the gleam in your eye back there."

"I couldn't help it," I said. "If I don't have a piece of candy soon, I'll probably *die!*"

"I was afraid you were going to smack that kid and take her chocolates!"

I started laughing so hard that I slipped off my stone perch into the water. "*Darn* you! Now look what you made me do."

"I don't know if I can keep you out of trouble all the way to Georgia or not," Bump said, reaching out a hand. He pulled me ashore, wet and still laughing, and we headed for the Old Stage Road. The lean-to in which we found our night's lodging was in the worst condition of any we had seen. It was without a floor and full of bugs. After we had eaten and made the lean-to as habitable as possible, we explored the area. Near the spring we unearthed an old quart bottle. Its twisted neck suggested hand blowing. Realizing its potential value, I stowed it in my pack. We tried to imagine what it was like, perhaps a hundred years ago, to live and work here. We discovered no further traces of those remote lives, and somehow I wasn't sorry.

Fortunately, since Monson is one of the two places in Maine where Appalachian Trail hikers can get supplies without leaving the trail, the people were not unaccustomed to sights such as we presented. We wore our trail clothes—dirty shirts, slept-in jeans, high boots—for we had no other clothing. We had been thoroughly chewed by various bugs and the bites looked bad. My hair was dirty and untidy. Bump was unshaven. Lingering over coffee, we speculated about the way people might look at us farther along, in places where we would have to leave the trail to procure supplies. Would they dismiss us at a glance as "hippies"? Would they be repulsed by what showed on the surface? I hoped not. I hoped they would look beneath the trail dirt and find the people there. Bump said this hope I had for finding humanity in human beings was an incurable disease.

Sated at last, we turned to our errands. Our one change of clothing was washed and dried in a laundromat instead of a brook and a branch. We bought food, including plenty of chocolate bars. I ate three of them as we walked back to the rooming house. For $5 we had a room, a bed with a real mattress and clean sheets, and a bathtub. Luxury! Ready for the tub, I was horrified to see that I looked very much like a scarecrow. We knew we were losing weight, but I was unprepared for this. I had lost 10 pounds, at least! We luxuriated in hot bath and shampoos, but when we took a nap we found the bed too soft.

It was still dark outside when I began reviewing some of the "we can get by without its," and Bump began to toss and turn. It was amazing how the human body adapts itself, I thought, as I shifted on the fluffy mattress. How quickly our backs had adjusted to their log and bough beds on the trail! Air mattresses and shorty pads had been on our "rejected" list, along with other items such as tents, stoves, swimsuits, and pajamas. And shaving equipment, I suddenly remembered, as Bump rolled over and his whiskers scraped my arm.

Nudging him, I asked, "How come you didn't bring a razor?"

"Because I'm gonna raise a beard. Besides, you didn't bring any hair curlers, did you?"

"I'm gonna raise pigtails."

He yawned, rolling over again at the same time I did. We both sort of slid downhill and collided in the feather bed. I stopped worrying about the things we had left behind.

At daybreak on June 24 we put our nemesis behind us. We hiked on and off the highway, in and out of the woods, through Blanchard, across the Piscataquis River, then back into the woods again. The walking was good, with very little climbing. We had covered 17 miles between Monson and Moxie Bald Mountain by the time we stopped. The area around the lean-to was littered with garbage and the evidence of a recent bear killing. Inside the shelter there was perhaps 50 pounds of salt in a box, left over from curing hides. It wasn't a pleasant place to curl up for the night, but we were tired. With miles of trail behind us and a mountain ahead, we were in no position to be choosy. At dusk, having performed our usual chores, we were settling in when I heard a strange sound. "What's that noise?" I whispered.

"What noise?"

"That *swishing*."

"I don't hear a swishing."

We were near the edge of a pond, and I said, "It sounds like someone swimming. If you won't get up and look, I *will*."

"All right." He didn't budge.

"All right, *what?*"

"All right, go look if you want to." *My hero.* I crawled out of my sleeping bag and tiptoed outside, just in time. In the mirrored stillness of the water I saw a giant moose. For several moments he remained perfectly motionless. Then, apparently refreshed by his evening swim, he moved into the night. It was a rare moment for me. As I returned to my bed, Bump said sleepily, "See any water-skiers?"

"I saw a moose, and it could have been a *bear!*"

He chuckled. "Wasn't, was it?"

No argument could jar that of logic. I gave up.

We broke camp early and headed for Caratunk, a small town with a country store and post office. We mailed postcards, bought supplies, ate Italian sandwiches, and learned the whereabouts of a ranger who could tell us how to cross the Kennebec River. We were told that the river was being dragged for the body of a man killed in a log drive. The ranger located a man to take us across the river, and for $5 we were transported in an aluminum rowboat across the Kennebec. I was glad when we reached the opposite shore and could put the dead logger's river behind us.

Pierce Pond was one of the loveliest places we had seen. We would have enjoyed staying in the new lean-to but there was half a day's hiking time left. We had to be satisfied with sitting on the bank, eating peanut butter and jam sandwiches, and dangling our feet in the cool clear water. We made East Carry Pond by nightfall. A pleasant evening and restful night turned into a dismal morning. We woke to the sound of rain drumming on the roof. I rolled over in my sleeping bag and asked Bump what time it was.

"I don't know. My watch broke."

I thought about that for a while. It was a peculiar feeling, lying there in the half-dark as the rain beat down around us, not knowing what time it was. Time, as measured by a watch, had governed most of our lives, but here on the trail that sort of time had no real meaning.

Finally there was an easing in the downpour so we ate a hurried cold breakfast and moved out. The trees and grasses were wet and dripping. Every branch we jostled gave us an additional shower. After a few miles we looked and felt as if we had been swimming. The slashing rain eventually tapered off to dripping and drizzling. When we reached the lean-to at Jerome Brook we stopped for the day.

Inside the lean-to we discovered packs but no people. It was a little eerie, but we began to concentrate on our most desperate need of the moment—a fire. How wet and cold we were! My teeth chattered furiously as we searched for dry wood, bits of bark, twigs—anything that would burn. At last the tiny carefully nurtured flame caught and began to blaze. We were sitting almost on top of it, warming ourselves, when we heard a thrashing in the brush. We looked through the mist to see a rather large woman carrying a little red lantern emerging from the bushes. Behind her came another woman, slipping and sliding across the log bridge. Here was the answer to the unattended packs.

The women were teachers from Maryland who spent their vacations exploring the Appalachian Trail. They were tremendously excited to learn that we planned to go the entire trail. The four of us shared the warmth of the fire and the shelter of the lean-to. We couldn't have asked for more pleasant company. In the morning Miss Willis, whom I would always picture peering out of the bushes clutching her little red lantern, cooked breakfast for us. She and her friend were carrying fresh eggs, something we hadn't seen for some time. The fireplace grate was uneven and the eggs persistently slid into a heap on one side of the pan. Trying to be helpful, Bump attempted to straighten the grate and burned his fingers. I admired his efforts at self-control and solicitously dug out the bag balm for him, then dug into my eggs. They were delicious, and I could have eaten a dozen of them.

Miss Willis had told us Bigelow Mountain would be the longest 11 miles of the trail we would find, and she certainly knew her mileage. It was the roughest going we had encountered. On Myron H. Avery

Peak, at an elevation of 4,088 feet, we came to a sign: 95 MILES TO MAINE-NEW HAMPSHIRE LINE. I promptly sat down.

Bump grinned. "Quitting?"

"Resting," I retorted, glaring at him.

"Come on," he laughed, pulling me to my feet. I'll buy you a Coke and a Baby Ruth at the very next roadside stand we hit." A bottomless source of inspiration, my husband.

We made it over Bigelow by suppertime. It was the most exhausting day yet. That evening we were joined at our cozy retreat by a Boy Scout troop. "Ah, the solitude of the Maine Wilderness," Bump sighed, but I knew he enjoyed having the youngsters around.

We were thoroughly soaked by the time we reached Spaulding Mountain Lean-to. We had been at the shelter just long enough to build a roaring fire, change, and hang up our wet clothing when we were joined by another hiker, a lone man who obviously was happy to find the lean-to inhabited.

"That fire feels just great. You don't know how glad I am to find someone here. I've lost my guidebook and was getting worried."

"Afraid we can't help there," Bump said. "We don't have a guide-book, either."

"You don't? Lose yours, too?"

"No. Just didn't bring any."

"Well—maps, then. You must have maps."

"No."

"Compass?"

Bump shook his head.

"How far are you planning to go?"

"Springer Mountain."

"Springer Mountain, Georgia? That's the whole trail! How can you go the whole Appalachian Trail without guidebooks or maps—or a compass?"

"Well, we're depending on markers and on meeting people who'll give us tips," Bump explained.

The clean woodsy smell of the night, laced with the aroma of frying hot dogs and boiling coffee, was heady as wine. We ate with our backs to the fire's warmth, lulled and contented. Suddenly Bump said he smelled something burning that shouldn't be burning, and we discovered that Bump's boots, set by the fire to dry, were not only dry but had shrunk, and the toe of one boot was burned completely through.

"What'll you do?" the man asked. "You can't walk to Georgia barefoot!"

"He'll think of something," I said, and Bump was already setting margarine to melt over the fire. He soaked the boots in margarine for some time, and finally pushed stones in to stretch them and left them overnight. In the morning they were wearable again.

The Saddlebacks were tough, and again we were moving through heavy fog that cheated us of any view of the surrounding country. Most of the approaches were thick with what we had come to call "moose muck." It smeared our boots and legs like salve, making walking difficult. Around noon we reached Piazza Rock Lean-to. Water, wood, a fire, and food. Our routine was quickly executed now without discussion or direction. When Bump returned to the site with an armload of wood his free hand was filled with daisies and buttercups and Indian paintbrush. "This is July 2, isn't it?"

"Oh, Bump, they're beautiful! Thank you." I poured water into my coffee cup and arranged the flowers. "I didn't think you'd remember."

He laughed. "Not remember 20 years in double harness? Fat chance!"

I passed him my last treasured Milky Way. "Happy anniversary!"

"Thank you," he said. Then, grinning, "Don't worry. We'll share it."

Another hiking couple stopped by the lean-to and we were able to record a special moment. Dirty, shaggy-haired, Bump's beard scraggly, both of us with moose muck all over, we had our picture taken. Deciding we had ample reason for celebration and goofing off, we spent the rest of the afternoon lazying around, happy just to be alive.

The good weather stayed with us the next morning as we geared up to head for Notch, Old Speck Mountain, and ultimately, the Maine-New Hampshire line. Following Frye Brook was like walking in a great gorge. It was shady, cool, and green—refreshingly different from the ledges and blueberry bushes of the Baldpates. We were still in the mountains, though, and soon we were climbing the East Peak of Baldpate, topping off at over 3,800 feet. The view stretched over many miles and let us appreciate the great beauty of the mountains we were crossing. We were at Notch Lean-to before noon and Bump wanted to go on and take Old Speck, the third highest mountain in the state at over 4,000 feet. I was for saving it until morning. As in many of our compromises on the trail, we did it his way. The approach to Old Speck was rocky and made for slow going. When we were perhaps halfway up we came to an empty shack. It looked to me like a good place for an early supper and bedtime. We got in plenty of wood, built a nice fire, and cooked Kraft macaroni and cheese. We were quite comfortable when two people came down the mountain and told us of the fantastic view from the huge fire tower on the peak. I shot a quick glance at Bump. Sure enough, it wasn't bedtime yet. When we reached the summit at nine o'clock there was nothing to admire except the thickening darkness. The great roofless fire tower was fine for daylight viewing but useless for shelter.

"*Now* what?" I asked.

"Might as well go on down and see what's on the other side of the mountain."

"I *know* what's on the other side. Dark, just like here!"

"Got a flashlight, haven't you?"

"Well, yes, but where's the trail? Where are the blazes?"

The dependable white trail blazes we had followed all the way from Katahdin seemed to have disappeared. All we could depend on now were the two small flashlights and instinct. My instinct said to bear in one direction; Bump's said to go in the other. We stumbled around in the dark, arguing.

Bump said, "This way seems to be the most traveled."

"That doesn't make it the right trail. I think we should take the other one."

"Those lights way off there must be a city—maybe Gorham. We have to hit that."

"You don't know if those lights are Gorham or not. They're miles and miles off."

Silence. Then he said, "I'm going this way. Are you coming?" End of discussion. For better or worse, two flashlight beams bobbing along Old Speck's night-blackened backside. We went down through the darkness, picking our way along, hoping we had the right trail. Finally, after nearly two hours, we knew we were on the right trail when we reached Speck Pond Shelter. We were thankful, and Bump even had the grace not to say "I told you so." The lean-to was spilling over with Boy Scouts whose counselor wanted to move them out to make room for us but we were so happy just to know where we were that we gratefully spread our bedrolls on the ground.

The next morning we came to Mahoosuc Notch. The Appalachian Trail is one thing; Mahoosuc Notch is something else. Forsaken by the sun, it is almost a mile of snow, ice, sheer ledges, caves, and moss-covered rocks. Walking in Mahoosuc Notch isn't something you expect your feet to do by themselves. We clambered, slipped, clung, slipped again, and eventually emerged into the sunshine. Some time later we reached the Maine-New Hampshire state line. Hallelujah! That porcupine-chewed sign, surrounded by bright blue-topped little spruce, was a most welcome sight. It was July 9 and we had been on the trail 27 days and had traveled 279 miles. I wanted to cheer, and we did. I persuaded Bump to pose by the sign and it was a fine shot: the gnawed wooden signpost and Bump beside it, grinning through his whiskers and wearing Steve's University of Maine beanie, which served time as a pot holder. Now Maine, and home, were really behind us.

On the Carter-Moriah Trail we had thunder, lightning, and beating rain. On the summit we stood beneath a leaky fire tower for protection until the shower slackened, then walked on to a ski lodge where we stopped for hot chocolate. After a hearty supper at the foot of Wildcat we headed for Mt. Madison and soon lost the trail. It was late and the weather was threatening again. There was nothing to do but make camp and try again in the morning. We put up the tarp by a small stream and tried to make ourselves comfortable. We're not lost, I told myself, just temporarily misplaced. Sometime before daybreak I awoke to the sound of rushing water. Worse than the sound was the *feeling*! Water seemed to be coursing all around us!

"Bump!" I shouted. "Wake up!"

Our innocuous gurgling brook had swelled to overflowing and was drenching us, soaking our sleeping bags and creeping into our clothing. Suddenly, it was just too much. "Bump *do* something," I cried, on the verge of tears.

"What shall I do? Build you a castle?"

I decided I might as well laugh as cry. We pulled the jumbled mess of our equipment up onto higher ground and tried to get a fire going. Wet. Soggy. Cold! At last, a fire, hot coffee, and oatmeal. Simple comforts, but all we asked at the moment. With daylight, after finding no signs and no blazes, we climbed about six miles up the mountainside and finally met some people who set us straight. Not only were we on the wrong trail; we were on the wrong mountain! The man and woman gave us their map and pointed us back down the mountain to the road and the spot where the sign, perhaps now hanging in some souvenir-happy citizen's recreation room, should have been. They probably wondered what kind of people would start out to walk a couple of thousand miles without maps. I was beginning to wonder, myself.

We walked a swinging bridge across a brook toward Mt. Madison and faced 3,500 feet of water-slicked ledge, with scarcely a toehold to be found and nothing to grasp but slippery roots. Twice during our upward struggle we stopped to pull off our packs and stand under the space blanket, at the mercy of thunderstorms that were accompanied by crackling lightning and punishing hail. I thought of the sign we had seen earlier, warning against traveling in these mountains in bad weather. Particularly haunting was one terse statement: MANY HAVE DIED ABOVE TIMBERLINE.

When we reached the summit we were wet through and chilled to the bone and another storm was close on our heels; we felt it might have been December 25 instead of July 12. Finding shelter, warmth, and hot food at the Madison Huts represented all the security in the world. Bunks and blankets were furnished. Men slept on one side of the hut, women on the other. We could have purchased paper sheets and pillow-cases as well, but decided there was no sense in starting to be fancy now. We learned a lot from the other hikers, including "Moose," who was a jolly man full of stories, and the most interesting person I had met so far on the hike. He had once attempted to do the whole trail with a friend, but the friend inconsiderately broke his leg, thus ending the venture. When Bump and I mentioned our confusion concerning the trail blazes since we had left Maine, he explained that through New Hampshire and Vermont we would have orange and black blazes, compliments of the Dartmouth College Outing Club. Orange and black were Dartmouth's colors. No wonder we couldn't find a white blaze!

In the morning we paid $14 for the supper, lodging, and breakfast for two. Reasonable, but not something we could afford to do often. We were in the Presidential Range, following a cairn-marked trail over crests draped with fog. We knew we had more than 20 miles of hiking above tree line as we crossed the flanks of Mts. Adams, Jefferson, and Clay. It was cold and there was no wood for fires. We stopped only once, to change into long pants. Though it isn't part of the trail, we climbed to the top of Mt. Washington. Rising 6,288 feet, it is New Hampshire's highest point and we couldn't pass it by. We saw the Cog Railway and the weather observatory on the summit. Best of all, from the highest telephone in the northeastern United States, we called home!

We followed Crawford Path to the Lakes of the Clouds. No other name could so aptly describe it! At one unnerving spot on the path we peered down into some 5,000 feet of sheer space. As far as we could see in every direction there were mountains and more mountains.

Real reassurance came with the morning. It was a brisk sunny day just made to be greeted with enthusiasm. From Webster Cliffs we looked down on the highway, running like a zipper along the back of a billowing green dress; then we hiked Zealand Ridge and the Ethan Pond Trail. Whitewall Mountain was rough, with loose rocks that rolled under our feet. After about 18 miles we camped outside Gale-head Hut. That evening we met a teacher from Massachusetts who had a two-man mountain tent to sell. It had a rain fly and was waterproof and practically new. To me it looked like a palace. Bump told the man we didn't have enough money with us to buy it.

"Try it for the night," he said. "If you like it, send me a check later."

Bless him! In the morning he took our tarp to send home for us and we packed the tent, shook his hand, and set out. Still in the Presidential Range, our mountains for the day were Garfield and Lafayette, with other less formidable heights in between. Fog was settling in and other hikers were few as we started up Mt. Lafayette. On the mountain's top, at over 5,000 feet, there was fog so dense we could barely see the cairns, and they were the only way the trail was marked. Great gusts of wind were so strong that we were nearly plucked from the ground. It was frightening, and I had a new reason to be grateful for my 35-pound pack.

It was still miserably foggy and raining hard when we made it down to Liberty Spring. The shelter was already overflowing with campers, and the roof was leaking to boot. Several hut boys, who had been packing in lumber for reconstruction, were staying here. One of them came to our rescue, letting us change our soaked clothing in his tent. He insisted that I use his sleeping bag because the wind had torn my impromptu plastic pack cover and rain had seeped into my bedroll. Then he loaned us his Coleman stove so we could make hot chocolate. In the morning the boys offered to take us to town to buy the small Svea stove we had decided would be worth carrying. Terrific people, these lads. During the ride they delved into the "whys and wherefores" of our journey. We tried to explain how we felt about the wilderness, about wanting to see it and live in it before it was polluted and super-highwayed out of existence.

"You know," said one boy, "I have the same feeling sometimes. Guess that's why I like this job. How were you able to get so much time off? You teachers?"

"No," Bump said. "My wife has five months leave without pay. I had to quit my job."

Their admiration was obvious. "You quit your job to do the trail? That's terrific!"

"It probably won't be so great next winter when we're eating snowballs," Bump said dryly. The boys were impressed, nonetheless. We had sort of kicked the establishment in the teeth to "do our thing."

On July 31, our forty-fourth day on the trail, we entered Massachusetts and reached a shelter in a cool and quiet pine grove at sunset. It was a time and a place for retrospection. We had traveled through three states, had been on the trail 44 days, and had hiked more than

550 miles. We had been chewed by blackflies, jabbed by mosquitoes, stung by horseflies; we had been sticky and smelly with sweat, and dry with thirst; lost; footsore; our hands had swelled and our backs had been weary; we had been pommeled with hail; starved for fresh fruit and beefsteak and candy bars—yet right now we probably were healthier and more relaxed than we had been at any time in the last 10 years.

Our basic diet of oatmeal, peanut butter, and Kraft dinners, although not very appealing aesthetically, seemed to be providing enough protein and vitamins. Although we had been wet and chilled at times, we had developed no colds. We had used water from unreliable sources without harm. Our feet were toughened and our shoulders strengthened. Though our hands still swelled, sometimes quite a bit on extremely hot days, they produced no real discomfort. Bump, still smoking two packs of Camels a day, was feeling their effect less and less. The insects that had put us through purgatory at first had now lost their punch. We were winning. The dream was one-fourth reality.

We gave a full day and night to Mt. Greylock. Parts of the trail were narrow, almost like tunnels through the hardwood and spruce. How human the trees seemed! Old and gnarled, or youthfully supple; thickset, slender, balding, hirsute; some raucous in the wind, some whispering; many prolific with seed; a few diseased, waiting quietly for death. Such places always stirred an echo of Thoreau: *It is not their bones or hide or tallow that I love most . . . but the living spirit of the tree . . . it is as immortal as I am.*

The view from Greylock's summit held us. To the west, ridges plunged into ravines; to the east there were wide ribbons of hills; deep valleys reached north and south. In our immediate vicinity there was a huge fenced-in stone monument, with an eternal light on top, honoring the Massachusetts war dead. Here, too, was Bascom Lodge, an old building, big and rambling, faced with stone and weathered shingles. Here, for a brief moment, we lived in style of a sort, eating chicken cacciatore and sleeping in actual beds. Consensus: for us, style was not only too expensive, but it didn't seem to fit us, either. By 6:30 the next morning, we were on the trail again. Coming off Greylock we were hailed by two hikers camped in a blueberry field near the trail. They had seen us at the lodge and were waiting for us. We gathered round and toasted each other with wine, which was heady fare so early in the morning.

At the next shelter we overtook Jay Smith, whose name we had seen in the registers. He had left Katahdin a week before we did and the blackflies had nearly eaten him alive. Now he was taking his time, trying to get healed. How we could sympathize! Farther along the trail we met a Mr. Herring, 66 years old, hiking alone from Georgia to Maine. Stalwart folk, these backpackers!

Next day, after going through Dalton, we ran onto more of the bushes, six to eight feet in height, that we had thought would bear juicy pears. We now saw that they were highbush blueberries, the likes of which we had never seen! We picked and ate our fill. On a steeply descending section of trail Bump tripped over a rock. Down he went and down he stayed. His pack probably weighed 45 to 50 pounds and it held him flat. Looking like a derailed train, he glowered at me. "For @!#*! Help me *up!*"

"I will if you stop raving," I said, trying not to laugh.

"Dammit, Margaret, it's not funny!"

"You'd think it was if you could see yourself." I giggled until finally he began to laugh, too.

"OK, it's funny," he agreed. "Now get me out of this."

"And you were going to keep me out of trouble," I said, pulling at his pack.

We had magnificent weather, clear and warm, through the shires of western Massachusetts. I began to catch myself singing bits and pieces of *Mountain Greenery*. One nice day we had lunch with Mrs. Hutchinson, a kind lady who spends her summers in a circa 1811 farmhouse near the trail, often feeding Appalachian Trail hikers. We camped overnight by beautiful Finerty Pond, but later learned that it was a public water supply and definitely taboo as a camping spot. We crossed Mt. Wilcox and went down and across the tonic River. We had several 20-mile days, took coffee and cookies with an artist from Greece, and climbed up and down, mostly up, over Jacobs Ladder Highway. On Bump's birthday, August 6, we were in Connecticut. Bear Mountain was our first climb that day. At the top I saluted my 42-year-old husband. "Happy Birthday to the Old Man of the Mountain!" I shouted. He was beginning to look the part, slightly stooped against the weight of his pack, one big hand clenched around his moosewood walking stick, his gray whiskers shaping into a beard. Jokingly, I said, "You don't look a day over a hundred."

"For that *you* get to start the stove and make the coffee tomorrow morning."

"Oh, I didn't mean it," I said, with mock contrition. "You'd pass for fifty easy."

"I *feel* about twenty," he roared, "so you'd better look out!"

Speed being the better part of discretion, I moved right along down the mountain. Later, in Salisbury, I bought him a birthday present—six Three Musketeers candy bars, his favorite, and a pound of brown sugar. A little sweetening never hurts.

We went through the hushed majesty of Cathedral Pines, with the sun slanting on a quiet needled carpet. It was like being in a church that had no need of doors or statues or preaching. We went over mountains and more mountains, not terribly high, but there.

By August 14, when we had been on the trail two months, we were leaving the shelters very early in an effort to beat the heat. One morning we walked across the Bear Mountain Bridge over the Hudson River. At the other end of the bridge we were confronted by a rather cranky looking fellow. "You just cross the bridge?" he asked testily.

"How do you think we got here?" Bump wanted to know.

The man scowled. "Ten cents."

Right.

At the entrance to Bear Mountain State Park we were confronted again by the long arm of authority. "Can't go in yet. Isn't nine o'clock."

Turnstiles and stop watches. Life measured in dimes and minute hands. *Do you know*, I wanted to shout, *that we have walked through hundreds of miles of timelessness? Do you know there is another life out there where you have mountains for breakfast and trees for friends and nine o'clock means nothing?* Instead of shouting I bit my tongue and kept the peace.

"We'll go around, then," Bump said, and we did. Farther on we came down into the park. There were no signs or blazes, and we were not sure of just where we were. There was a tourist area, a huge parking lot, an inn and souvenir stand, and a small police station.

"We'll go in and ask where the trail is," Bump decided.

I looked at him for a long moment. "Are you going to leave your pack outside?"

He shook his head. "Wouldn't want them to think I have something to hide."

In we went. There seemed to be policemen all over the place. We explained our problem and the desk sergeant answered our question. "You're on the Appalachian Trail right now," he said pleasantly.

"Good enough," Bump said, turning to leave. "Thanks a lot."

The sergeant's voice stopped us cold. "You come all this way without weapons?"

Bump laughed, slapping his hip. "No, sir. Got my hunting knife right here."

The sergeant looked steadily at us and finally nodded. "Okay." As we left, I tried not to think about the loaded revolver in Bump's pack.

We moved due south along Kittatinny Mountain. We were on the ridge crest most of the time and our feet, in boots with the soles worn thin, were beginning to complain. The weather remained indulgent, though, helping us make good time. I experienced a moment's disillusionment at one of the familiar Appalachian Trail signs. This one read: MAINE 927 MILES—SPRINGER MOUNTAIN, GEORGIA 1,673 MILES.

"No matter how you add it," I said, "it comes up 2,600. That's almost 600 extra miles!"

"Well, there's been a mistake somewhere, so don't get your fluffer down," Bump said.

"All right," I said wearily. "But I'm going to set it down temporarily pretty soon. My feet are sore." They surely were and Bump's were, too. We would have to get new boots soon.

On August 20 we had 20-odd miles of rocky climbing over Rattlesnake Mountain and Mt. Mohican. We passed Sunfish Pond where the area was strewn with scantily clad people in variegated clusters of blacks and whites, to all appearances stoned on something. We went down through a deep ravine and finally, late in the afternoon, came to the Delaware Water Gap. This must be where the word breathtaking was coined. We were struck by the beauty of it, with the Delaware River, blue and sandy-beached, gently curving between the steep rocky walls of mountains rising over a thousand feet on either side.

We climbed up and out of the Delaware Water Gap onto Blue Mountain and went on to Wind Gap. Here we found a fine spring and an ideal campsite. While we were scouting for the best place for our tent, we came upon a small grave with fresh flowers on it. The words *Hi Punkin* were written on a piece of broken slate. Suddenly everything seemed very still. The power of imagination! We looked slowly around us. Off to one side was a fireplace with an open can of meat on the grate. On the other side there was a tarp, with boughs beneath it. I looked at Bump. Puzzled, he shrugged his shoulders. "We might as well eat."

I couldn't shake the feeling that someone was watching me. Just as I was finishing my sandwich I noticed the sneakers, a huge pair neatly placed beside the tarp. They must have been size 12, at least. That did it for me. We picked up and moved on, and eventually were forced to set up camp near a highway, where the distant buzz of traffic disturbed the stillness of the night.

In Pennsylvania we had rocky climbing with rain and rocky climbing with heat, and rocky climbing with high humidity. The rocks plus the new boots equaled tender feet, but the knowledge that we were halfway to our goal gave us new determination and kept us going. At the Allentown Hiking Club Shelter we found the spring dry and discovered that we had lost the key to our stove. At a highway diner the lady in charge asked if we were Mr. and Mrs. Smith. We confessed that we were. She said that about an hour earlier two boys had been looking for us. One had been a redhead; the other had lightcolored hair. Steve and Ken! We realized the boys must be hitch-hiking and a truck driver on a neighboring stool volunteered to drive to the intersection and look for them. When he returned shaking his head, the woman's husband drove farther down the highway. Kind gestures, but to no avail. The boys were gone. We could only hope that we would see them when we reached the next town.

We came to Rausch Gap and then to an abandoned village where building foundations and wells had apparently been buried long ago by rock slides. There must have been a recent windstorm as well, for the surrounding vegetation was bent to the ground and many of the trees had been violently uprooted and flattened. All told, the place had an eerie chilling effect on us, and we didn't dawdle.

Stony Mountain was appropriately christened. We decided there must be more rocky terrain in Pennsylvania than in all the other states combined. We were through Clarks Creek Valley and coming up to the Earl Shaffer Shelter when we heard gunfire. Thinking we were being shot at, Bump yelled. Two boys appeared, guns in hand. They had been target shooting. They asked if there was anything they could do for us.

"Sure is," Bump said. "Got a pair of pliers you don't need?"

They were happy to oblige. Within moments they presented us with the needle-nosed pliers they used for tinkering on their Volkswagen and we had a new key for our stove. We dined rather well on beef Stroganoff and Kool-Aid while a storm built up around us. We opted for the shelter, but it leaked like the proverbial sieve. We were awake most of the night, watching the lightning strike and dodging raindrops.

At dawn it was clearing, cool, and breezy. We went along the beautiful Susquehanna River using a small branch with leaves on it to brush away the hundreds of webs spun across the trail by spiders. We picked up supplies in the village of Duncannon and went on past Cove Mountain and Conodoguinet Creek into the Cumberland Valley. At a fruit and vegetable stand near Churchtown the proprietor insisted that we help ourselves to anything we wanted. We gratefully loaded up on plums. At a dairy bar the kids laughed at Bump's ragged pants, but we ignored them as we stuffed ourselves with ice cream and milk shakes. Unable to find Dark Hollow Shelter, we camped beside a peaceful brook. Over breakfast Bump complained about the coffee-soaked edges of his mustache. I fished out my all-purpose sewing scissors. A little dull, but they would do.

He inched backward. "Don't know if it bothers me *that* much."

"Only take a minute," I said, starting to snip.

"Ouch! That pulls!"

"Sit still and be quiet."

Snip, snip. Again the *ouch*.

"There. See? Told you it wouldn't take long."

"Good thing it didn't." He gingerly put his fingers to it. "You're a beautician by trade. Do you make all of your customers yell?"

"Of course not," I said, "but I don't do many mustaches."

As we were leaving I noticed a funny little stick attached to a tree trunk. As I watched, it began to move! Obviously it was some of living thing, one with which we were totally unfamiliar. We began to keep an eye out for these little sticks and saw many more of them. Our cool weather, good for walking, was heating up again. We passed South Mountain, Piney Mountain, and Pine Grove Furnace Park. The Pine Grove furnace was constructed of stone and had been used at one time for smelting lead. As usual, we were most aware of the trees in the park. What was there about a stand of mature pine that made me feel so good? Tall and straight, enduring the passage of years with quiet strength, they were like men grown old with time's buffeting, somehow stronger and more resolute for the experience. Walking in the woods was conducive to such introspection. On this point my husband and I were in complete accord. The only time he glanced at me as if I'd been in the sun too long was when I compared the personality of a particular tree with the personality of some person we'd known.

On September 5 we were still following the ridge of South Mountain when we entered the state of Maryland. About noontime we stopped at a fish and game installation and were invited to lunch. The men were very kind and helpful, but their Southern accent was so heavy I had difficulty in understanding them. Bump managed, though, and assimilated enough information so that farther on, confronted by a roadside telephone and a PLEASE CALL FOB CLEARANCE sign, we knew we were passing Camp David. Should we have elected not to dial the prescribed numbers and check in, there was a possibility that we would be picked up and interrogated. We called.

Just beyond Greenbrier Park we met Tom and Ruta Rose and accepted a kind invitation to stay at their farm for the night. How gratifying it was to meet such friendly and helpful people, who accepted us as we were, for what we were. We had barbecued steaks with all the trimmings. *Ohhh!* And melon. I knew I was being piggish, but I couldn't stop eating the melon. You have a new appreciation for the flavor and just plain *goodness* of a food when you haven't tasted it for a long time. Tom, a science professor at Hood College in Frederick, telephoned a fellow teacher, a hiker who had walked many sections of the trail. The teacher turned out to be none other than Miss Willis, the lady with the little red lantern at Jerome Brook back in Maine! How nice it was to see her again! She brought us maps, told us where to look for the springs, and advised us to take an 8-to 10-day supply of freeze-dried foods for our hike through the Smokies.

In the morning the Roses took snapshots they would send to Steve. It wasn't long after we were back on the trail that my stomach started giving me the business. Too much melon? In Washington Monument State Park we stopped to talk with another couple and their children. They wanted to feed us, but for once I couldn't eat a thing. Incredible! We thanked them, and as we were leaving Bump shook the fellow's hand. They were a black family and the man looked at Bump with surprise. He said, "You're the first white man to shake my hand in seven or eight years!" It was a sad commentary and I could think of no adequate response. Perhaps there was none.

After five or six more miles I was feeling nauseous and light-headed. We had stopped along the trail to rest when we heard a terrible squawking racket. Buzzards! We watched them, two black, red-wattled, scrawny-necked buzzards fighting in the top of a tree. Holding my stomach, I asked, "Do you think they know something I don't?"

Bump laughed. "The winner gets to pick your bones!" I quickly became ambulatory. A few more miles put us in Gathland State Park and we decided to stop. It was a small park, clean and well kept. I was too miserable to enjoy it properly, so I eased myself into bed. Next day the park ranger urged us to stay, offering us the softest piece of ground he had. He also wanted to take me to a hospital, but I assured him I wasn't that ill. After we had left the park we realized we were being followed. A basset hound, long ears flopping, was trailing along behind us. We told him to go back, but nothing doing. It began to look as if we had been adopted.

Through the morning I had intermittent nausea and sporadic attacks of diarrhea. Oh, how I cursed my greediness! At last we were in sight of the Potomac. It was dirty and edged with campers. In Sandy Hook the basset took an abrupt left turn and trotted off down the street. I watched him go, hoping he was as sure of his destination as he seemed to be.

We climbed high to cross the bridge, then skirted Harpers Ferry. My head continued its spinning spells. Along a narrow path I saw and felt it all at once—*a copperhead was striking my boot at about ankle height!*

I yelled, and then Bump had a pole and was beating the snake. At last it was dead. The copperhead had a strong odor; to us it smelled like cucumber. Bump notched the copperhead's length on his walking stick and then tossed the lifeless snake into the bushes. The episode didn't help my nausea any, but we kept pushing along the ridge, having determined from earlier signs that we were traversing the Virginia-West Virginia boundary. At Keys Gap we stopped. I was too sick to travel farther. After settling me in, Bump left to find medicine. He was gone for a long time. Between dashes to the outhouse I flopped on my sleeping bag, gagging, fighting nausea, my head whirling. What if Bump got lost? What if he didn't get back? My head went round and round. After what seemed like hours, I heard him coming. He had some Pepto-Bismol, which I began taking immediately. We holed up the next day and night, and by the following morning I felt able to travel. A little woozy, but ready to go. Crossing a highway, we saw some men working on the road and Bump asked if they had a tape measure. It was a peculiar request, but one of the men pulled a steel tape measure out of his pocket and passed it over. Bump measured his walking stick to the notch he had put on it to indicate the copperhead's length. $38^3/_4$ inches. "Thanks a lot," Bump said. He handed the tape back and we continued walking. They must have thought we were crazy.

The next day we tramped on the highway and the heat was like a heavy pressure. Water was nil. As we plodded on our thirst became a real threat. We attempted to hail passing motorists but the only one who even slowed down shouted something unintelligible and hastily sped away. There was nothing to do but keep moving.

When I saw the water, I thought it must be a mirage. It was running from the piece of pipe sticking out of the roadside bank. We drank by turns, then filled our jug. A little later on night forced us off the road and into a rocky pasture. The accommodations weren't the best, but at least there was a vacancy. To have our breakfast served to us at a small restaurant in Rockfish Gap was a rare treat. Afterward we telephoned Jack Stewart and he brought our food and cash and took us to lunch. Just before entering the woods again we came upon a group of workingmen who were booted to the knees as a protection against snakes. They told us the section we were heading into hadn't been cleared since hurricane Camille. One man looked pityingly at us. "I wouldn't put my hound dog through where you're going!"

It can't be that bad, I thought, but it was, with fallen trees, brush, tangles of vines, and briers that grabbed our legs. And so hot! We pitched the tent under the humid breath of a fast-approaching thunderstorm. We got the rain fly up just in time, and sat cross-legged eating canned sardines while the storm snapped and stabbed at us. Bump paused between sardines and looked at me. "Aren't we stupid? Sitting here like two idiots when we could be home in a nice dry living room watching TV."

"So which is better?" I asked him. "Here or there?"

Indecision. Then, "Here."

After a night of rain the air was cooler next morning. Humpback Mountain was a climb of over 3,000 feet, and we crossed others nearly as high. After a night at Harpers Creek we went down to the Tye River and over the bridge. Evidence of Camille's destruction could still be seen in the tumble of boulders and the marks of floodwater high up in the birches. Our food was running low as we climbed The Priest, some 4,000 feet of mountain. We clambered over the ridges of several other mountains and finally bedded down, only to arise and start another day hungry and discouraged. We didn't know where we would find the next store; we were only sure that we would find a great many more mountains. In a picnic area we met a family from Maryland who invited us to eat with them and told us where to find a store about four miles off the trail. We went to the store and restocked. When the owner of the store drove us back to the trail we found a plastic bag full of shrimp packed in crushed ice. A postcard addressed TO THE HIKERS was attached. It told us the shrimp were a gift from some people from West Virginia. It seemed that whenever we were down, someone came along and gave us a boost.

It was hot again, and the mountains seemed to rise higher and become more demanding. One blistering afternoon, when we had been without water for a long time, we came to a lean-to with a brook running by it. Into the cool beautiful water we went! It was pure enjoyment. The lean-to was tucked into a stand of hemlock, and the trees seemed like old friends from home. As we drifted into sleep, listening to the splashing chatter of the brook, I remembered a line from one of Loren books: *If there is magic on this planet, it is contained in water.* At that moment I believed it.

There had been a distinct change in the weather. The air was chilly, nippy. We would need long pants soon. These were beautiful mountains, with huge rocks and views of trees, farms, factories, mills. From the top of Tinker Mountain we looked out over a lovely lake that, judging from the unnatural perfection of its edges, must have been man-made. We seemed to wind around and around it, first on one side, then on the other. Coming down off Catawba Mountain, on a stretch of sheetlike ledge, we watched a small plane. It circled, tipping its wings. We waved, feeling a communion with the pilot, and inexplicably, with the whole world.

We followed paths around giant pointed rocks and skirted wide crevices that looked eerily bottomless. The weather really was becoming cold and it felt good. Through the Skyline Drive area most of the shelter floors were of concrete and we had avoided them like the plague. Now we were finding wooden floors again, in lean-tos with steeply-pitched tin roofs and wide overhangs. At Niday Shelter, named for a family who had homesteaded here in 1865, we drew water from the same spring the Nidays had used and walked among gnarled trees from which they had gathered apples. We hiked along the same ridge that the Nidays' six children must have walked to school some hundred years ago. Here, at least, the land had not changed much.

On the first day of October we talked for a time with a slightly inebriated gentleman who was accompanied by his hound dog Maggie. I didn't tell him that was my nickname, too. With a thick tongue he explained the intricacies of making moonshine and said we weren't far from the spot where he once ran a still. He said I looked like an Indian, and I told him I was one. I tan quickly and by now my face and arms were a deep nut-brown. I suppose the coloring, coupled with rather high cheekbones and long black braids, fitted his image of an Indian, especially when viewed through rum-shot eyes across a campfire. Sometimes I wished I could lay claim to more than my one-eighth American blood, but in doing so now I seemed to have made the man uneasy; I wondered if he expected me to let fly with a tomahawk. In any event, he soon whistled for Maggie and moved unsteadily into the deepening shadows and was gone. A pity, I thought, that we so often see only stereotypes instead of individuals.

The mornings were cool but they warmed up nicely. The leaves displayed colorful hints of autumn. In Pearisburg I bought new boots, and we each got a pair of light gloves. Bump invested in insulated underwear and I settled for long pants that fit. I had found that extremely loose-fitting clothes were as uncomfortable as clothes that were too tight. Tired of drinking from a tin cup, I bought a china coffee mug. Bump had carried his coffee mug all the way from Maine without breaking it; with any luck at all I thought I might make it the rest of the way to Georgia. Guided by a card left in a lean-to by Ed Garvey, we went to Mary Finley's rooming house in Pearisburg. The lady was just leaving for the beauty shop when we arrived. "Go right in and make yourselves at home," she urged us. Price? Two dollars each. Mr. Garvey had known what he was recommending when he said it was a clean and economical place.

In the morning we climbed Pearis Mountain and went on to Sugar Run Gap and Sugar Run Mountain. It was a comparatively easy day except that my feet were sensitive because of the new boots. The weather was cool, and the trail went by black walnut trees and yellow birches. At Dismal Creek Lean-to that night we were awakened by the cold, and what a frosty morning! At a store in the next settlement we were told it had been cold enough for ice to form. They gave us hot coffee and told us that the Dismal Creek Lean-to hadn't been used for months because the area was so thickly infested with snakes. We hadn't seen any snakes, but perhaps they had been all around us? I had a case of belated shivers.

Before we went to sleep that night we got into a discussion of "what we should have had" and "what we should have done." Hindsight is an amazing faculty.

"We should have had a double sleeping bag," Bump said. "Think of the lost body heat."

I agreed. "But who would have carried it?"

"I would, of course," he said generously. "At least half the time anyway."

"We should have had good raingear," I said. "Something light but durable, not tearing on every little twig. And waterproof pack covers."

"Right. And we really should have had the tent and stove to start with. We made out okay, but they would have been nice."

"How about maps?" I asked. "They would have been nice, too."

Bump pooh-poohed that. "Now, how many times have we been lost?"

"Plenty!" I exclaimed. "As soon as we left Maine—"

"Oh, it hasn't been that bad. Those topographical maps are fine, but you'd need a mule train to carry them."

"I'd like to stop at a shelter or come to a road and have some idea of how far it is to a store—and know what direction to take!"

"And miss all that adventure?"

"Some adventure!"

"Seriously, though—a better arrangement for money is what we really should have had. But all in all, we haven't done too badly, have we?"

"No." I twisted in the bedclothes, wondering if I would have to relearn sharing a bed my husband. "But we've been lucky," I said, remembering that we had suffered no snakebites, no sprains, no broken bones. Would we continue to be lucky? Growing sleepy I rolled over, taking my share of the blankets with me and making Bump complain. "We have about four hundred more miles of mountains, including the Smokies." I said. The Smokies. I fell asleep to dream of those mountains.

On October 10 we went up Holston Mountain and hiked the mountain crest in the Cherokee National Forest and the state of Tennessee. Each time we crossed a state line it seemed like a momentous occasion. Nearing Double Springs Gap Lean-to at dusk, we saw a big bonfire. As we came closer we could see three men, all wearing side-arms. What now? We went ahead to the lean-to and in five minutes Bump had become fast friends with Elmer Jones and his two boys. They were in the mountains gathering ginseng roots, which they told us could be sold for $50 a pound. The pistols were for protection from snakes.

The Jones boys gave us their leftover supper beans and treated us to candy. We all sat around the fire and talked awhile. Checking out the lean-to I found a dirt floor with wall-to-wall chicken wire about a foot above the ground, and several fleeing mice. Could we sleep in here with the Joneses? Thinking of the snakes outside, I decided we should try. From experience we knew that the custom in wire-bed sleeping is for every other sleeper to reverse his direction, so that there is a head, then feet, then a head, and so on. This seems to keep the whole precarious business somewhat stabilized. We rolled out our sleeping bags. The Joneses had burlap bags. Not wanting to sleep near the wall because of the rats and mice, I ended up with my head between two pairs of feet, Bump's and Elmer's. It was impossible to get upwind of everybody. Oh, well, I thought. You can't have everything. It was a night of snoring and scratching sounds; one person rolling over jiggled four others; mice scampered indiscriminately across the lot of us. I slept with my head tucked into the sleeping bag and the first thing I saw when I emerged in the morning was a tiny mouse sitting on Elmer's shoulder. Hiking surely makes strange bed-fellows.

We joined Elmer and his boys for a breakfast of Spam and eggs, then moved out. We followed the crest of Holston Mountain for a long time, then there was Locust Knob, Iron Mountain, and pen Gap. We spent a night on a mountaintop overlooking Watauga Lake. The moon was full and we stood on a huge rock near our lean-to and looked down on the sleeping village. The scene, the smell of the night, and the sharp fleeting sense of being a part of everything that ever had been or ever would be brought quick stinging tears to my eyes.

In Laurel Gorge we came to what must be the most beautiful spot in all of Tennessee. Laurel Fork Lean-to was in a shady gorge with abundant rhododendron and mountain laurel and a stream that plunged and splashed over rocks. During the night we heard a bobcat howling in the distance. Sunlight streamed into the gorge in the morning, highlighting the leaves, playing on the water. It was a place I would like to come back to in early summer to see it alive with blossoms.

We had tough going as we scrambled up White Rocks Mountain. It was an appropriate monument for the end of our fourth month on the trail. We stopped at a little country store for candy bars and were warned that it was dangerous to hike in the Roan Mountain area, particularly Grassy Ridge, when it was foggy. We went up and down, into gaps and over tote roads. Occasionally, as in the past, one of us would stay at a blaze while the other went ahead to search for the next one. We put up the tent in an apple orchard which was fine until the middle of the night when it began to rain and the wind blew so hard I thought it would tear up the tent and us with it. We rolled up our bags, pulled down the tent, and ran to a rickety apple shed for shelter. As soon as we were inside we got our stove going and then sat on crates under the space blanket and dozed fitfully for the rest of the night.

The Pisgah National Forest, with its hills and gaps and mountain folk, was hiking country that reminded me of the book *Christy*. In Devil Fork Gap we were invited into a shanty by a woman and her brother, both chewing tobacco, both eager to do something for us. The woman took a box of raisins from a meagerly stocked shelf and insisted that we take them. She then pressed two pot holders into my hand. Impoverished as they were, these people's need to give was greater than their need to possess.

We passed Flint Creek Gap, Gravel Knob, and Big Butt. It rained but we were dry and warm in a cozy lean-to with an inside fireplace. Then came Bald Mountain, Bearwallow Gap, and more rain. At Alien Gap we found a store and selected supplies to the beat of country and western music. Paying, Bump said to the cashier, "You've sure got some pretty mountains in North Carolina."

"What's the matter with the mountains in Tennessee?" she asked pleasantly.

"Not a thing. Why?"

"Well, that's where you are right now."

We had been crisscrossing between the states of North Carolina and Tennessee. Outside, I gave Bump the elbow. "Next time you hand out a compliment find out what country you're in first!"

Buzzard Roost Ridge, Deep Gap, Spring Mountain, all dismal with rain. Dry out, eat, sleep, get up and do it again.

Through the gap, over Bluff Mountain; climb, climb, climb. Higher and higher.

For a couple of days we seemed to climb steadily through autumn foliage that surpassed anything a painter could ever put on canvas. At long last, on October 24, we were in the Great Smoky Mountains National Park. We stopped at the Davenport Gap Lean-to, the first in the park. Across the front of the lean-to there was heavy chain link fencing with a gate that could be kept closed and bolted. It was put there to keep bear out of the shelter. Garbage was not supposed to be carelessly tossed aside here, as we had seen it in some places. Such precautions led us to believe that bear were as prevalent in the Smokies as moose had been in Maine. Surely we would see a bear, at least I hoped so.

As the lean-tos would be close together through the Smokies, and as we could expect the cold weather to have a numbing effect on snakes, we decided we no longer needed the tent. In any case, with its waterproofing worn off, our once reliable home on the trail had become pretty much deadweight. When the men with whom we were sharing the lean-to offered to pack our tent out to a post office and send it home for us, we let it go.

We went over Mt. Sequoyah and Eagle Rocks and through gaps and around the sides of mountains. Unlike the Blue Ridge with its profusion of side trails and fire roads, there was but one path to follow here. We went through spruce and fir and colorful hardwoods and around the starkly treeless Charlies Bunion. Newfound Gap was a popular tourist stop, and near the gap we came upon a nature study group. Some of the members eyed us as if we were new and strange specimens.

We had long since learned that the best assurance of a quiet uncrowded spot was to find a place that couldn't be reached by automobile. People who won't go to a place if they can't drive to it don't know what they are missing. Roadside picnic areas are sometimes nice and drive-in campgrounds are sometimes fine, but they both often attract people who bring a noisy transistorized world with them. To turn your back on the macadamized beehives and go into the forest, to walk the quiet footpaths and hear nothing but bird songs and animal sounds, to see the colors, the shapes of trees and mountain streams, is to evoke a sense of life that is often forgotten in the business of living. The serenity of the forest can rejuvenate the body and restore the soul.

On October 28 we left the crest of the Great Smokies. How it did rain at the lean-to at Birch Spring Gap! We passed the evening in the lean-to talking with other hikers. There was no letup in the rain the next morning, but knowing we were within six or eight miles of Fontana Village and real food, we struck out in the downpour. Late in the forenoon, very wet, we crossed over Fontana Dam. The dam was almost

500 feet high, and at that time was the highest of over 40 dams in the Tennessee Valley. It was an impressive sight, the only thing it lacked was a little sunshine. A man who worked for the TVA gave us a lift to the village. We rented a little cabin, then went to the cafeteria where we met a reporter who wanted a story and pictures for his paper. We told him OK, but we had to eat first. He waited patiently, even when we went back for seconds.

We picked up some welcome mail, but there was no check. It was still raining when we made our way to the cabin. It contained a tiny kitchen-living room, a bedroom, and a bathroom with a tub. *Ahhh!* How marvelous it was to be wet and warm and soapsudsy instead of wet and cold and shivering. We had all manner of good things to eat, mail to read, a bed to crawl into. What did it matter if rain drummed on the roof? Tomorrow we might have problems, but tonight we had none.

There were about 1,850 miles of trail behind us now and we slept easily under any circumstances except concrete floors. On logs, boughs, boards, chicken wire, the ground; alone in the forest or jammed in a shelter like with a dozen other people; in stifling heat, sky-ripping thunderstorms, or foggy chilling cold, we slept. This soft bed wrapped us in comfort and we slept as though tomorrow would never come—of course it did, and with it, more rain. Rain, *rain*. There was still no money at the post office so we asked that it be forwarded to Suches, Georgia, when it did come. The cabin cost $13; there was an additional cash outlay for supplies, and more for breakfast. We had really splurged, eating like mad, filling our packs with all the food and every last candy bar we could carry. We left Fontana with $3, and laughed like fools in the spattering rain because there was no place to spend it in the woods.

Entering the Nantahala National Forest I remembered reading somewhere that Nantahala was an Indian word meaning *Land-of-Noon-Day-Sun*. How I wished we might see a little sun at noonday—or any time. It was miserable to be wet all the time.

Rain dimmed the autumn beauty of the walnut and maple trees. We walked across a half-dozen balds and wondered about their origin. The rain stopped and we kept going over Sheep Knob to Panther Gap, to Swinging Lick Gap, to Winding Stair Gap, to Rocky Cove Knob, to Buck Knob. I found these names intriguing and tried to imagine how each place had earned its name. At Rock Gap Lean-to it rained again. Besides being wet it was cold and the temperature was still dropping. There was very little wood and fire building was discouragingly difficult. We shivered as we blew on the fire with smoke in our eyes; we were hungry and longed to be *warm*. Eventually, after several false starts, we had a blazing fire. What had been dismal and wet became warm and cheery. Reluctant to let the fire die, we tended it spasmodically through the night. In the morning we were glad we had made the effort. It was *cold!* As we walked along that morning we plucked icicles from ledges and sucked them. The day was clear and it warmed up a little. We made about 20 miles, climbing Big Pinnacle, Albert Mountain, the Ridgepoles and Little Bald. Below Standing Indian there were banks of clouds that made the other mountaintops look like islands in the sea. The lean-to and its nearby brook were all ours. It was cold, but there was plenty of dry wood, so we settled in comfortably. Tomorrow we would be in Georgia.

In the night I had a dreamlike sensation of discomfort, of cold. I fought my way up through layers of sleep, and saw *snow*. Snow everywhere! It actually was *snowing*! I poked Bump, and he reared up, the snow flying off the foot of his sleeping bag. "What————?" he began, but the "what" was grimly obvious. We were caught in a blizzard.

Our boots were frozen stiff. Our hands felt the same way. The thin cotton of our gloves and our pants gave us little protection from the snow and cold. Bump built up the fire, piled on wood, and set our boots close to the fire to thaw out. We covered ourselves with the space blanket, but the wind was blowing hard and driving all the heat out into the snowy darkness. Our boots thawed enough so we could get them on. My shoes had been too close to the fire and the laces had burned. With numbed fingers Bump replaced them with pieces of our clothesline. I cooked some oatmeal and we ate, standing over the fire with snow blowing all around us.

We were afraid that if we stayed we would surely freeze to death, so we threw the dirty dishes into our packs and started hiking. We were at an elevation of some 6,000 feet. If we could work our way down we might be able to walk out of the storm. It was almost daylight now but we could see very little. We crept along, hair and eyelashes caked with snow, boots like chunks of ice. The soles on Bump's boots were worn smooth and he kept slipping and half-falling. I was terrified, afraid he would fall and injure his already weakened back. We had said we would finish the trail or drop trying. I began to get angry. In frustration I shouted to Bump, "If we die I'll come back and haunt this damn Standing Indian!"

For hours it seemed that we barely moved over the slippery covered trail. However, we gradually made our way down out of the wind and the blinding snow, and off the mountain. Finally, a long way off, we could see buildings and smoke curling into the frosty air. Half-frozen, we moved toward that smoke. It was a farmhouse, and when we reached it we met Willard and Elva Rogers, who get our vote for being the best people in the world. Willard took off our packs; we couldn't. Elva took care of our wet jackets and boots and huddled us around the stove. They listened to our story and told us we were to stay with them until we could buy warmer clothing. We agreed wholeheartedly with this idea, but we had no money. We started making phone calls, but no one was home—not Steve, not Bump's parents or his sister, not my mother—*no one!* Then Bump remembered Howard Bridges, a friend who had said, "If you run into trouble, just call." Howard was at home. "No problem. I'll wire the money. It's as good as there."

We were in Titus, which was a very small place. The nearest town was Hiawassee, and Mr. Rogers said he would drive us over in the morning. The Rogers fed us a hearty supper, and bedded us down with an electric blanket! I was too weary to think about the extremes of our fortunes. It was enough that we were under cover, warm, dry, and fed.

We awoke with itchy peeling feet, a result of the chilblain we had suffered. We ate a breakfast of squirrel and hot biscuits and eggs. Sitting around the table with the Rogers and their little boy and girl, Keith and Brenda Jean, we felt like part of the family. Later Willard drove us to Hiawassee. We got our money, bought hooded sweat shirts, heavy woolen pants, and rubber pacs. The weather was a little better, but it was still frosty. We needed little coaxing when the Rogers urged us to stay another night. I had heard about Southern hospitality, but these people had taken us in and cared for us just as if we were a part of the family. We would never forget them.

In the morning we left, almost regretfully, but we still had miles to travel. We went through Park Gap and over Mule Mountain; over the ridge from Hellhole Mountain to Dismal Mountain. How appropriately named they were! When we came down off Rocky Mountain into Unicoi Gap our legs were cruelly chafed and our feet were blistered. The rubber pacs hadn't worked out too well.

At the highway we started thumbing. It was almost dark when a college student picked us up and drove us back to the Rogers' home. They greeted us warmly, glad to see the bad pennies turning up again. We called Steve and told him our estimated time of arrival at Springer Mountain. He said he would be there to pick us up. We had another nice evening talking with Elva and Willard Rogers and playing with the children. When we left the next morning we wore our old beat-up boots, leaving the parboiling behind. Again we went over the mountains and through the gaps.

There was a clear sky and the air was brisk. The mountain green was enriched with autumn bronze and red and yellow. Climbing, we began to see dugouts and foxholes. Finally we were stopped by a man in uniform and learned that we were in a Green Berets' training area. We kept walking, too near the end of our journey to stop for anything now. I was busy unwrapping a candy bar when I almost stepped on a snake. I yelped and Bump swung his walking stick. The snake slithered away. We went on up a mountain, along a ridge, down again, crossed a road and had another mountain to climb. But this mountain was different—it was the last one! It was Springer Mountain. On the summit we dropped our packs in a sudden tumble of feelings—triumph, exhilaration, fulfillment, gratitude, regret. I was between a smile and a tear as I looked at the sign: SOUTHERN TERMINUS OF THE APPALACHIAN TRAIL. A MOUNTAIN FOOTPATH EXTENDING 2,000 MILES TO MT. KATAHDIN IN MAINE. We signed the register: *Bump and Margaret Smith. 1:20 P.M. November 9, 1970.* One hundred and fifty days, with mountains every morning. Bump put his arm around my shoulder and grinned. I grinned back at "Yes, we did it. We made it all the way."

Georgia to Maine on the Appalachian Trail

By Thomas McKone

Started at SPRINGER MOUNTAIN on April 1, 1971
Finished at MT. KATAHDIN on August 5, 1971

Fitful gusts of wind swept across the summit during the night, shaking the forest to its roots and flapping the sides of the tent so violently I thought they would collapse. Toward dawn the wind subsided and as the sun rose on Springer Mountain on the morning of April 1, 1971, Bob and I broke the first of many camps we would make on our way to Maine. We were not yet in condition and laboriously plodded along the overgrown woods roads with 35-pound packs on our backs and sweat on our brows. Sometimes the trail slabbed the side of a mountain instead of going over the top, and during those first days we loved to see "slab" in the guidebook trail descriptions. We agreed that it was the most beautiful word in the English language.

There were still patches of snow beneath the laurel and rhododendron bushes, but the days were warm and sunny. An ice storm had hit the area the previous week, leaving much of the trail in shambles. Climbing through the fallen trees with full packs was an extra strain on our city-soft muscles. We hiked 10 miles the first day and spent the night at the Hawk Mountain Lean-to. After dark I walked out to a nearby field and strolled around in the moonlight, playing the harmonica and singing and whistling, and listening to the music echo off the next mountain. Four deer came to the edge of the field, then ran back to the protection of the woods. Storm clouds began to move in, gradually covering the moon and stars. I walked back to the lean-to and went to sleep. I had not been sleeping long when I heard Bob ask, "What are you doing in my pack?"

"I'm not in your pack. I was sleeping."

"Well, somebody's in my pack!"

I fumbled for the flashlight. A moment later the beam was shining on a black-and-white animal that had its paws in the open zipper of Bob's pack. I thought it was a raccoon and reached out to push him away, but just before I touched him I realized that it was a skunk. I yelled, then Bob and I both yelled. The skunk, hardly disturbed, waddled out of the lean-to. He visited us twice more that night, each time leaving the air as fresh as it was before he came; he must have realized that we were more afraid of him than he was of us.

Mice scampered around all night, and ate a hole through a nylon sack to get at some peanuts. After that experience we hung our food out of reach of the various animals that were interested in it and slept more peacefully. The mice continued to scamper around the lean-tos, and sometimes ran over us, but at least they didn't get any more of our food. With the appetites we had developed, we were not willing to share our food with any nocturnal visitors. The next night we stayed at Gooch Gap Lean-to. Like many of the lean-tos in Georgia and North Carolina, it had a Bible in it. After supper I read aloud the account of creation in Genesis, including the line about God making "little creatures that crawl upon the face of the earth." We laughed at the line, but we also refrained from swearing at the mice that night.

On our third day on the trail we climbed Blood Mountain, which at 4,461 feet is the highest point on the Appalachian Trail in Georgia. The mountain gets its name from an Indian legend to the effect that the Cherokees and Creeks once fought such a horrible battle there that the mountain ran with blood. Now Blood Mountain runs only with the sweat of hikers.

There was some snow beneath evergreen bushes and behind rocks, but when the temperature reached 74 degrees on the summit we thought that Spring had come. On our way down the mountain, when Lucy Rogers of Newton, Massachusetts, showed us how to make snow cones by putting snow in a cup and flavoring it with Tang, we thought it would be a one-day treat. Two days later, however, we had more snow than we could eat in a lifetime. That was the day we crossed into North Carolina, and it was the worst day we had in our four months on the trail. The day started calmly; then in turn it rained, sleeted, and hailed. The cold forced us to keep our coats on under our ponchos and the temperature difference between our bodies and the outside air caused moisture to condense inside our ponchos and soak our clothing. However, we were less wet, and warmer, than we would have been if we had walked without our ponchos. After we had gone about 10 miles the sky began to clear. We stopped for lunch by a side trail that led to a shelter and discussed the situation. We could go to the nearby shelter and build a fire and dry our clothes, or we could continue hiking and let our clothing dry as we walked. The next shelter was 10 miles away, but it looked like the weather was going to be good. We decided to hike another four or five miles and camp out. Half an hour later the sun went behind clouds and we never saw it again that day. We should have gone back to the last shelter, but we had already developed an aversion to hiking in the wrong direction. We continued on, not knowing that the weather would soon get worse. It began to sleet, then to snow. We had expected cold weather during the first part of April, but not snow; we were not outfitted for winter camping. We had a floorless tent, no axe, no pads to put under our sleeping bags, no mittens, no scarves; we would have to keep going until we reached the next shelter. The snow continued to fall as we climbed our first 5,000-foot mountain; the wind howled through the naked forest and snow beat against our rosy faces. We grew tired and began to dread each footstep, but we had gone halfway to the next shelter, so nothing would be gained by turning back. We dug towels out of our packs and wrapped them around our necks for scarves, and put socks on our hands for mittens. The snow piled up quickly and tramping through it exhausted us. We were so weak that we decided not to take breaks, fearing that we would not be able to start again.

Late in the afternoon the wet snow began sticking to the trees and covering the blazes. The snow also obscured the trail, and at times a white blanket covered even the rocks and bushes. Visibility was very poor. With only a few minutes of daylight remaining, we came to a clearing which was the junction of six or seven woods roads. We knew one of these roads led to a shelter, but the guidebook description was too ambiguous to be of any help. Guessing that the shelter was on the Appalachian Trail rather than on a side trail, we found the road with white blazes and followed it into the forest. Earlier in the day we had seen bootprints in the snow, so we expected to find someone at the shelter. With our last reserves of energy we called into the white blindness for help, but our Maydays got no answer. The last bit of twilight was fading, and still there was no sign of the shelter. There were only white trees against a white sky, white ground, and white air—a terror of whiteness. Suddenly fatigue overcame me and I wanted to sleep, nothing mattered except sleep. Then we heard a sound that was almost lost in the louder sound of the wind in the trees, and the next moment a shelter appeared through the snow.

The two hikers in the shelter were Bill Finucane, of Bucksport, Tennessee, and a man named Arnold from Washington, D.C. Like us, they had been surprised by the storm, but they had reached the shelter before it got too bad. I was hungry, but too tired to eat. Putting on all the dry clothes I had, I got into my sleeping bag. Since lunch-time we had walked six hours through mountainous terrain without taking a break, and much of the time we had been in the snowstorm with high winds. Somewhere in the midst of that storm we had crossed into North Carolina.

Bill Finucane was tall, slim, and long-legged. Nicknamed the Tennessee Ridge Runner, he was probably the strongest and fastest walker we met on the Appalachian Trail. In the 18 weeks we were on the trail we met only two or three people who could out-hike us with full packs on. Bill was one of them. I don't mean to say that we were fast hikers, or that Bill rushed. Most people seem to think that because we walked 2,000 miles, we walked fast. We walked no faster than most people, but we were not slowed down very much by hills or mountains, and we didn't need many rest breaks. Once we were in condition, we could walk all day without tiring. Although we could have hiked 30 or 40 miles a day in some areas, we never did more than 27 miles. Our average was 15 or 16 miles. Speed was never one of our goals. Bill was not particularly interested in speed either, but he had a helluva stride. We appeased our 2,000-miler pride by telling ourselves that he could out-hike us because we were not in shape yet, but the Tennessee Ridge Runner was not in shape, either.

Arnold taught conservation law at George Washington University. He hoped to be the first person to hike all of the Appalachian Trail in winter. He told us he began hiking only after Labor Day and stopped before Memorial Day. At the time I thought he was crazy, but after hiking through New England in summer I changed my mind.

The morning after the snowstorm we sat in our sleeping bags and watched the snow melt. The storm had left about six inches of snow where we were, and more in the higher mountains. Arnold took a side trail to the highway and started back to Washington. Bill stayed with us. By lunch the sun had melted almost half of the snow, so the three of us decided to hike eight miles to the lean-to at Carter Gap. The first day after bad weather is always enjoyable, and now our worst day on the trail was followed by one of our best. During the afternoon, with the sun shining brightly, we went over Standing Indian (5,498 feet). The snow averaged three or four inches, but there were drifts up to our knees.

At the end of seven days we had gone 92 miles. We had estimated that we would do only 75 or 80 miles the first week, so we were quite content with the 92 miles. For several days I wore only one pair of socks; I had never gotten blisters wearing one pair of socks on day hikes, and I wanted to see if I could do without a second pair on a long hike. My feet were fine when we were doing 10 or 12 miles a day, but as soon as we increased our mileage I got no less than 10 blisters, including 2 on my heels that were larger than any I had ever seen. Deciding that the one-sock experiment was a failure, I began wearing a pair of Wick-Dry socks under my wool socks. During the next four months of hiking I had a total of only three blisters, all small.

The section from Wesser to Fontana has the reputation of being one of the most challenging parts of the Appalachian Trail, so we split the 25 miles up into three days of walking. We entered the area in the middle of one day, completed 13 miles the next day, and hiked the final five miles and went on into the Smokies on the third day. The trail was all up and down; however, because of the way we divided it up, we didn't find it too bad. A scarcity of water was the only difficulty we encountered.

We left Fontana Village with heavy stomachs and overflowing packs. We had stuffed ourselves with the sort of food we couldn't get on the trail, and loaded our packs in a rather futile effort to carry enough food to satisfy our ravishing appetites. One bad thing about towns, as every bloated hiker knows, is that they are always in gaps or valleys. Every time a hiker resupplies at a grocery store, or gorges himself in some small country restaurant, he starts off again by going uphill. At Fontana Dam the Appalachian Trail crossed the Little Tennessee River and entered the Great Smoky Mountains National Park. From the dam the trail climbed steeply until it reached the crest of the ridge, then wove along that ridge for the next 70 miles, with not more than two or three difficult climbs. In many places, the ridge fell off sharply on either side, and since there were no leaves on the trees yet, we often had fine views on both sides. We had been hiking for 12 days and were getting into good condition, and most of the park trail was well-graded and rather easy.

On our first night in the Smokies we shared the Birch Spring Lean-to with four people from North Carolina and Georgia. This lean-to was large enough for 12 people, and had a heavy wire fence across the front to protect the occupants from bears. Someone said that a bear had been seen there two nights before, but our only visitor was a deer. In fact, we didn't see any bears in the Smokies; we were told that it was too early for them to be so high in the mountains.

Clingmans Dome, with an elevation of 6,643 feet, is the highest point on the Appalachian Trail. Until recently, Clingmans Dome was thought to be the second highest mountain in the eastern United States, but the May, 1970, U.S. Geologic Survey showed Mt. Craig, which like Mt. Mitchell is in the Black Mountains of North Carolina, to be 6,647 feet, or four feet higher than Clingmans Dome.

Clingmans Dome was the first summit we shared with tourists. A paved road brings people to within a short walk of the top. In one hour we saw more people than we had seen in two weeks on the trail. People in high heels, skirts, and dress shoes seemed like an awful insult to the mountain, to the trail, and to hikers. In our opinion the tourists had cheated themselves, for we felt that no one could really appreciate a mountain if he had not climbed it.

We arrived at a shelter late in the afternoon and were relieved to find only three people there—Scott and Judy from New York, and a girl from Michigan named Linda, who was hiking alone in the Smokies for a week. Like Lucy Rogers, whom we had met in Georgia, Linda found solitary hiking lonely and discouraging. She was the last lone female backpacker we met until we reached Maine. Soon after we set down our packs and removed our boots, a couple from Michigan, Bruce and Liz, arrived. Although most of the sheltermates we had along the trail were companionable, we occasionally had to put up with a misfit. I described Scott in my journal: "For company in our shelter tonight we are fortunate enough (?) to have a 22-year-old, know-it-all backpacker-hiker-camper-walker-thinker-philosopher-psychologist-sociologist-writer-mathematician-critic-of-all-trades who besides knowing everything, understands everything, has an answer to everything, and believes nothing he reads unless he wrote it himself."

After suppers were finished and the sun had set, Scott, Judy, and Bill engaged in a long and noisy argument on religious and social matters with Bruce and Liz. Linda and Bob were in their sleeping bags trying to sleep. When I finished writing in my journal the five were still at it, so I mentioned that they were breaking shelter etiquette and disrupting the social order, which earlier in their argument they had all agreed was necessary. Bruce and Liz acknowledged that it was late and got into their sleeping bags. Scott, Judy, and Bill continued to talk, at first in quieter tones, but then in normal voices again. A little later one of them said something about having nothing against the Asian (Vietnamese) people. In the middle of the sentence I interrupted him with "Well, what have you got against us people?" Again I reminded them of how inconsiderate they were being, and for the first time in five hours of nonstop talking, Scott had no come-back. After a few private whispers, they got into their sleeping bags. The following day we ran into Bruce and Liz at Newfound Gap and they asked where I got those rules about shelter etiquette. I told them I had made up the rules because I wanted to get some sleep.

Bill Finucane had intended to hike to northern Virginia, but now he decided to leave the trail as spontaneously as he had started it. He was good company, and I was glad to have met him, but I was relieved when he was gone. He liked to hike longer days than we did, and he did not like to stop as often to look at views or flowers. Traveling in a twosome is difficult enough, but traveling in a threesome is impossible, to my way of thinking. Often, when one person wants to stop, the others want to go on, and when this is repeated often enough, company becomes a burden. Hikers can hike separately and meet at the end of the day, but this is not always comfortable, either. Going it alone may be the best way to make the hike. There are always people on the trail, so a hiker can have company when he chooses, whether it is for an evening or a week or two. As Bob and I discovered, being with the same person 24 hours a day for several weeks is extremely difficult, even for the best of friends.

April 17 was our last day in the Smokies and the first day we didn't see snow or ice. As Bob observed, we had been seeing juncos (snowbirds) and robins on the same mountainside. That day we caught up to Jim Wolf, also on his way to Maine. Jim had left Springer Mountain on March 23 and planned to reach Katahdin about Labor Day. He had started planning his hike a year ahead of time, and had figured his stops, pickups, and stay-overs much more precisely than we had. Jim wore a brimmed hat, carried a camera and binoculars, and had an "office" on the front of his shoulder strap. Two days before, someone had asked him if he were Colin Fletcher!

After the Smokies we moved into the Pisgah and Cherokee National Forests. The beauty of these forests was inferior to that of the Smokies, but they were still nice. Here we began a month of solitude. For the next 500 miles we had the Appalachian Trail almost completely to ourselves. After spending the night with Jim Wolf at a lean-to, we shared shelters with hikers only two more times before reaching the Shenandoah National Park, and in that whole time we met only a handful of people on the trail.

Coming from the south, the first town the Appalachian Trail passes through is Hot Springs, North Carolina, population 721. Hot Springs actually has hot springs, and was once famous as a health resort. The springs are still warm (110° F.), and are still open, but they are not as popular as they once were. The town used to be called Warm Springs, but the name was changed in 1888. The townpeople seemed to be very proud of the fact that the Hot Springs area was one of the largest producers of burley tobacco in the country. Life in Hot Springs, and in almost all the areas we passed through on the Appalachian Trail, was much slower than life in cities. After we bought our groceries we sat in front of the store, eating lunch and repackaging our food. The owner of the store came out to sit with us, and so did the man in the hardware store across the street. The four of us sat there in the center of Hot Springs, North Carolina, just passing the time of day, as though there was nothing in the world more important to do.

Two days after we left Hot Springs, high in a remote section of the southern Appalachians, we passed the graves of two Civil War soldiers, William Shelton, Co. E, 2 N.C. Inf., and David Shelton, Co. C, 3 N.C. Mtd. Inf. Since we were in the South, and since their military identification included N.C. for North Carolina, I assumed that these men were in the Confederate army, but later I learned that although they lived in North Carolina, the men were in the Union army. They were killed by Confederate soldiers when they came home to visit their families while the war was still in progress. Millard Hair, a 13-year-old boy who was with them, was killed and buried, too. However, since he was not in the army, the government didn't give him a marker. The Shelton tombstones were erected in the early part of this century by two local preachers, Rev. Frederick Webb and Rev. Monroe Shelton. They obtained the gravestones from the government, but did the work themselves. That afternoon we walked across the farms of two Shelton families. We talked with one of the Mrs. Sheltons, who told us that the soldiers buried on the mountain were distant ancestors of hers. As in many backwoods communities, one or two family names dominate the census lists. Most of the people in this area, she told us, were either Sheltons or Hensleys.

On April 22 we completed our third 100-mile section of the trail. It was our second consecutive rainy day. We had read that many 2,000-milers encountered weeks of rain in April or May, and we were pessimistically anticipating that we were about to get ours. We were right. For the next $2^1/2$ weeks we had rain almost every day. Fortunately, it usually came in the form of showers, and the sky was clear for a part of each day.

There was supposed to be a spring about a hundred feet off the trail on the way up Big Bald. I kept my eyes open and spotted a very green area with several kinds of plants and mosses. I bushwacked over and found a beautiful little spring. The water was shallow and clear, and the bottom was covered with small pebbles. Rhododendron grew nearby. Moss covered many of the rocks, and it also covered a fallen tree which lay across the stream just below the spring. Bob identified the pleasant aroma that filled the air as coming from wild peppermint. I could not get the scent out of my mind. When we left I wanted to take it with me and regretted that, although I could preserve a sound with a tape recorder and a scene with a camera, there was no way I could preserve the smell of the wild peppermint. The best I could do was to put a few leaves in my pocket and keep them until they lost their aroma.

When we reached the summit of Big Bald I forgot all about the peppermint. The trees stopped well below the summit, so the top of the mountain was a huge field. Southern balds are actually too far south to be above timberline at 5,000 or 6,000 feet. Some of the summits were cleared by man, but what made the old balds remains a mystery. Big Bald rises to 5,516 feet and is much higher than any of the neighboring peaks. It provides a 360-degree panoramic view. We sat on the grassy summit for three or four hours, gazing at the valleys and the smaller mountains below us, and at the larger mountains in the distance. What a place it would be to watch the sun rise and set, and see the stars shine! For the man with an eye for the stars, the summit of Big Bald might be as close to heaven as anywhere on earth.

As we sat on top of Big Bald we watched clouds form and disappear. The entire sky was blue (we saw a complete hemisphere) but the air mass coming from the northwest was moist and clouds formed when the air reached the cooler temperatures over Big Bald. After going over the mountain, the air mass would descend to lower warmer altitudes and the clouds would dissipate. The process was exact. We knew precisely where to look to see clouds form, where they would reach their greatest size, where they would begin to disperse, and where they would disappear completely.

The next morning it rained as we were walking down a beautiful ridge from No Business Knob. The ridge was supposed to offer spectacular views, but the visibility that day was only a hundred yards. During the rest of the rainy spell we made weather forecasts by reading the guidebook. When the guidebook mentioned spectacular views, we predicted it would rain. After the rainy spell we became more scientific weathermen and began forecasting according to clouds, weather patterns, and "how it felt." In New England I often gave weather forecasts to hikers and did quite well. One night on the Long Trail, just after I had completed my Appalachian Trail hike, I told a shelter full of people that I could predict the weather fairly well because I had been in the open for four months. As a demonstration, I predicted that it would rain the next day. In the morning the sky was blue, and I felt a little foolish. However, the sky soon turned dark, and it began to sprinkle. It rained all that day and into the next. For once I was glad to see rain; my honor as a weather prophet was at stake. I would have hated to leave those hikers with the impression that someone who had hiked all the way from Georgia to Maine didn't know what he was talking about!

A weekend Naturalist Rally was in progress near Erwin, Tennessee, when we passed through. As we hiked up the dirt road on Unaka Mountain (5,180 feet), a string of cars on their way to the outing passed us. One of the cars stopped and the driver told us he was Charles L. Johnson of WEMB radio in Erwin. He asked us some questions and taped two interviews to use on WEMB in connection with the Naturalist Rally. I was slightly taken aback when, in one of the interviews, Mr. Johnson called us "strange characters with beards." However, later on, when I looked at a picture Bob took of me on Unaka Mountain, I was surprised that Mr. Johnson had stopped at all. It had been laundry day, which meant that we had semiclean socks, T-shirts, fishnet shirts, and underwear hanging on our packs. We always tried to look respectable, but without Amy Vanderbilt to guide us, we occasionally forgot the rules. A new etiquette manual is in order, for there is a subculture in America in which it is perfectly proper to carry your dirty underwear wherever you go.

The next day we went over Baldtown Mountain, Roan Mountain (6,150 feet), and several other nice balds. Roan Mountain is famous for its rhododendron gardens, but we passed by too early in the season to see them in bloom. Coming down the north side of the mountain we saw more patches of snow and ice, and the trail was muddy. To avoid stepping in mud I sometimes stepped on rocks four or five inches in diameter and some of these sank so deep that most of my boot disappeared with them. The day after we went over Roan Mountain we went over two more large bald mountains—Big Yellow and Hump. On Hump Mountain we encountered the strongest winds I have ever known. A great portion of Hump was bald and afforded no protection at all. Each time we lifted a foot to go forward we would be blown sideways and end up making twice as much progress to the side as we did forward. Eventually, however, we reached the summit, and after lunch we left North Carolina for the last time and headed into Tennessee.

We stayed at a lean-to high in Laurel Fork Gorge, and during the night we had torrential rains, brilliant flashes of lightning, and tremendous crashes of thunder. The storm was right on top of us. In the morning everything was peaceful, and the violent storm of the night before seemed like a bad dream. After breakfast we continued through Laurel Fork Gorge and passed near Watauga Dam and Watauga Lake. From there we followed the top of a ridge and had good views all afternoon. On our last night in Tennessee, from the rock behind the Vanderventer Lean-to, we watched the shadows of the mountains crawl over the valleys. The lights of civilization came on one by one until it seemed as if there was a field of stars on the earth below us as well as in the heavens above us. It was the best view we had yet had from a lean-to.

Damascus stands in the area which was once known as Mocks Mill, after a man named Mock who came from North Carolina and built a home and mill. There in the undeveloped Virginia wilderness Mock raised three families, having three wives and 33 children. In 1890, Gen. John D. Imboden, a pioneer in the coal, iron, and lumber industries of southwestern Virginia, came to Mocks Mill to promote a town. He named it after Damascus, the ancient capital of Syria, "because of the confluence of beautiful mountain streams there." On our way into town we went across a Mock farm. A young man in a jeep, presumably one of Mock's many descendants, waved to us.

The Appalachian Trail goes down the main street of Damascus, passing the town hall, post office, grocery stores, laundromat, and ice-cream stand. Our first stop was the post office. The postmaster and two other postal employees were delighted to see two Georgia-to-Maine hikers. They had us sign the register they keep for long-distance hikers, and showed us a file folder full of newspaper clippings about Appalachian Trail hikers and letters and postcards they had received from some of the hikers who had been through Damascus. After the post office, we made our regular visits to the laundromat and supermarket, and finished our morning in town with a stop at the ice-cream stand.

A few days earlier two hikers had told us that Virginia forests were closed because of fire danger, and signs posted outside of Damascus confirmed their warning. We didn't stop because of the signs; we hiked on, perhaps going a little faster than usual when we crossed roads. Since neither of us smoked, the only adjustment we made was to have no campfires. As always, we were extremely careful with our stove, so all in all we felt that we were not a fire hazard.

On the morning of May 3, two or three days out of Damascus, we were surprised when we awoke to find an inch of snow on the ground. If it had rained during the night we would have heard it, and hence wouldn't have been surprised in the morning, but the snow came on "cat's-feet" and never made a sound. Most of the snow melted within a few hours, but a few patches remained until the next day. It was the last snow we saw until we reached Mt. Washington in New Hampshire. The following night was one of the coldest we experienced on the trail. When we awoke in the morning the water bag was frozen to the floor of the shelter and there were chunks of ice in the water. Spring seemed to be late in coming. It was the first week of May, yet the trees in the mountains were bare. It was only when we went down into a valley that we saw signs of spring.

The first day the Virginia forests were officially reopened we met a ranger sitting in his truck on a secondary road. He told us he was driving past the next shelter, the Wapiti Shelter, and offered to give us a ride. We explained that we were walking the entire Appalachian Trail, therefore we couldn't take a ride. However, keeping our ponchos, we let him take our packs. He told us that several years ago this area had been stocked with elk and that a hunting season on them had been opened. (The name of the shelter we were headed for, Wapiti, means "elk.") However, the area was not suited for elk, and the animals had been destructive to crops on nearby farms. Although all of the elk had not been accounted for, the rangers were fairly certain that all of them had either been taken by hunters or had died.

In some ways rainy days are good for walking. They are often very good days for thinking and for getting things in our heads straightened out. When it is raining it is very easy to get into the rhythm of walking and let the mind wander. There are few distractions, no views, fewer animals, no sunny springs, no dry places to sit, and over-all, nothing to do except walk and think. On rainy days our mileage was good, and it helped make up for the lower mileage we had on sunny days when various distractions slowed us up. Several successive days of rain, however, are hard to take. After the first two days, the weather becomes monotonous and discouraging. On May 6 the rain was especially hard and was accompanied by a strong wind. The wind blew our ponchos around so much we got soaked to our waists. Everything around us was wet. There was nothing we could do but walk—and after several days of rain, walking bored us to death. The longer it rained, the muddier the trail became. The treads on the boots I had bought in North Carolina were almost worn off, and when we came to a series of steep descents I kept falling on the muddy trail, often sliding for quite a distance on the seat of my pants. Soon I was a human mud pie. When we reached a road near Pearisburg we didn't discuss whether or not we would go into town—the only question was where we would stay. We were directed to Mary Finley's boardinghouse, and for two nights we slept on the convertible sofa bed in her parlor at the anti-inflationary rate of $2 each per night. We forgot about the trail, and spent our time in Miss Finley's parlor and in the Pearisburg Public Library. We ate our meals in restaurants and washed our clothes at the laundromat.

It was in Pearisburg that I realized that I had been making a mistake by not living each day for itself instead of constantly thinking about the length of the hike and how far it was to Maine. The more backpacking I have done, the more I have come to understand that the hiker's reward is not in reaching his destination, but in the journey itself. I think the best way to hike is probably the way Averill and Takaro, who were a few weeks ahead of us, were hiking. They had no specific goal, but were just following the Appalachian Trail for the length of time they had to spend. They put their destination in registers as "seven weeks north." If our society were not so goal-oriented, this would be the way most of us would hike. If we hiked without a deadline and destination, there would be no pressure to move on when we found a place where we would like to spend some time. Every 2,000-miler faces the dilemma of wanting to slow down in a favorite area but at the same time wanting to get to the other end of the trail as soon as possible.

When we returned to the trail after our stop in Pearisburg we were refreshed and in good spirits. Except for a few warm days in Georgia and the Smokies, May 10 was our first springlike day. That night we stayed at the Niday Shelter. It was on the site of the homestead where the Niday family had settled about 1865. The shelter was clean and new, with a grassy area in front of it and a clear cool spring nearby. In the yard there was a huge apple tree, the largest I have ever seen. The tree, planted by the Nidays a hundred or more years ago and still bearing fruit, was in bloom when we were there. The next morning, May 11, was the first time it had been warm enough for us to get out of our sleeping bags for breakfast. For the first 40 days we had eaten breakfast while still in our sleeping bags, with our coats on.

Through the southwestern part of Virginia we met no hikers to tell us what the trail ahead was like, and the guidebook for this section was out of print at the time. We never knew what to expect. Although this sometimes caused problems, it also made many of our discoveries more enjoyable. When we reached the top of Cove Mountain we had one of these pleasant surprises. The top of the mountain was made up of huge rocks resting in bizarre positions—many were on end, reaching high into the air. Without a second thought we put down our packs and started climbing on these rocks. We later learned that the place was called Dragons Tooth, after the highest of the vertical rocks. Just after Cove Mountain the trail went along the top of the cliffs of Tinker

Ridge. One huge slab of rock extended beyond the face of the cliff, hanging in the air with nothing underneath except the trees far below.

As we approached the road to Snowden we spotted a red pack on the trail ahead, and knew we were going to meet more backpackers. We caught up with this group quickly and when we overtook them it was easy to see why. Al and Melinda Boyers of Raleigh, North Carolina, were accompanied by their three children—a third grader, a first grader, and one in nursery school. They were all very friendly and we enjoyed talking with them. It was the first backpacking trip for the children, and they seemed to be enjoying it and doing well—except for the smallest who sometimes had to be carried. All the way from Georgia to Maine, when we had to go off the trail to pick up supplies, we met people who went out of their way to help us. Now Al Boyers offered to drive us to Snowden. This side trip should have been a short one, but as it turned out, was one of those towns that you can drive through without even knowing you have reached it. The town consisted of four buildings: three houses set back from the road behind many trees and almost impossible to see, and a small store with a post office in it. The store was closed because it was Saturday. The Boyerses drove us 10 miles to Glasgow, waited for us to do our errands, and then drove us back to the trail. A few weeks later we learned that Al Boyers had written to our parents and gave them an "unbiased account" of how we were. He wrote that we "smiled freely, looked good, and smelled bad, liked to talk, and could walk fast with long strides," and he predicted that we would achieve our objective of completing the trail.

The next day we hiked a rough trail of some 20 miles from the Brown Mountain Creek Lean-to to The Priest Lean-to. That afternoon painters had painted the ceiling and half of the floor of the Priest Mountain Lean-to. They had not intended to paint any of the floor, but I suspect they were really foresters, not painters. Fortunately it was a clear night and we did not need shelter. Except for rainy nights, we did not stay in lean-tos much, anyway. We usually camped near a lean-to because that was where the best campsites and water sources were, and if the weather changed the lean-to roof would be available. We carried a two-man tent which we used in a few emergencies, but we hated sleeping under such claustrophobic conditions. Most nights, whether we slept outside or in a lean-to, we would be in the woods, so we seldom had a good view of the stars. Our nights in the woods made us treasure a clear night in the open when we had one. An astounding number of stars were visible when there was no moon and you were far from civilization. It was almost like a different sky; there were so many stars that some of the common constellations were hard to pick out. The sky out here was not like the one we saw in urban and suburban areas; here it was filled with stars all the way to the edges of the sky. The Milky Way stretched from horizon to horizon, and was so distinct that it looked like a cloud. Meteors fell and quickly burned out in a streak of light as they raced toward the earth. When sleeping under the stars I liked to wake up every couple of hours to see how much the sky had changed, and what stars were rising and setting. Some nights the moon rose. If it was only a crescent, the moon added to the show, but if it was any larger it made it impossible to see so many stars.

One evening at dinner we sat through an invasion of whippoorwills. First we heard one in the distance, then he came closer. Others followed. Without being able to see any of them, we could hear whippoorwills on three sides of us. Then one landed near the fireplace, 25 feet away. Another flew into the tree beside us and a third flew into a tree behind the shelter. We could see and hear all three of them at once, and we could hear many others in the distance. One or two whippoorwills were delightful to listen to, but a flock of them could almost drive you crazy.

When we reached Rockfish Gap we had been on the trail for 50 days. For seven weeks and a day we had been living peacefully in the woods. Our visits to towns had been brief. We had become more accustomed to the quiet and calm than we realized, and Rockfish Gap gave us a severe shock. The trail came out near the parking lot of a Holiday Inn, crossed a busy highway with all of the usual travel facilities, and then went through an area where an interstate highway was being built. Civilization was with us again—motels, hotels, restaurants, gas stations, highways, construction, cars zipping by, trucks rumbling, dust flying, horns honking, everyone hustling and bustling. As quickly as we could we went to Waynesboro, picked up our mail, bought our food, and hurried back to the tranquility of the woods.

The stretch from Rockfish Gap to the northern end of the National Park was the easiest 100 miles of the Appalachian Trail. The trail was well-graded and cleared, and such easy walking that we never noticed whether we were going uphill or downhill. We would complete our daily quota of 15 miles by 11:30 or 12:00 and spend the afternoon on a nature trail, horseback riding, bathing, writing, or talking with people we met. This section, and the areas north and south of it, was no challenge. As far as we were concerned there were no mountains from a few days south of the park to Connecticut—an opinion which upset many sweaty hikers who thought there were. Although the low fertile mountains in the Shenandoah National Park were pretty, and abounded in flowers and wildlife, the trail was overcivilized and overcrowded. The park was packed with tourists, and the excessive crisscrossing of the Appalachian Trail by the Skyline Drive gave the tourists access to all parts of the trail. In 104 miles the trail crossed the parkway 25 times. No backwoods hiking here—just a pleasant stroll through the crowded woods. We saw more deer in the park than anywhere else on the trail. Since hunting was prohibited, the deer were rather tame and often allowed people to come quite close to them. Bob almost got one to eat out of his hand.

One morning I started ahead of Bob. (We often hiked separately and met at lunchtime or suppertime.) About 15 minutes after I left camp I heard a rustling noise, then saw a large black bear in the bushes 75 or 80 feet ahead of me. He walked out onto the trail, turned abruptly, and ran the other way. The trail curved and he was soon out of sight. The only other bears I saw along the trail were in the zoo at Bear Mountain State Park in New York.

Because of construction at Swift Run Gap, the trail followed the Skyline Drive for almost a mile. While I was walking this section two drivers stopped, at different times, to ask me questions. The first asked directions to the Appalachian Trail, which we were on. The second asked where he could get a permit to hike the Appalachian Trail. At the time this question seemed absurd, but considering how overused the trail is in summer, it may not be as farfetched as it sounds. A permit system has already been started in the Smokies.

That day we finished hiking at the South River Shelter before noon. Bob took a hike and I planned to spend the afternoon alone, writing. It was a Saturday and the shelter was only a half-mile from the Skyline Drive, so I should have known better. Shortly after lunch I started getting visitors. Before supper a dozen people had arrived to stay for the night, and another two dozen had stopped by on their hikes in from the road. I met several interesting people, but did not catch up on my journal and letter writing.

We had made camp at Byrd Shelter No. 3 when a woman came up the trail from the Skyline Drive with a box on her shoulder and an armful of pots. She told us that her husband and four friends were hiking on the Appalachian Trail, and she had come ahead in the car to make supper for them. We spent a pleasant evening with the Greists and their hiking companions. They invited us to dinner and Mrs. Greist proved to be an excellent cook. It was the best meal we had on the trail. Over the years Ned Greist had hiked all of the Appalachian Trail, with the exception of one 50-mile stretch, from Katahdin to this point. He had also hiked Vermont's 260-mile Long Trail, had climbed all 46 of the 4,000-foot peaks in the White Mountains, all 46 of the 4,000-foot peaks in the Adirondacks, all 3,500-footers in the Catskills, all 4,000-footers in New England, and the 100 highest mountains in New England. He had been at it for 40 years. During the same period he had raised five children and saw them through college, had been a scoutmaster for many years, and was active in the Appalachian Mountain Club.

Immediately north of the Shenandoah National Park several landowners had closed the trail across their land, so for 20 or 25 miles we had to walk on roads. We spent 28 days in Virginia—then in one 25-mile day we left that state, hiked through the easternmost tip of West Virginia, and crossed the Potomac River into Maryland. West Virginia was the only state in which we didn't spend at least one night. Incidentally, West Virginia, with some 20 miles, has less of the Appalachian Trail in it than any of the other 13 states through which the trail passes.

We spent our first night in Maryland at the Weverton Shelter, a converted bathhouse located on the northern bank of the Potomac between the river and the C&O Canal. Camping by a river was totally different from camping in the mountains. Our conversation turned to Mark Twain and Huckleberry Finn, and our minds kept drifting downriver with them. We wondered how anyone living on the bank of a river could resist building a raft and going with the current. As Huck said, "Other places do seem so cramped up and smothery, but a raft don't. You feel mighty free and easy and comfortable on a raft."

The Chesapeake and Ohio Canal is now a national monument. It extends 184.5 miles from Washington, D.C. to Cumberland, Maryland. The first 22 or 23 miles out of Washington are navigable, but open only to boats without motors. The towpath, where the mules once walked to pull the barges, runs parallel to the canal for the entire 184.5 miles. It is wide, flat, and smooth, and open to bicyclists and walkers. Along the way there are a number of hiker-biker stops with water and picnic tables. In 1954, United States Supreme Court Justice William O. Douglas, with others, made a walk along the towpath to help save the C&O Canal. The effort succeeded. Justice Douglas made the walk in response to a newspaper editorial proposing the construction of a scenic highway through the area. He invited newspapermen and others to take the hike with him and, by showing them the natural beauty which would be destroyed, convinced them that a scenic highway would not be as valuable as other uses to which the canal and the towpath could be put. The Appalachian Trail follows the towpath for only a short distance.

We hiked the 38 miles of the Appalachian Trail in Maryland during the Memorial Day weekend. On Friday and Saturday the trail was crowded, but showers reduced the crowds for the remainder of the weekend. Near Hagerstown, Maryland, the Appalachian Trail has its own footbridge over Interstate 70. This bridge is similar in construction to the regular concrete bridges over highways. Just as other bridges have the names of the streets or routes that cross over them, so this bridge has a large green-and-white sign that says: APPALACHIAN TRAIL. We stood on the bridge for several minutes watching the cars race by below us. They were covering as much distance in an hour as we covered in four or five days. We spent the night at the Pine Knob Shelter with several people from Hagerstown. Like many others we met on the trail, these people assumed that we lived in either Georgia or Maine and went to college in the other state.

On a topographical map the Appalachian Trail in Pennsylvania looks easy. According to the map there is not a single difficult climb, and only relatively small changes in elevation. Moreover, the trail usually follows the tops of long low ridges. When actually walking the trail in Pennsylvania, however, the hiker finds that the path is not as simple as it looks on the map. It is never really flat; in fact, it is more like an obstacle course across miles and miles of loose jagged rocks. When someone asks me what part of the Appalachian Trail I liked least, I usually mention Pennsylvania, noting how low the mountains were, how dry it was, and how I got shinsplints from walking on hard surfaces and sore ankles from the uneven rocky trail. These were the unpleasant aspects of our hike through the state, however, and in looking back through my journal, I find that interesting things happened there, too. We encountered a great deal of small wildlife in Pennsylvania, including an abundance of snakes. During my four months on the Appalachian Trail I saw 32 snakes, and most of them were in Pennsylvania. Of these, only two were poisonous—both copperheads; 12 were garter snakes, one was a puff adder, and a half-dozen were blacksnakes. The rest were either grass snakes or snakes I couldn't identify. I was disappointed because I didn't see any rattlesnakes, but I did get a good look at both copperheads. One of them was actually between my boots when I noticed it.

June 5 was county snake-hunt day. All the local people who liked to catch snakes were out for the annual competition. The judges tallied all varieties of snakes, but the serious hunters brought back only poisonous ones. One hunter we met had three copperheads which he had captured without going off the Appalachian Trail. He showed us where he had been bitten on other hunts, and told us about a friend who had lost the use of his hand because of a snakebite. He then reached his bare arm into his bag and pulled out one of the copperheads. Despite the danger and the bites he had received in the past, he continued to hunt snakes and said that at the end of the day he would be working in the snake pits in town. Most of the hunters we met carried two sticks: one had a hook for pulling snakes out of holes and crevices; the other had a leather loop which could be put around the snake's head and tightened by a cord which extended to the upper part of the pole. Each hunter wore high boots and had a cloth sack in which to carry the snakes he caught.

One morning we met a young woodchuck who had taken it upon himself to guard the Appalachian Trail from all human intruders. We found him sitting in the middle of the trail. He let us come close enough to photograph him, then he ran 100 feet down the trail. When we caught up with him, he ran another 100 feet and waited. Now his Spartan blood was in a rage and he made his stand. This time, when we reached him, he charged toward Bob. We both started laughing. This little woodchuck was no larger than a boot, yet he seemed ready to fight the two of us to protect his section of the Appalachian Trail. Actually, he was only trying to get back to his den, so eventually we stepped aside and let him run back down the trail to where we had first seen him.

Occasionally we met wild dogs in the woods. To call them "wild" is misleading; they are more appropriately called "homeless." We never encountered a pack of these dogs, and the individual homeless dogs, we met were timid. The only animals that gave us any trouble were hostile domestic dogs. In rural areas we often met small packs of these dogs. I never had to strike any of them with my walking stick, but having the stick gave me assurance and helped keep the bolder dogs a little farther away. One of the common questions we were asked was what we carried for protection, and many people seemed to think we should have been carrying a gun. City people, and even some rural people, think it is safer to spend a night in the city than in the woods. What they really fear is the darkness and the unknown, for there are far more dangerous "animals" in any large city than there are in all the woods of North America.

On June 3 we crossed the Cumberland Valley. This was not the longest day I spent on the trail, but it was my best day for mileage. I did 14 miles by 11:00 A.M. and 27 miles for the day.

All morning on June 6 we wondered how close we were to Castleman and Weirich. We had been following them since Georgia—more than two months and over 1,000 miles. We knew we were close to them. We had never met either John Castleman or Dan Weirich, nor had we seen a picture of them. However, we had been hearing about them from postmasters and store clerks all along the trail, so we knew a great deal about them and could easily identify them. As we approached Applebee Shelter we saw Dan returning from the spring. He glanced up and saw us coming, but of course he didn't know us. From the register entries we knew that John was now hiking in moccasins, and that he had sore feet. As we came to the shelter I said, "How are your sore feet, John?" Bob turned to Dan and said, "Hi, Dan." We then rattled off their life histories and an account of their adventures along the trail. They just sat and stared at us! After they got over the initial shock, the four of us had plenty of trail experiences to share, and we talked for many hours into the night.

By modern backpacking standards, Castleman and Weirich were the two most unorthodox long-distance hikers we met. Actually, there was nothing truly unorthodox about their methods and equipment except that they were old-fashioned. They had decided to hike the trail on the spur of the moment, with little time or money for preparation, planning, or equipment. Although they did have packframes, they used canvas packbags and carried regular kitchen pots. I don't think they had any lightweight equipment at all, and I know they had no maps or guidebooks; they simply copied information from the guidebooks of hikers they met along the way. These two hikers proved, better than anyone else I met, that very little money is needed to hike the Appalachian Trail, or just to take to the woods for that matter.

When we left the next morning, John and Dan were getting ready to bake bread. Through the central part of their hike, they baked in the morning, starting hiking late, and quit early to bake again. However, the baking was just an excuse: after 1,000 miles they were tired of walking. They continued getting slower and slower, until they finally split up in New York. After they separated, John and Dan got back into the swing of steady hiking.

At Dans Pulpit in Pennsylvania we spent an hour reading the register. Many registers, especially when the entries were written under difficult conditions, contain some unique trail-made humor. This register was filled more with complaints than with humor, but the entries were still amusing. Most of the accounts were written by out-of-shape day-hikers who thought they were going to die. One man complained that the guidebook did not warn readers that the trail was not fit for older people. Another wrote: "You should have been honest and put in the guidebook that this trail is treacherous and should not be traveled." A third hiker gave an elaborate account of how he had started out with a group of over 100 hikers; then he told of the disasters that had over-taken all of the others. He concluded by saying that only he and his dog had made it through alive.

We spent our last night in Pennsylvania at the Kirkridge Shelter. The shelter was on a ridge with a good view of the valley below. Mos-quitoes were out in full force and we built a smoky fire for protection as we didn't have any insect repellent. During the night we had the unpleasant choice of leaving the sleeping bags open and enduring the mosquitoes or leaving the bags closed and roasting. We had lightened our packs by a few ounces by waiting to buy insect repellent until we actually needed it—a mistake we would not make again.

As the southern Appalachians were never covered by glaciation, they lack the glacial ponds that are so numerous on the northern part of the trail. Sunfish Pond in New Jersey was one of the first natural lakes we came to; it was also the first opportunity we had to swim in anything larger than a stream. From this point on, the farther north we went the more abundant the natural bodies of water became. In Maine we sometimes passed half a dozen ponds in a day. At Sunfish Pond I started the day with an early morning swim. Although there were at least 60 people camped nearby, only a few were awake. As I stroked across the smooth surface of the water, I could see no one and could hear no man-made sound except for someone chopping wood in the distance. For a few moments I was back in the days of the pioneers, for my ideal was to travel on more than just one level of consciousness; the Appalachian Trail can lead to more places than one would think. On my best days I traveled the Appalachian Trail as Thoreau traveled the Old Marlborough Road:

> If the fancy unfurled
> You leave your abode,
> You may go round the world
> By the Old Marlborough Road.

On our second day in New Jersey, after a morning rain, I slipped on a wet rock and fell directly on the end of my spine. The lower part of my back hurt for only an hour or two but my spine remained sore and tender. After about 10 days the pain flared up and the bottom of my spine started to hurt intensely. I was reluctant to go to a doctor because I was afraid he would tell me to stop hiking. However, the pain persisted and I finally decided to leave the trail the next morning and seek aid. To my surprise, the pain disappeared that night, and I never had any spine trouble again.

Considering all that our bodies went through, we had very few health problems and never had to stop because of an injury or illness. Except for blisters in the beginning and my injured spine, neither of us had any aches or pains that lasted more than two or three days. Occasionally we would get sore ankles, a sore leg, or a sore foot, and periodically, sore hips from the weight of the packs. However, we never had anything serious or anything that lasted long. We were each sick one day in the beginning of the hike, and I had diarrhea three times, but most of the time we felt exceptionally healthy. Minor aches and pains are taken in stride when you are in good condition, and active and happy.

We had hardly entered the Garden State before we left it. We entered the Empire State at Unionville. As we walked through town we watched the storm clouds brewing and knew we were in for a rainy night. There were no lean-tos in the area, and we avoided using our tent whenever possible. Under these circumstances the large barns of the neighboring farms looked especially attractive. We approached one of the farmers and after a little good-natured bargaining we won a luxuriously soft night on Mr. Cosh's piles of hay by simply promising that we wouldn't set up our stove or make a fire inside the barn.

The next day was rainy and we had to walk several miles on hard-top roads. Late in the afternoon we lost the trail for the second time that day. As we walked along a dirt road we came to the New Jersey state line again. We were supposed to have left that state for good, so we turned around and went back. Shortly before dark we found the overgrown entrance to the trail. Back in the woods we made a lean-to with our tent. It kept us reasonably dry through the night's showers, but we had no room for our packs inside. There were no large trees from which to hang them, so we simply leaned the packs back to back and covered them with a poncho. Except for the interruptions caused by two persistent raccoons who kept trying to get into the packs, we slept very well.

Although New York and New Jersey were the most populated areas through which the Appalachian Trail passed, the walk through these states was more pleasant than I had anticipated it would be. I had expected to weave in and out of shipping centers and along freeways for 158 miles, but we found that most of the trail was in the woods. Even the occasional stretches on roads had a rural flavor. I didn't know there were as many wooded areas in the whole state of New Jersey as we saw just in the northwest corner.

Bear Mountain State Park, by the Hudson River, is a playground where frustrated New Yorkers go to recreate on Sunday afternoons. It was also the most atrocious place the trail took us: noise, herds of people, outlandish prices, extreme apathy and self-centeredness. We made the best of the situation and followed a nature trail through the park. We stopped by the statue of that great exponent of the open road, Walt Whitman, and passed the bear den which, at 115.4 feet above sea level, is the lowest point on the trail. The only bargain I got at Bear Mountain State Park was on a set of scales where I learned both my weight and my fortune for a penny. After 2½ months on the trail my weight was down to 147 pounds, some 22 pounds less than it had been on Springer Mountain. By the time I reached Katahdin I had lost 30 pounds.

One evening I couldn't find the water source near the lean-to so I took the canteens and went down a dirt road to a boys' camp. At the camp I met a middle-aged counselor who directed me to their pump. We talked about backpacking for 10 minutes, then for some reason he started talking about the Vietnam War, social problems, racism, poverty. He did all the talking; I had nothing to say and had no interest in the conversation. That night I wrote in my journal: "Those were problems of another world. Now I live in a new world. At college I could have talked about those things all night, but they are meaningless to me now. If he wanted to talk about the dry spring up the road, the terrain or trail conditions, or about how healthy and pleasant it is to be living close to nature, I would have had plenty to say. This episode made me realize for the first time why Thoreau did not vote, and why he would not attend a political or social gathering, although he might attend a meeting to save endangered species of pine."

On our last night in New York we camped on the rifle range of a Boy Scout camp. We had received permission to sleep there from the ranger's wife, and she told us that the ranger probably would come over to visit us when he got home. When we saw a man coming over the hill, we figured it was the ranger. However, it turned out to be Ned Greist, whom we had met in the Shenandoah National Park. Ned was dropping off Tom Kern, whom we had also met in Virginia, for a few days of hiking.

The next morning the sky was clear and it promised to be a beautiful day. Ned fixed fresh eggs and hot chocolate for us. By 6:30 we were on the trail, with only 2½ hours of hiking to the Connecticut state line on top of Schaghticoke Mountain. I am a native New Englander, and after traveling for three months on foreign soil, so to speak, I relished this return to my own land. We reached the Chase Mountain Lean-to shortly after noon and met the Winslows there. We had lunch with them, then Bob went home to Avon for a day. I stayed on the trail, and the next day, June 20, my family and a friend drove out from Hartford and I met them in Macedonia Brook State Park for a picnic. That afternoon the Winslows brought Bob back to the trail. After a couple of hours at the picnic grounds, Bob headed up to the lean-to and his family started back to Avon. Later my own family left for Hartford. As I walked through the darkening woods I felt a little lonely. When I reached the lean-to, being very conscious of the weight of my freshly loaded pack, I introduced myself as Colin Fletcher—"because I don't know of anyone else who is crazy enough to carry such a heavy pack." One of the people sitting by the campfire went along with it: "Well hello, Colin Fletcher. I'm Sam Prentiss." Soon I felt good again. I had my pack, I was at a lean-to with a white Appalachian Trail blaze on the trail beside it, and I was sitting by a campfire with good people. I wondered why I would ever want to go back to the city.

The next day we hiked 12.5 miles with Sam and his son, Bard, over St. Johns Ledges, Calebs Peak, and along the bank of the Housatonic River. Northwestern Connecticut and southwestern Massachusetts are noted for an abundance of beautiful ravines. At Dean Ravine we came to a section of the Appalachian Trail that we had hiked the previous fall. There was much more vegetation now, and it was like walking a different trail. It occurred to me that with every change in the season, and even on each new day, we did indeed walk a different trail—even if we covered exactly the same ground. There is really no need to go far away for variety. If we look closely there is as much to see in one mile of trail as there was in 2,000 miles.

Bear Mountain (2,316 feet), which is only a few miles south of Massachusetts, is the highest peak in Connecticut. Although we enjoyed sleeping on mountaintops, wind and lack of shelter prevented us from doing it very often. In fact, Bear Mountain was the first summit we had camped on since Springer Mountain in Georgia. After breakfast we descended through Sages Ravine and entered Massachusetts, our eleventh state on the trail. After going through the ravine, we went over Race Mountain (2,365 feet) and Mt. Everett (2,602 feet), then had lunch at Guilder Pond.

Late that afternoon I left the trail to make a telephone call. Bob waited by a road, and while I was gone he met Eric Agar, a 15-year-old who lived on a nearby farm. Eric gave us permission to sleep in one of his family's fields. The field was covered with deep wet grass, so we set up camp near the road where the grass was shortest. A row of trees sheltered us from the road. Soon a green truck pulled in. The driver jumped out, and without saying a word to us, dumped several gallons of gasoline on a large pile of tree trunks and branches nearby and lit a fire. We were stunned by his reckless and inconsiderate action. We were especially surprised because Eric had made a point of telling us not to have a fire. After lighting the fire, the man leaned against his truck and watched the blaze with childish fascination. We returned to our dinner, but kept an eye open for the fire-happy fellow's next move. A little later he asked if we would watch the fire for him. Although I told him we didn't want to do it, he got in his truck and left anyway. The flames were very high and the fire smoked heavily. People driving along the road slowed down to look, and we were afraid people would think the fire was ours, and that it would give them a bad impression of backpackers.

An hour later another green truck, similar to the first one, drove up and stopped. This man looked concerned, and asked us if we had a permit for the fire. Bob and I thought he was joking, but he wasn't. He told us he was with the Dutch Elm Patrol, and said he had received complaints about the fire. After hearing our story he decided that the man who had started the fire was actually one of his own employees who had not been scheduled to work that night. He told us that the grass was wet enough to contain the fire, and that it wouldn't be dangerous for us to sleep there.

Sam Prentiss came by while we were eating lunch—and told us that on the previous afternoon he had passed Washington Town Hall and Mrs. Hutchinson had asked if he had seen us on the trail. He said a newspaper article about us was hanging on her dining room wall. When we arrived at Mrs. Hutchinson's house we found her dozing on a couch on the porch—or the veranda, as she would call it. We stood there for a moment, afraid to wake her up, and wondering what to do. She solved the problem by opening her eyes and very calmly saying, "Oh, it's you," even though she had never seen either of us before, except in the newspaper photograph. Mrs. Hutchinson was a very active and interesting woman. At 88 she had so much life and energy that she made a younger person feel ashamed that he was ever tired. She lived in a beautiful old house that had been built during the Revolutionary War period. It was called the Country House because around 1811 it had been used as a tavern with that name. We camped behind the Country House for two nights, and on our second evening Mrs. Hutchinson's daughter and son-in-law, Mr. and Mrs. Allen, who lived across the road in a more modern home, invited us over for hot showers and to wash our clothes in their washing machine. The two homes stand with the old Washington Town Hall on top of one of the Berkshire hills, but regardless of altitude, this was one of the high points of our journey along the Appalachian Trail.

On both mornings Mrs. Hutchinson invited us in for breakfast and afterward read us Robert Frost's poems. She had known Frost for 20 or 30 years, both through a poetry society she belonged to and as a neighbor in Amherst. She had several volumes of Frost's poems that had been autographed by the poet. When they were living in Amherst, Mrs. Allen went to Frost to ask his advice on how to read his poem, "Death of the Hired Man," which she was going to read in an oratory contest. Frost told her that each person had to decide how to read it himself, but he did say he regretted that a time limit would force her to leave out sections of the poem. "Everything I put in there I put in for a reason," he told her.

Mrs. Hutchinson had kept a diary for each of the 51 years she had lived or summered in the Berkshires, and all 51 volumes were in a bookcase in the Allens' home. She had also kept a guest book since before the trail was routed by her home, and had entertained many of the 2,000-milers as guests or visitors.

After our day with Mrs. Hutchinson we hiked an easy 10 miles to Dalton. Frost's poems were running through our heads, and when we went through a grove of white birches, we had to swing them. I was 21 years old, yet had never swung a birch. Despite my many years of schooling, this was a part of my education that was lacking. How could I have understood the poem, "Birches," before? Any literature student who has not spent some time in rural New England can hardly be expected to understand Frost or any other New England writer. In school you can analyze Frost, but only when you are in rural New England can you understand him.

Back on the trail we again met the Bad-Off Appalachian Jug Band, a good-hearted group we had first encountered a few days before at Benedict Pond. Mike, Ed, Wes, Pete, and Mark had several instruments, including kazoos, harmonicas, mouth harps, and a recorder, and with these instruments they made some of the strangest sounds ever heard on any trail. The band was not very concerned with camping~dos and don'ts and simply took things as they came. One of their outstanding characteristics was their lack of organization. Now, at this camp, no one cleaned the pots or put the food away. In the morning they were missing eight chocolate bars, wrappers and all. During the night I had seen a raccoon making trips up and down a tree to the picnic table, but not until morning, when I heard about the missing candy bars, did I understand the reason for the raccoon's trips. The one member of the group who had already eaten his two bars had a good laugh, and the others learned something about camping.

We reached the top of Mt. Greylock (3,491 feet) early in the morning. In every direction it was totally undercast with morning fog and our only view was of the clear blue sky above. Many of the trails on Mt. Greylock were so wet they could best be described as mudways or mushways. This was a preview of the Appalachian Trail in Maine. The worst parts of the mudways were usually made passable by log walks; some of these walkways were made with long logs laid lengthwise along the trail, but usually they were made with short logs laid parallel across the trail.

Soon after Greylock we went through Blackinton, then entered Vermont. From the Massachusetts state line to Sherburne Pass we followed about 95 miles of the Long Trail before the two trails separated with the Long Trail continuing through Vermont to Canada, and the Appalachian Trail turning east toward New Hampshire and Maine. One of the many hikers we met on the Long Trail was a quiet youth named Russ. He was a slow walker, was afraid of nonexistent bears, and said he preferred going from town to town rather than staying in the woods. I could never figure out why he was in the woods in the first place. Russ told me repeatedly that he could not believe how much I ate. He said that the most amazing thing he had seen on his whole trip was my appetite. As a matter of fact, on the trail I did eat about three times what I normally ate, but with the energy I burned up, even that was not enough. Whenever Bob and I were not hiking, we were eating. Two days after picking up food we would usually have to start rationing ourselves in order to make the food last until the next pickup. On the northern half of the trail, where stores were more common, we sometimes ate a full week's supply of food in three days and then had to load up again.

On the night of July 3 the temperature dropped to 40° F. in a nearby town, so we figured it was probably in the thirties in the mountains. (We had already broken two thermometers and no longer carried one.) Our sleeping bags were comfortable to about 10° F., so we kept warm. The next day we crossed four peaks: Bromley Mountain (3,260 feet),

Styles Peak (3,394 feet), and Peru Peak (3,429 feet), and Baker Peak (2,850 feet). Rock-topped Baker Peak offered very interesting views of Otter Creek Valley, and the views from the observation tower on Bromley Mountain were good. The ski lift was running on Bromley, bringing people to the summit for $3.50 per person.

We passed Little Rock Pond the next morning. If we had known how beautiful it was we would have walked an extra six miles the day before and camped there. The pond was small, clear, and clean. It was surrounded by forest, and there was an impressive rock cliff on the west, and a rocky mountain above that. An ideal Walden Pond, if you could chase all the people away. After a boat ride and a visit with some campers, we hiked on to Sunnyside Camp. (On the Long Trail a "camp" is a four-sided closed shelter which usually has a stove and bunks.) The next day I had a long conversation with a farmer who had motioned from his tractor for me to wait for him. He started the conversation by asking, "How come everyone has red packs?" After talking about the trail for a while, he started quoting me all sorts of farm prices for the past 15 years. He told me he had 660 acres, most of which he didn't need. Even though he had had many good offers, he refused to sell because "neighbors only mean trouble."

A half-mile after Sherburne Pass the Appalachian Trail and the Long Trail separated. At this junction we stood only 166 miles from Canada by the Long Trail, but still 490 miles from Katahdin by the Appalachian Trail. When we came to the first register after Sherburne Pass we were surprised to find that Dan Weirich, the 2,000-miler whom we had passed in Pennsylvania, was the last person to sign it. Apparently he had passed us while we were off the trail for supplies.

Bob's camera broke for the third time the day we went through Gifford Woods State Park, and we went to the ranger's office so Bob could call his parents and make arrangements for another one. While Bob was on the telephone I talked with the ranger about backpackers who had stopped there in recent years, and the conversation turned to hippies. The ranger was about 55 or 60, with short hair and no beard or sideburns, so he was far from what anyone would call a hippie. He told me that the park commission had sent out a warning to state parks to the effect that 200,000 hippies would invade Vermont during the summer. "When one of the hippies came in I waited for him to do something wicked. From the warning, I thought they were supposed to come in dancing on their heads, but they just walked in like anyone else. I've had a hundred longhairs in here and they're very nice people. In my report to Montpelier, under the section on hippies, I said they had been 100 percent perfect, and that I hoped I got a lot more of them."

Late in the afternoon of one of our last days in Vermont we met Arthur Wood of South Woodstock. Mr. Wood had never met Bob or me before, but his daughter worked with Bob's mother. He took us out for supper, then to his house for the night. Arthur's brother Clyde, who lived across the road, was a beekeeper. He also trained chipmunks. At various times he had worked with 23 chipmunks that he called "educated." The chipmunks lived behind his house in the natural state, and he had constructed an elaborate trap to catch any cats or raccoons, that tried to interfere with his "students."

The next morning we met our first Maine-to-Georgia hiker, Jim Rutter. When we shook hands with him, Katahdin and Springer Mountain met. We had no golden spike to drive, but we did have much to talk about. Bob and I had less than 500 miles to go, but Jim still had over 1,500 miles of hiking before he reached his journey's end.

Later in the day we picked up food and mail in West Hartford, and before supper we were in New Hampshire with 12 states behind us and only New Hampshire and Maine ahead. As we approached the main street of Hanover, another fellow 2,000-miler, Jim Ross, greeted us. Jim passed us while we were off the trail at Mr. Wood's house. Long-legged and fast-walking, he had left Springer Mountain on April 26. Jim's family was driving up from Massachusetts to meet him and to drop off his sister, Andrea, who was going to hike with him for about 50 miles—from Hanover to Glencliff. Jim's family invited us out to dinner and we dined with them on the patio of the expensive Hanover Inn. Bob and I had on dungaree shorts, dirty wrinkled shirts, and hiking boots, and our legs were dirty. However, despite our appearance, we were happy and in excellent physical condition. Several of the clean well-dressed obese diners, who could not see beyond our clothes, gave us indignant looks. Two nights later, when we stayed with a Outing Club trail crew, they were overjoyed to hear that we had eaten at the Hanover Inn while wearing hiking clothes. One of them told us he had once been asked to leave the inn because, although he was wearing a sports jacket, did not have a tie.

Three days after leaving Hanover, Bob and I split up. Being with the same person almost every hour of the day is very tiring, no matter who the person is. Since we were not getting along well there was really no reason to continue hiking together. I climbed Mt. Moosilauke, my first 4,000-foot peak in the White Mountains, with a new feeling of independence. For weeks I had been hearing about how rough the ascent of Mt. Moosilauke was. When I got there I discovered that going north, it was the *descent* that was steep. Several places had ladders or steel cables to help the hiker. The following day I climbed South Kinsman (4,363 feet) in the rain. The climb was hard but interesting. I had to use my hands constantly. Sometimes I threw my walking stick ahead because I needed both hands to climb. As always, I was intrigued with the clouds and how quickly they moved and changed. I went into a cloud halfway up the mountain, and when I reached the summit I found myself in a thunderstorm. Fearing the lightning, I hurried along the trail to the woods.

I arrived at the Appalachian Mountain Club's Lonesome Lake Hut in pouring rain and found only two hut boys there. Although 13 people had made reservations and paid, no one else came, except for a third hut boy. Since the AMC huts are inaccessible by automobile, supplies are carried in on hut boys' backs. Getting one of these jobs is hard, just as the work is, but a hut boy holds a respected position in the White Mountains. The hut boys take pride in how much weight they can pack in to a hut and how fast they can do it. The hut boy who arrived after I did was carrying 122 pounds. His record load was 130. The four hut boys at Lonesome Lake were all trying to get up to 130 pounds before the end of the summer. They told me that the boys in another hut had set their goal at 150 pounds. The alltime record, they said, was 180 pounds.

The next morning I went down through Franconia Notch, then up across the shoulder of Mt. Liberty and followed the Franconia Ridge Trail over Little Haystack Mountain (4,560 feet), Mt. Lincoln (5,108 feet), and up to Mt. Lafayette (5,249 feet). Much of the walk from Little Haystack Mountain to Mt. Lafayette is well above tree line and has some of the best views in the White Mountains. Little Haystack Mountain, although it rises to 4,560 feet, is not included in the AMC list of 4,000-foot White Mountain peaks. To be on the list, a peak must rise 200 feet above the ridge from any neighboring 4,000-foot peak, and this stipulation disqualifies several mountains. As I followed the Appalachian Trail through New Hampshire I climbed 19 of the recognized 4,000-footers, including all of the ones the trail goes over, and a few on side trails.

On the Franconia Ridge Trail, I met Steve Gorman of Long Island, New York, who was hiking the Appalachian Trail from Maine to Georgia. As far as I know, Steve and Jim Rutter were the only Maine-to-Georgia hikers I met who made it to Georgia. In New Hampshire and Maine I met over 20 people who said they were going all the way to Springer Mountain. However, I could tell that not more than four or five of them had any chance of making it. Most of these people had the money, the time, and the equipment to complete the trip, but they lacked the determination. One morning at 10:30 I met three young men who were just finishing breakfast. The trio thought they were going to Georgia and told me so, but I knew they would never make it. I had already climbed three mountains that morning; if they were determined to go to Georgia, they would have been doing the same. Another day I met three women who were physical education teachers and they told me they were going all the way to Georgia, but they were not hiking that day because it was raining. A backpacker who does not hike in the rain would never get out of Maine.

One late afternoon I reached Crawford Notch after going over South Twin Mountain and Mt. Guyot. From the notch I had a 2000-foot view-filled climb up the Webster Cliff Trail to Mt. Webster (3,910 feet). Coming down Mt. Webster I started to slip occasionally. Although I still felt strong and alert, I knew that this slipping was a sign of fatigue. Soon my feet started to feel sore every time I put them down. When I reached the Nauman Shelter I realized why I was tired. I had walked 19 or 20 miles—nothing exceptional in most areas, but a good day's hike in the White Mountains.

The next day was July 17. The weather was beautiful and I spent most of the day above tree line, following the old original trail to the summit of Mt. Washington. First I went to the summit of Mt. Clinton (4,310 feet), then across the shoulder of Mt. Pleasant (4,761 feet), over the summit of Mt. Franklin (5,004 feet), across the shoulder of Mt. Monroe (5,385 feet), and finally to the summit of Mt. Washington, which at 6,288 feet is the highest mountain in the northeastern part of the United States. Walking above tree line on a clear day is one of the most extraordinary and fulfilling experiences I have known. There is a feeling up there on the rock-strewn summits that is as close to perfection as a feeling can be. In bad weather these treeless summits are a danger and sometimes a killer; but in good weather they are a giver of life. We climb mountains more for our mental health than for the physical exercise. From tiny alpine and subalpine plants to miles of aged rocks and broad flat tablelands and piked peaks, to scattered cumulus clouds and brisk winds and blue skies, to the welcoming and friendly valleys below, to the beckoning summits in the distance, and most of all to the sacred mountains themselves, everything fills us with exhilaration and wonder.

The Appalachian Trail misses the summit of Mt. Washington by 0.2 mile, but a short side trail leads to the top. The summit is in clouds 60 percent of the time, so I was pleasantly surprised when I found it clear.

After Mt. Lafayette and other spectacular summits, the summit of Mt. Washington is a letdown. It is too wide to get a panoramic view in all directions at once, and the buildings further limit and break up the view. Also, Mt. Washington is located in a less interesting place than many other mountains. It is on the edge of the White Mountains and in one direction the view is of lower, flatter land. The summit buildings, besides being obstructions to the view, are so commercialized as to be disgraceful. The weather station is the only respectable enterprise on the summit. Meteorologists have been living there the whole year around for many years in order to record weather conditions. As the White Mountain National Forest's signs warn, the area has some of the worst, fastest changing, and most unpredictable weather in the world. The highest surface wind speed ever recorded in the world—231 miles per hour—was recorded on Mt. Washington. The average wind speed on the summit is 35 miles per hour. The highest temperature ever recorded at the station is 71° F. The lowest temperature recorded there is -49° F. The average temperature is 27° F. The record snowfall is 97.8 inches (just over 8 feet) in about one day. Although record snowfalls occur in winter, it is not uncommon for some snow to fall during the summer months.

I have read that more people have died on Mt. Washington than on any other mountain in the world. Most of these deaths were caused by underestimating the weather possibilities. The hiker in the valley below often does not realize that the valley weather bears little relation to the weather on Mt. Washington. If an ascending hiker finds that the weather is bad, he should turn around and go back down; conditions are only going to get worse the higher he goes. The stubborn hiker who refuses to do this may pay with his life, or endanger the lives of others who go to search for him. It is no disgrace to turn back because of bad weather on Mt. Washington, Mt. Katahdin, or any other mountain.

Most of the people at the Madison Huts were out for the weekend and were staying at the huts each night, so they carried only day packs. My bulging pack stood out. Someone asked where I had come from, and as soon as "Georgia" was out of my mouth, several people looked up. Soon I had a large audience and held, as one person called it, a "press conference." The Madison Huts are in the col between Mt. Madison and Mt. Adams, and are well above timberline. From the inside of one of the huts we could see the shoulder of Mt. Adams and a bright orange tent that was pitched less than 100 yards away. Suddenly a dark cloud came up over the side of the mountain and within a few minutes we could see neither the shoulder of Mt. Adams nor the tent. In three or four minutes visibility had been reduced from good to zero.

From the safety of the hut this was an amazing scene to watch—but outside in the storm it would have been a frightening experience for most people. As we looked on in amazement, two hut boys with huge packs appeared out of the dense fog and calmly walked in. Who knows the trail better than the hut boy who walks it all summer long with a heavy load on his back? No other hiker has to watch and plan each step as carefully as he does.

After having eaten with the hut crew at Lonesome Lake, I was disappointed with the breakfast at the Madison Huts. At Lonesome Lake I had a satisfying breakfast—a quart of orange juice, a quart of fresh whole milk, hot cereal, pancakes, eggs, bacon, toast, and hot cocoa. At the Madison Huts they served me only a glass of juice, hot cereal, a bun, and hot cocoa. When they cleared the tables I thought they were preparing for the second course, but when it didn't come I realized that at Lonesome Lake I had been served *a hut boy's breakfast* but at the Madison Huts I was getting only a *hiker's breakfast*.

At Pinkham Notch I met my family and went with them to their campsite at Moose Brook State Park. The following morning my father dropped me off at Pinkham Notch at 6:30 so I could hike the 19.9 miles to the Gorham-Shelburne Road (U.S. Route 2) and meet him there that evening. The guidebook said that three days should be allowed to traverse this section. I allowed myself 13 hours, and told my father I would meet him at 6:30, but carrying only a day pack I was able to make it in only 8 hours. After the first two hours I did not push, and late in the afternoon I even loafed. That day I went over six 4000-foot peaks and 12 peaks in all, including Wildcat E (4,041 feet) and Wildcat Mountain (4,397 feet). From both of these summits I had excellent views of the Presidential Range. The morning was exceptionally clear; there was no haze and not a cloud in the sky. Visibility on Mt. Washington that morning was said to have been 100 miles. Beyond Carter Notch I went through the Carters—Carter Dome, South Carter, Middle Carter, and North Carter. When I was on Middle Carter it began to get cloudy, and after Mt. Moriah it began to rain. When my family met me at U.S. Route 2, my mother was surprised that I was wearing my poncho since it had been clear that morning. I told her that I was used to mountain weather and was prepared for almost anything.

After a day of rest, I got back on the trail at U.S. Route 2 and entered the Mahoosucs. As I left North Road I met Jim Ross again. We hiked together and just after lunch we found ourselves shaking hands on the Maine-New Hampshire state line. Maine was no longer a dream—it had become a reality. Except to backpackers and hikers the Mahoosucs are an unknown mountain range, for the only way in is on foot. I had never even heard of the Mahoosucs before beginning my hike on the Appalachian Trail, but once on the trail, even as far south as North Carolina, I started hearing stories about the steep cliffs, the snow and ice in summer, and the mile of trail that takes many hours to traverse.

The Mahoosuc Range has several difficult ascents and descents, but what gives it uniqueness is the Mahoosuc Notch. The trail descends steeply into the notch, then goes between impregnable rock walls for almost a mile before coming out at the other end. The walls on both sides are almost vertical. There are no significant changes in elevation on the floor of the pass, but the area is covered with huge boulders which make normal walking impossible. Often the trail climbs over these rocks, and several times it goes through gaps beneath them. I went through Mahoosuc Notch during the third week of July, yet snow and ice remained in some of these chilly shaded passageways. I could have avoided climbing under some of the boulders by going over them, as I could see others had done, but climbing under them was a new experience which added variety and adventure to the hike. To get through some of these passages I had to take off my pack and push it ahead of me. Once I tried to save a few seconds by leaving it on, and then lost several minutes trying to get myself unstuck.

Maine proved to be a very wet state. It showered almost daily. There were few level campsites. The cleared areas near lean-tos were about the only places where a tent could be pitched. The sleeping platforms in many of the lean-tos in Maine were made of two-inch logs, and these bumpy little logs made the worst bed I have ever tried to sleep on. They made me feel like I was really roughing it in the wilderness!

In both Georgia and Maine the Appalachian Trail went through some lumbered areas and sometimes followed dirt logging roads. In addition to being ugly, newly lumbered areas often obscured the trail. Trees with blazes on them were sometimes cut down. Places where the trail left the road and entered the woods were obscured by piles of branches, gravel, and rocks. After following the unblazed trails of New Hampshire I was out of the habit of watching for blazes. This, together with the disruption of the trail by logging, caused me to lose the route several times. I made a conscious effort to reprogram myself to the valuable habit of watching for blazes. Losing the trail occasionally is almost inevitable, but the hiker who is watching for blazes knows very quickly when he has strayed, and hence loses less time in finding the trail again.

I had looked forward to the quiet and solitude of the Maine woods. I had anticipated experiencing "perfect natural silence," but I never did find it. Chain saws were the worst offenders. I could hear them for hours at a time, although I seldom saw the workers who were using them. Occasionally I saw or heard lumber trucks or tractors, and sometimes I heard the drone of an airplane, but even when these reminders of civilization were completely absent, the wind and rain insured that I never found total silence.

I reached the 1,800-mile mark at Sabbath Day Pond Lean-to. This shelter was in a beautiful location on a small isolated pond which had an excellent triple echo. Two loons made quite a racket during the night, but they were more interesting and amusing than disturbing. Near the pond I found moose tracks, but did not see my first moose until several days later.

Many of the Maine peaks were engulfed in clouds a great deal of the time. In the southern Appalachians I had walked in mountain fogs on many mornings, but here I walked in fog on summit after summit for days at a time. I went over Saddleback (4,116 feet) and The Horn (4,023 feet), both in the clouds. The next day I went over Spaulding Mountain (3,988 feet), Mt. Sugarloaf (4,237 feet), and West Peak of Bigelow (4,150 feet)—all enveloped in clouds.

When I arrived at the Myron H. Avery Memorial Lean-to, between the main peaks of Bigelow, I found a group from a boys' camp already there. It was beginning to rain, and when I walked up to the lean-to the boys asked me where I was going to stay. I said I was going to stay in the lean-to. There was not enough room, they said, and suggested that I go back three miles to The Horns Pond Lean-tos. I told them that there was enough room in a lean-to for as many people as came, and besides, I never hiked south. I had never refused anyone room in a lean-to, and with this one exception, no one ever tried to refuse me. I stayed, but made no friends. Between Georgia and Maine I met several well-organized and happy Scout groups, but only one such camp group. Most of the group from the boys' camps were on a required overnight hike. Usually the leaders knew little or nothing about camping and sometimes hated it; the trips were not organized, and the routes were too strenuous for the children taking the hikes. I felt that such an experience could only lead to a lasting dislike of the outdoors; many of these middle-class city kids would never again voluntarily set foot in the woods.

The next morning I climbed Myron H. Avery Peak (4,088 feet), but missed seeing Katahdin because of clouds. At West Carry Pond I met two men who were surveying beside a dirt road. One of them asked how I would like a Coke. "A Coke?" (Tom Dickson later told me that I sounded like I didn't believe there was such a thing in the Maine Woods.) He directed me to his camp on West Carry Pond, where Mrs. Dickson invited me inside—wet boots and all. I sat with Mrs. Dickson and Mrs. Storey and had soda and cookies until Mr. Dickson and Mr. Storey joined us. They had met several 2,000-milers, including Branley C. Owen. They were the only people I met who had seen Owen stop; it seems he couldn't turn down a soda, either. Tom Dickson had been born in Scotland, but his family had brought him to Maine when he was still an infant. He had been summering at the Carry Ponds since 1927. Back in the thirties he had been a supervisor of the Civilian Conservation Corps camp at Flagstaff Lake when the CCCers built several trail lean-tos in the area, as well as part of the original Appalachian Trail in Maine.

Every hiker has his own story of how he crossed the Kennebec. The river is about 1,000 feet wide and has no bridge, and from the south, no ferry service unless it is arranged in advance. Each morning, usually at about 9:00, a dam upriver is opened and logs are floated down. Southbound hikers I met had used various methods of crossing. Some had hired a boat or canoe in Caratunk and had been ferried across, but most of them had forded the river. Some hikers waded across bareboot and said that method worked well; some went barefoot and cut and bruised their feet. Some wore boots and suggested wearing them; others wore boots and said it was better not to wear them. Most suggested using a walking stick or pole. Some used a rubber raft for their packs; one made a log raft. Few people agreed on what time the logs started coming down the river, or whether the water level rose.

I got into a long conversation with a southbound hiker and reached the Kennebec later than I had planned. Just as I got to the river one of the fishermen on the other side hollered that the water was coming up, and I was surprised to see all 10 or 12 fishermen get out of the water immediately. Hoping that I was not too late, I started into the river. I was wearing my boots, socks, shirt, and shorts. The current was quite strong. When I was about 50 feet out into the river I decided to turn back, and when I reached the shore I was glad I did. Looking out across the river I saw scores of logs where there had been only a few of them two minutes before. I decided that the Kennebec would have to wait until another day. I climbed up on the bank, found a good campsite, and spent the day reading and watching the cars on the highway across the river.

The next morning I had a leisurely breakfast and watched two hikers ford the Kennebec from the other side. They inched across the river, pulling and pushing an air mattress they were using as a raft for their packs. When I had welcomed them to the southern shore I started across myself. This time I wore only my boots, without socks, and my shorts. I carried my pack on my back as usual, except that I put the sleeping bag *above* the packbag instead of below it. I made my crossing about 100 yards upstream from where the Appalachian Trail comes down to the river. Rapids extended two-thirds of the way across, so I only had to worry about the depth of the water for the last third of the crossing. The current was strong and the bottom was covered with small, slippery rocks. Each time I took a step I made sure I had found secure footing before I put my full weight down. My walking stick served as a third leg and helped me keep my balance. Most of the time the water was only up to my knees; in the deepest places it rose to the lower edge of my shorts. The surging current reminded me of how easily I could be washed downstream, but overall, the crossing was easier than I had expected.

At the general store in Caratunk I was surprised to learn that Jim Ross had been there only an hour before. I wondered why I had not seen him cross the river, but when I reached Moxie Bald Lean-to in midafternoon I found Jim there and learned that he had crossed 300 yards downstream from my camp.

The next morning I hiked into Monson with Jim. He set the pace and I got to Monson quite a bit sooner than I would have if I had been walking by myself. We were in Monson at about 11:15 with 16 miles behind us. Monson is a friendly town some 1,912 miles from Springer Mountain or 116 miles from Katahdin, depending on your point of view. For Jim and me it was a major landmark—our last food and mail pickup on the Appalachian Trail.

Monson has one of the best inexpensive restaurants along the Appalachian Trail. Hikers rave about it when writing in the registers or when you meet them on the trail. Jim and I ate there, or rather, we *overate* there. We started with a full dinner, then had lunch, then several desserts. The waitress was shocked with each new order. The table was intended for four, but was not large enough for the two of us, even when we stacked the empty plates and dishes. Eventually the waitress had to take some of the empties away before she could bring our next order. Jim and I camped outside of Monson that night and the next morning he left before I did. That was the last time I saw him on the trail.

Late the following afternoon I went over White Cap Mountain. Hoping to get a glimpse of Katahdin I took a side trail to the summit, where there was a fire tower. It was hazy, so I still didn't have my first view of Katahdin. I also missed seeing the celebrated moose who "lives" on the trail on White Cap Mountain, the moose that *everyone* sees. Two days later, however, I finally did see my first moose. I was walking along an open road and heard a sound behind a clump of bushes 100 feet ahead. As I walked closer, taking care to be quiet, I saw a brown back in the bushes and knew it was a moose. Looking like an awkward and mal-formed horse, she started trotting down the road away from me. I had assumed she would run off quickly, as most deer would, but she stopped a short distance down the road, turned her head, and looked at me over her shoulder. Then she stood politely while I got out my camera and took a picture. After that she ambled off into the woods.

By the end of the day I was over the 2,000-mile mark—some 2,003 miles, by my calculation. I spent the night at Rainbow Lake Lean-to, where I met two friends of Mark and Pete of the Bad-Off Appalachian Jug Band. They were waiting to meet Mark and hike to Katahdin with him. They told me some elaborate stories about the wolf they had seen the night before, but long ago I had learned that only inexperienced backpackers tell wolf stories, and only even more inexperienced back-packers believe them.

August 4 was another rainy day. It was not until late in the after-noon of this last day before climbing Katahdin that I got a view of the mountain—first with its summit in the clouds, then from Katahdin Stream Campground with the summit clear.

The next morning was beautiful. I had a leisurely breakfast and started for Baxter Peak at 8:30. As I walked through the woods I savored each beautiful moment. By the time I reached timberline I was bubbling over with a joy that I had felt only once or twice in my life. The sky was perfectly blue except for some snow-white cumulus clouds in the distance. Above me were some huge granite boulders, and beyond them I could see a point that I thought was the summit of Katahdin and the end of my long journey. As I got closer I realized by looking at the neighboring 4,000-foot peaks that I was not high enough, but I could see no higher peak ahead of me. I continued to be puzzled until I reached the crest of the ridge. Then I was amazed to see that the summit was still a mile or more away across a broad flat table-land. The summit of Katahdin had been hidden by the ridge. In the excitement of the last few days I had neglected to look at my maps and no one had described the top of the mountain to me.

More than any other kind of mountain, I love rocky primitive summits; not the gentle forest-protected peaks, but the ones that soar to the
heavens. Katahdin is as near to perfection as a mountain can get. As I
neared the summit I recognized the brown weather-beaten sign that
marked the northern terminus of the "endless" footpath through the
Appalachian Mountains, an endless path to which I had found an end.
Four people were on the summit when I got there. Although I knew it
was the end, I cried in an incredulous tone, "Is this the end of the
Appalachian Trail?" Without waiting for a response, I rather compul-
sively started telling them my story, "I've hiked the whole Appalachian
Trail from Springer Mountain. I left Georgia on April 1, and. . . ."

I stayed on the summit of Katahdin for a long time. I couldn't think
of anywhere else to go or anything else to do, but Pamola[1] finally drove
me off. Perhaps too many people had climbed Katahdin that day and
he was angry. The clouds moved in and darkness hovered over our
heads. Raindrops fell and the wind howled. From my experience with
mountaintops I knew that Katahdin would soon be engulfed in clouds.
I discovered that my hands were numb. I had spent much time in the
heavens and it was time to return to earth. I could not hike the Appalachian Trail forever. For four months I had lived a whole life, and a
great one, but when we reach the end of one trail, it is time to look for
the beginning of the next one. There is not so much life in what we did
yesterday, or in what someone else did, as in what we do today.

[1] "To the Indians, Pamola was the deity of the mountain. In awe of Pamola's wrath, the
Indians never ventured too near Katahdin. Those who accompanied Charles Turner Jr.
in 1804 told him how had destroyed a party of Indians who had previously ventured
into the fastness of Katahdin."—Myron H. Avery, in KATAHDIN SECTION, GUIDE TO
THE APPALACHIAN TRAIL IN MAINE.

What are some of the things I remember now that the trip is over? I remember awakening at daybreak on a mountaintop and watching the world transform itself into miles of rolling forest-covered hills. I remember having my faith in humanity renewed. I remember asking myself "Why?" about things I couldn't understand, and I remember not being able to answer in words, but knowing the answers, just the same.

Bradley W. Grueling
"There and Back"
Hiking the Appalachian Trail, Vol. 2

Appalachian Trail Maintaining Clubs

The 2175-mile-long Appalachian Trail is maintained by volunteers. The following is a list of the hiking clubs that work on the AT; there are 30 clubs maintaining sections of the Trail in each of the fourteen states through which the Trail passes. These clubs welcome anyone with an interest in keeping the Trail open, safe, and in good repair—a never-ending job.

Information on meetings and how to join are available through their Web sites.

Maine Appalachian Trail Club (MATC)
www.matc.org

Appalachian Mountain Club (AMC)
www.outdoors.org

Dartmouth Outing Club (DOC)
www.dartmouth.org

Green Mountain Club (GMC)
www.greenmountainclub.org

AMC-Berkshire Chapter
www.amcberkshire.org/at

AMC-Connecticut Chapter (AMC-CT)
www.ct-amc.org/ct

New York-New Jersey Trail Conference (NY-NJTC)
www.nynjtc.org

Wilmington Trail Club (WTC)
www.wilmingtontrailclub.org

Batona Hiking Club (BHC)
www.batonahikingclub.org

AMC-Delaware Valley Chapter (AMC-DV)
www.amcdv.org

Philadelphia Trail Club (PTC)
www.zanger.tripod.com

Blue Mountain Eagle Climbing Club (BMECC)
www.bmecc.org

Allentown Hiking Club (AHC)
www.allentownhikingclub.org

Susquehanna Appalachian Trail Club (SATC)
www.satc-hike.org

York Hiking Club (YHC)
www.yorkhikingclub.com

Cumberland Valley Appalachian Trail Club (CVATC)
www.cvatclub.org

Mountain Club of Maryland (MCM)
www.mcomd.org

Potomac Appalachian Trail Club (PATC)
www.potomacappalachian.org

Old Dominion Appalachian Trail Club (ODATC)
www.odatc.net

Tidewater Appalachian Trail Club (TATC)
www.tidewateratc.org

Natural Bridge Appalachian Trail Club (NBATC)
www.nbatc.org

Roanoke Appalachian Trail Club (RATC)
www.ratc.org

Outdoor Club at Virginia Tech (OCVT)
www.outdoor.org.vt.edu

Piedmont Appalachian Trail Hikers (PATH)
www.path-at.org

Mount Rogers Appalachian Trail Club (MRATC)
www.mratc.pbworks.com

Tennessee Eastman Hiking and Canoeing Club (TEHCC)
www.tehcc.org

Carolina Mountain Club (CMC)
www.carolinamtnclub.com

Smoky Mountains Hiking Club (SMHC)
www.smhclub.org

Nantahala Hiking Club (NHC)
www.maconcommunity.org

Georgia Appalachian Trail Club (GATC)
www.georgia-atclub.org

For more information on the Appalachian Trail, visit the Appalachian Trail Conservancy at *www.appalachiantrail.org*.